CRYPTOCURRENCY
QuickStart Guide ®

CRYPTOCURRENCY

QuickStart Guide®

The Simplified Beginner's Guide to
Digital Currencies, Bitcoin, and the
Future of Decentralized Finance

Jonathan Reichental, PhD

Editors: Bryan Basamanowicz, Jesse Hassenger, Marilyn Burkley
Cover Illustration and Design: Katie Donnachie, Nicole Daberkow, Copyright © 2023 by ClydeBank Media LLC
Interior Design & Illustrations: Katie Donnachie, Brittney Duquette, Nicole Daberkow, Copyright © 2023 by ClydeBank Media LLC

First Edition - Last Updated: July 4, 2023

ISBN: 9781636100401 (paperback) | 9781636100425 (hardcover) | 9781636100449 (audiobook) | 9781636100418 (ebook) | 9781636100432 (spiral bound)

Publisher's Cataloging-In-Publication Data
(Prepared by The Donohue Group, Inc.)

Names: Reichental, Jonathan, author.
Title: Cryptocurrency QuickStart Guide : the simplified beginner's guide to digital currencies, bitcoin, and the future of decentralized money / Jonathan Reichental, PhD.
Other titles: Cryptocurrency Quick Start Guide
Description: [Albany, New York] : ClydeBank Finance, [2023] | Series: QuickStart Guide | Includes bibliographical references and index.
Identifiers: ISBN: 978-1-63610-040-1 (paperback) | 978-1-63610-042-5 (hardcover) | 978-1-63610-043-2 (spiral-bound) | 978-1-63610-041-8 (eBook/ePub)
Subjects: LCSH: Cryptocurrencies--Handbooks, manuals, etc. | Bitcoin--Handbooks, manuals, etc. | Investments--Handbooks, manuals, etc. | Electronic trading of securities--Handbooks, manuals, etc. | LCGFT: Handbooks and manuals. | BISAC: BUSINESS & ECONOMICS / Bitcoin & Cryptocurrencies. | BUSINESS & ECONOMICS / E-Commerce / Online Trading. | BUSINESS & ECONOMICS / Investments & Securities / Analysis & Trading Strategies.
Classification: LCC: HG1710.3 .R45 2023 | DDC: 332.4--dc23

Library of Congress Control Number: 2022951131

Author ISNI: 0000 0001 2649 9477

For bulk sales inquiries, please visit www.go.quickstartguides.com/wholesale, email us at orders@clydebankmedia.com, or call 800-340-3069. Special discounts are available on quantity purchases by corporations, associations, and others.

Copyright © 2023
www.quickstartguides.com
All Rights Reserved

ISBN-13: 978-1-63610-040-1 (paperback)
ISBN-13: 978-1-63610-042-3 (spiral bound)

OVER 850,000 READERS **LOVE** *QuickStart Guides.*

Really well written with lots of practical information. These books have a very concise way of presenting each topic and everything inside is very actionable!

— ALAN F.

The book was a great resource, every page is packed with information, but [the book] never felt overly-wordy or repetitive. Every chapter was filled with very useful information.

— CURTIS W.

I appreciated how accessible and how insightful the material was and look forward to sharing the knowledge that I've learned [from this book].

— SCOTT B.

After reading this book, I must say that it has been one of the best decisions of my life!

— ROHIT R.

This book is one-thousand percent worth every single dollar!

— HUGO C.

The read itself was worth the cost of the book, but the additional tools and materials make this purchase a better value than most books.

— JAMES D.

I finally understand this topic ... this book has really opened doors for me!

— MISTY A.

Contents

PART III – CRYPTOCURRENCY IN ACTION

This book is dedicated to Satoshi Nakamoto. Whoever it is, whether a person or a group of people, they made history. I'm grateful that they made all of us think differently, that they challenged the status quo, and that—whether you agree with Nakamoto or not—they accelerated innovation in decentralized solutions.

No matter what the future holds for crypto and blockchain, Nakamoto made a dent in the universe.

BEFORE YOU START READING, DOWNLOAD YOUR FREE DIGITAL ASSETS!

 Major Cryptocurrencies Library

 Crypto Portfolio Management Workbook

 Crypto Research and Analysis Link Library

TWO WAYS TO ACCESS YOUR FREE DIGITAL ASSETS

Use the camera app on your mobile phone to scan the QR code or visit the link below and instantly access your digital assets.

 SCAN ME

or

go.quickstartguides.com/crypto

VISIT URL

Introduction

I was attending a tech-themed event in Austria in the early 2010s when I finally "got it." Until then the emerging crypto phenomenon had buzzed around the peripheries of my academic and social circles, but I'd neither understood it nor cared to.

My epiphany happened as I listened to a dinner speaker. Her talk didn't center on Bitcoin, which at that time was the only cryptocurrency with even modest name recognition. She spoke instead about a technology called *blockchain*: what it was and how it worked, and how blockchain was the rails on which cryptocurrency was moving through the world. What intrigued me, and what led to the permanent etching of this event in my memory, was the technical elegance of the idea.

She explained blockchain as a technology that could enable anonymous participants to connect and transact with one another without the need for intermediaries. I found blockchain to be compelling and I wanted to keep learning.

I came to cryptocurrency by way of blockchain as opposed to the other way around. Understanding how blockchain technology functioned made learning cryptocurrency far easier. It also created the wider context for how its various components and design could enable different types of value—monetary or otherwise—to be managed and exchanged over networks. Blockchain provided the basis for building deep knowledge about cryptocurrencies and crypto investing, non-fungible tokens (NFTs), decentralized finance (DeFi), and more.

In the decade that's followed that evening in Austria, I've been fortunate enough to share my growing knowledge of crypto and blockchain with over a million people across the globe through speaking engagements, training courses, and writings.

Cryptocurrency QuickStart Guide is my effort to wholly encapsulate the breadth of knowledge I've accumulated on this topic, and I'm glad you've discovered it.

Over the years I've purchased and read several books on the topic, including many that were well-written and well-informed. Many of the books took an overly narrow lens, focusing only on, for example, Bitcoin, or only on blockchain mechanics, or NFTs. What I felt lacking in the market was one unbiased, objectively positioned book that would tell the full story of cryptocurrencies and their ecosystem.

This book was written for those with or without prerequisite knowledge. It's beginner-friendly, but I trust that even the most seasoned enthusiasts will uncover new perspectives within these pages. I'm going to tell you the story of crypto, from the past to the present, and to a possible future. You'll learn how crypto works and how it is used in many contexts including investing, trading, digital assets, and much more. In addition, I'll describe in simple steps how you can fully participate in many aspects of the cryptocurrency ecosystem.

I'll introduce you to the fictitious Forrest family of *mostly* crypto-savvy individuals. As you work your way through this book, you'll get a glimpse of how the Forrests grapple with the various crypto opportunities that come their way. Their successes, challenges, frustrations, hopes, doubts, and dreams are similar to those of the many who choose to immerse themselves in this space. My hope is that, as a narrative tool, the Forrests remind you that this topic can be not only academic and technological, but also human and emotional.

Finally, I wrote this book not as an advocate for cryptocurrency, but as an educator. Without a doubt, this topic has strong contingents of enthusiasts and naysayers. I recognize that cryptocurrencies can stir up strong emotions on both sides of the argument. In this book I've tried as best I can to stay neutral on the topic. While I'll present different aspects of this wide-ranging subject, the final arbiter is you. You must decide, when all is said and done, whether cryptocurrencies represent the future. No matter what everyone believes right now, all of us will find out soon enough.

Enjoy the ride,
Jonathan

DISCLAIMER: The content of this book is for informational and educational purposes only. You should not construe any such information, my opinions, or other material as legal, tax, investment, financial, or other advice.

Chapter by Chapter

» I believe that historical context is important for understanding the "why" of the present, and even where the future may be headed. Chapter 1 is called "The Present, Past, and Future of Money." Here

I'll help you get your head around what money really is and how it functions, making it easier for you to understand how a mash-up of software and data has emerged as a viable currency with actual value.

» Chapter 2, "How Cryptocurrencies Work," provides a deep dive into the mechanics of cryptocurrencies and the blockchains that power them. Some of you will be inclined to skip the technical stuff, while others will find it fascinating and relevant to your overall goals.

» Chapter 3, "The Role of Cryptography," will show you how cryptography is used to ensure that transactions on the blockchain are secure and authentic. It's here that I'll introduce you to the concept of wallets and public and private keys. These are the essential tools of crypto ownership.

» Chapter 4, "Bitcoin," retraces the origin and meteoric rise of this signature crypto. I'll also discuss forks here and the many spin-off cryptos that have come into existence thanks to Bitcoin's source code. Finally, I'll offer my perspective on Bitcoin's future.

» Chapter 5, "Ethereum," is a profile of the cryptocurrency that changed the game in a multitude of ways—the scrappy, flashy runner-up that institutionalized smart contracts and dapps.

» Chapter 6, "Altcoins," will take you on an exploration of cryptocurrencies beyond Bitcoin and Ethereum. I'll break down the qualities that make these coins and tokens unique and I'll provide a deep dive on a few altcoin standouts.

» Chapter 7, "Tokens," explores an increasingly vital aspect of the crypto-verse, namely crypto tokens, in contrast to crypto coins such as Bitcoin and Ethereum. I'll explain the nature and uses of both fungible, interchangeable tokens and the non-fungible tokens (NFTs) that came to prominence beginning in the late 2010s.

» In Chapter 8, "Buying and Selling Cryptocurrency," I'll depart from the purely academic and enter into the practical aspects of crypto. Here I'll discuss the evaluation and selection of exchanges and wallets and the finer points of acquiring NFTs.

» Chapter 9, "Trading Cryptocurrency," provides the essential elements of the crypto trading game. I'll acquaint you with a host of different tactics and tools that are used by traders in the highly volatile cryptocurrency market.

» Chapter 10, "Investing in Cryptocurrency," looks at cryptocurrency as an investment asset and offers a means by which it can be assessed as such. For readers interested in acquiring and holding crypto for the long haul, this chapter has the goods.

» Chapter 11, "Mining Crypto for Profit," explains the means by which new transactions are added to a blockchain under proof-of-work, the original consensus mechanism. I'll take you through the details of the mathematical puzzle at the heart of this system and give tips on how to become a crypto miner.

» Chapter 12 introduces "DeFi," short for "decentralized finance," the term that describes blockchain-powered financial services. I discuss how this functions as a peer-to-peer approach, bypassing the need for third-party oversight and authority on the part of governmental and other institutions, such as banks.

» Chapter 13, "Different Countries, Different Approaches," will take you on a global tour of different nations' approaches to crypto regulation. Some countries take a laissez-faire approach, others are more restrictive, and still others have banned the use of crypto entirely.

» Chapter 14, "What's Next," is a forward-looking assessment of the possible future for cryptocurrencies and blockchain. From video games to identity management, I'll put on my futurist's hat and give you a glimpse of how I think the years ahead may unfold.

PART I

MONEY AND DIGITAL INNOVATION

I 1 I

The Present, Past, and Future of Money

Chapter Overview

 » Cryptocurrency and the Fourth Industrial Revolution
 » How crypto came about
 » Fitting crypto into the monetary system

There's a reason so many people are intrigued by cryptocurrency. Among other things, cryptocurrency (or "crypto" for short) is a revolutionary change in one of humanity's core tools: money.

The topic raises important questions. Is crypto "real" money, in the sense that it both stores value and serves as a medium of exchange? How is it similar to and different from the currency we're accustomed to and use in our everyday lives? Is cryptocurrency the future of finance or a passing fad?

To understand the future, it's often helpful to look at the past. How has money functioned through history, and what can this tell us about how it will function in the future? In this chapter, I discuss the larger cultural and social trends that affect crypto and examine how they relate to the history of money.

The Financial Sector Meets the Fourth Industrial Revolution

The debates in the Forrest household have been getting more intense in the last couple of weeks. Daughter Tori recently got her master's degree in computer science and landed a well-paid programming job at a Silicon Valley giant, but she already feels ready to move on from this position. She's talking to some friends about launching a start-up in the DeFi space. *DeFi*, or decentralized finance, refers to leading-edge enterprises whose mission is to provide financial services unmediated by central authorities such as banks and brokerages.

Tori's father Peter, a corporate lawyer, is worried. He thinks Tori has a great job and should stick it out for a few years. She'll be better equipped to go off on her own once she has some more experience under her belt. DeFi is highly speculative, he argues. Is it even going to be around in five years?

Tori's mother Lynn, meanwhile, a psychologist in private practice, has a different set of concerns. Tori's talking to her brother Alan, a high-school senior, about investing in crypto. But Lynn believes her son should be saving his money for college expenses and not investing in such a volatile market.

Sometimes patiently and other times less so, Tori tries to explain to her parents that the time to be getting into crypto and DeFi is *now*, when it's possible to get in on the ground floor of the revolutionary shifts happening now in organizations, which many are calling the **Fourth Industrial Revolution**.

There have been three industrial revolutions in the last three hundred years, each of which has fundamentally changed the nature of how humans live, work, and play (see figure 1). The development of steam power in the mid-1700s led to widespread mechanization and industrialization. The first factories opened, and mass production was born. A rural population became increasingly urban. A hundred or so years later, a second industrial revolution, powered by electricity, arrived. Inventions such as the electric light bulb transformed the way we live.

In the decades after World War II, a third industrial revolution ushered in the Information Age. The most important technology here was arguably the microchip, which paved the way for the personal computer, the smartphone, the internet, and so much more of our connected and digital world.

Today, we face possibly the most significant and rapid shift in the history of humanity—and that might be an understatement. Each industrial revolution has built on the ones preceding it, and that's certainly the case with this one. What's different is its scope, impact, and pace. The velocity with which change is occurring is accelerating. Like all revolutions, this one will be disruptive, and it will radically change the status quo.

This fourth revolution just getting underway will once more transform our world, including how we learn, how and when we work, how we make things, how we move from place to place, and how we produce and use energy. What may seem like many different trends—cryptocurrency and blockchain, artificial intelligence (AI), augmented reality (AR), self-driving vehicles, the Internet of Things (IOT), robotics, and much more—are actually all pieces of a single, rapidly assembling puzzle.

If the first industrial revolution ran on steam, the second on electricity, and the third on the microchip, what is powering the Fourth Industrial Revolution? The answer includes hyper-connectivity, digitalization, and data, with the swiftly evolving internet serving as the dynamo. In addition, it's been driven by the intersection of the physical and digital worlds—where atoms meet bits—and how that intersection creates new opportunities and ways of doing things.

THE FOUR INDUSTRIAL REVOLUTIONS

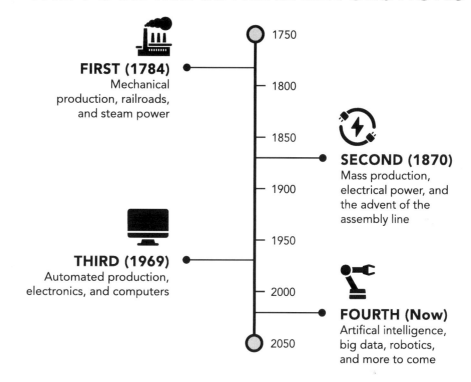

FIRST (1784)
Mechanical production, railroads, and steam power

1750

1800

1850

SECOND (1870)
Mass production, electrical power, and the advent of the assembly line

1900

1950

THIRD (1969)
Automated production, electronics, and computers

2000

FOURTH (Now)
Artifical intelligence, big data, robotics, and more to come

2050

GRAPHIC

fig. 1

The early days of the internet are now described as Web 1.0, which featured mainly static web pages. Around the turn of the millennium, Web 2.0 involved far more dynamic interaction, in areas like search, e-commerce, and social media, a trend further accelerated by the advent of the smartphone. Many people are convinced that *blockchain*, the technology behind crypto, signals the beginning of a new version of the Web, known as Web3, a platform far less centralized than the current Web. Web3 appears to be emerging as a critical component of the Fourth Industrial Revolution.

In other words, cryptocurrency is positioned within a much larger technological and social movement. It's captured popular interest and imagination partly because it's a type of money unlike any that's ever been seen before. In a world where rapid digitalization is impacting all aspects of life, crypto represents the digitalization of one of the fundamentals of our everyday existence: money.

Satoshi Nakamoto and Bitcoin

Unlike so many trends whose origins are lost in the sands of time and competing theories, cryptocurrency has a clear and definite starting point. However, a bit of mystery and intrigue persists.

A link to a provocative and compelling paper titled "Bitcoin: A Peer-to-Peer Electronic Cash System" was posted to a cryptography mailing list on Halloween 2008. The author was Satoshi Nakamoto, who then, three months later, implemented the software proposed in the paper and created (or "mined") the first bitcoin.

Who is Satoshi Nakamoto? That's the mystery. No one knows for sure. Various individuals have tried to claim credit, but none of their claims have been validated. Many believe it is a pseudonym. Nakamoto may be a man, a woman, or even a group of people. The paper was written in English; the author's Japanese name may have been meant to mislead. Or not.

fig. 2

Bitcoin: A Peer-to-Peer Electronic Cash System

Satoshi Nakamoto
satoshin@gmx.com
www.bitcoin.org

Abstract. A purely peer-to-peer version of electronic cash would allow online payments to be sent directly from one party to another without going through a financial institution. Digital signatures provide part of the solution, but the main benefits are lost if a trusted third party is still required to prevent double-spending. We propose a solution to the double-spending problem using a peer-to-peer network. The network timestamps transactions by hashing them into an ongoing chain of hash-based proof-of-work, forming a record that cannot be changed without redoing the proof-of-work. The longest chain not only serves as proof of the sequence of events witnessed, but proof that it came from the largest pool of CPU power. As long as a majority of CPU power is controlled by nodes that are not cooperating to attack the network, they'll generate the longest chain and outpace attackers. The network itself requires minimal structure. Messages are broadcast on a best effort basis, and nodes can leave and rejoin the network at will, accepting the longest proof-of-work chain as proof of what happened while they were gone.

1. Introduction

Commerce on the Internet has come to rely almost exclusively on financial institutions serving as trusted third parties to process electronic payments. While the system works well enough for most transactions, it still suffers from the inherent weaknesses of the trust based model. Completely non-reversible transactions are not really possible, since financial institutions cannot avoid mediating disputes. The cost of mediation increases transaction costs, limiting the minimum practical transaction size and cutting off the possibility for small casual transactions, and there is a broader cost in the loss of ability to make non-reversible payments for non-reversible services. With the possibility of reversal, the need for trust spreads. Merchants must be wary of their customers, hassling them for more information than they would otherwise need. A certain percentage of fraud is accepted as unavoidable. These costs and payment uncertainties can be avoided in person by using physical currency, but no mechanism exists to make payments over a communications channel without a trusted party.

What is needed is an electronic payment system based on cryptographic proof instead of trust, allowing any two willing parties to transact directly with each other without the need for a trusted third party. Transactions that are computationally impractical to reverse would protect sellers from fraud, and routine escrow mechanisms could easily be implemented to protect buyers. In this paper, we propose a solution to the double-spending problem using a peer-to-peer distributed timestamp server to generate computational proof of the chronological order of transactions. The system is secure as long as honest nodes collectively control more CPU power than any cooperating group of attacker nodes.

Source: https://bitcoin.org/bitcoin.pdf

The first page of the white paper that started cryptocurrency

Is it just coincidence that the paper was published right as the economy was collapsing in the wake of the subprime crisis, its unsustainable real estate bubble, and the beginning of the Great Recession? Again, nobody knows for sure. But certainly, enough was going wrong with the established financial system to motivate people to look for alternatives. On September 29, 2008, just a month before this fateful paper appeared, the New York Stock Exchange lost $1.2 trillion. Whether by design or by coincidence, the timing of Nakamoto's paper was remarkably good.

Understandably, people were scared, frustrated, and angered by the sudden economic downturn. And with those feelings, many started questioning the viability of the financial system as a whole. They saw governments bailing out banks that made bad home loans, but not bailing out the homeowners themselves.

Nakamoto's paper proposed an alternative currency that could operate independently of banks. There would be no money-issuing central banks like the Federal Reserve or other intermediaries. The paper faced the problems that plagued past ideas of a decentralized or "peer-to-peer" currency and came up with a viable solution.

Without more personal or background information about Nakamoto, it is difficult to assign clear motivations to the work. Nakamoto certainly didn't invent the idea of digital currency; there had been other attempts, with names like e-gold and eCash. None had survived.

Why create a new, digital form of currency anyway? The currently most widely used system of money—the system all of us are familiar with—is called *fiat currency*, which is government-issued and not backed by an underlying commodity such as gold. Fiat is a Latin word meaning "let there be" (as in *fiat lux*, "let there be light"), and fiat currency essentially means that governments and central banks, such as the United States Federal Reserve, declare the currency's value and promise to honor it. For a stable government and a smoothly running society, that seems like a reasonable promise. But, as the economic crisis of 2008–2009 illustrated, global markets and governments can't be counted on to keep economies afloat.

Enter cryptocurrency, which is both a form of money and an investment asset for the globalized, digitized world the Fourth Industrial Revolution has begun to reshape. Cryptocurrency is built on a set of technologies known as blockchain that's already inspiring major changes in areas such as banking and the supply chain. Although the word "blockchain" doesn't appear in Nakamoto's paper, the concept is fully spelled out as a way of solving what's called the *double-spend problem*.

The Double-Spend Problem

The issue is that without a central clearinghouse such as a bank, how can people be prevented from spending the same digital money twice? Or from claiming to have more funds than they actually have? In a digital context, what happens when someone who has $100 in their bank account writes two $100 checks to different people?

In the conventional banking system, the bank pays only the first check to be cashed. The second check is refused for lack of funds, and whoever wrote the checks is charged an overdraft fee. Outside the banking system, handling this problem becomes far more challenging. With direct or peer-to-peer payments, the individuals involved generally won't know (and therefore shouldn't be expected to trust) one another.

Satoshi Nakamoto described the use of blockchain technology as a way to solve the double-spend problem and enable cryptocurrency. A blockchain is a *trustless* system in which the participating parties don't need to trust one another because their transactions are mathematically validated. It's noteworthy that this technology is also a component of revolutionary change, as several of blockchain's properties solve problems in other sectors, too. As you'll see, the design of a blockchain, for example, significantly increases transaction integrity compared with traditional methods, although it isn't without some security weaknesses.

But to fully understand how cryptocurrency works and why it can be considered a legitimate form of money, you must first understand what money is and how it works. After all, if cryptocurrency is supposed to fulfill money's functions—as Tori Forrest would argue that it does—it is money, and part of a rich history that stretches way back before 2008. Before explaining further about the technical mechanics of cryptocurrency circulation in chapters 2 and 3, it will be helpful to first establish crypto's place in the broad history of money.

A Brief History of Money

Are Bitcoin and other cryptocurrencies considered money or investment instruments? Are they both, or is the whole premise an illusion? These questions can only be answered by being clear on precisely what money is.

There isn't a definitive story of the origins of money—just like there isn't a definitive history of the origins of agriculture or language. Before the appearance of money, trade was more likely carried out only with those whom you knew and trusted, which effectively meant members of your tribe—people you had known your whole life. Later, people would barter with strangers, but there were limits to how much different groups with different value systems could interact. The number of goods to barter was also quite limited.

People needed a way to trade goods and services with others that they didn't know. The development of money made it possible for people to travel, to trade, and to explore. It helped more people match their resources and their needs. Without money, commerce and society as we know them today would not exist.

Money didn't always resemble today's bills and coins. During the Neolithic Era, roughly 4000 to 12,000 years ago, people used shells, rice, salt, tea leaves, and other objects as tokens to exchange goods and services. These tokens had two functions. First, they were inherently useful. You could make jewelry and decorations from shells and precious metals; you could use seasonings to make food tastier. Second, they were scarce enough that people had to work to acquire them.

fig. 3

Cowrie shells: an early form of money.

Smaller items, such as cowrie shells (see figure 3) or metal tokens, were particularly useful for exchange because they were portable. Larger items, such as bushels of rice, were less portable; it may have sufficed to pay taxes with bushels of rice, but this form of payment would have made terrible pocket change. Another nice thing about shells, gold, and similar objects is that—unlike rice, salt, and tea leaves—their intrinsic value could be accessed without being consumed. You can make a statue or jewelry from gold and melt it down at some future time if necessary, but once you eat your store of rice, salt, or tea, it's gone forever.

The oldest known gold coins come from the kingdom of Lydia, located in what is now Turkey around 2,700 years ago. You can see what they look like in figure 4. These were made to be distinct from mere lumps of metal because they had a standard weight, contained a consistent amount of precious metal—a naturally occurring gold-silver alloy called electrum—and were stamped with a seal.

fig. 4

Source: Dosseman, CC0, via Wikimedia Commons
Lydian coins.

You can see the beginnings of a more interconnected world in these coins, in that their most likely uses were for trade with other kingdoms and amassing wealth, rather than buying goods in a marketplace. Archaeologists have found state-issued coins made from gold, silver, and electrum from around the same period throughout West and East Asia.

Why gold? Gold is valuable because of its rarity, malleability, and beauty. To have value, something must be relatively scarce. Gold, silver, and diamonds, for example, all derive their value from being scarce. Obtaining any of these requires an investment in resources and time.

Paper Money Arrives

It took about a thousand years for the next currency innovation to emerge. In China, during the Song Dynasty, around 3,000 years ago, tradespeople and merchants began using slips of paper to complete transactions, which were less onerous to carry around than bags of shells or metal coins. They left their money or goods with a shop designed for that purpose, received a paper receipt listing the details, and used that paper to complete the transaction. Over a period of about 200 years, local governments authorized and regulated the deposit shops, and the system evolved into paper money. The evolution from coins to paper money took a slightly different and longer route in Europe, with government-issued paper money emerging in the mid-17th century.

The value of government-issued paper currency was backed by gold and silver. This means that if a paper note indicated that it had $10 worth of value, there would have to be $10 worth of gold stored somewhere (think of Fort Knox in Kentucky) directly tied to the printed note. This is what's known as the gold standard. This system worked well as long as a country had enough gold to back the amount of currency it printed.

Over time, governments specified the nature of the link between their currencies and the value of the metals behind them and entered into treaties with other governments to fix exchange rates. For example, at one time, the United States set the standard so that $20 was equivalent to an ounce of gold. Similarly, a British pound sterling was at one time the equivalent of a pound of silver.

In the early 1970s, during the Nixon administration, the US had more paper currency in circulation than it had gold to back that currency. At that point, the government abandoned the gold standard and switched to fiat currency, which is a promise to honor that currency as a form of payment. This wasn't a new idea; similar systems have been seen as far back as 13th-century China, possibly invented by ruler Kublai Khan. Nevertheless, the 1970s marked the beginning of fiat currency's modern era.

Fiat Currency, Faith, and Credit

Fiat currency has no backing other than the government's and individuals' agreements to honor it. This drives home the point that money is fundamentally an abstract concept. It is ultimately whatever fulfills the following functions:

GRAPHIC

fig. 5

THE FUNDAMENTAL QUALITIES OF MONEY	
CHARACTERISTIC	**EXPLANATION**
Means of exchange	Will the seller accept your item as payment? If so, your cash, cowrie shells, or ultra-rare Charizard Pokémon card is a means of exchange.
Method of payment	This refers to the ability to use the item to pay off debts. The bank will take cash; it won't accept ramen noodles.
Store of wealth	If the asset can be set aside and used at a later date, then it is a store of wealth.

Standard of value	If everyone agrees that a certain amount of money buys a certain number of items, then it has a standard of value. For example, $2.00 equals one 20-ounce bottle of soda or one fast-food cheeseburger. The value of different Pokémon character cards may be understood in one school lunchroom but not another, so those are not a great standard of value.
Unit of account	Can the item in question be used to maintain records for calculating profits, losses, obligations, and account values? If so, it is a unit of account. Government-issued currencies fulfill this function especially well.

Money doesn't have to be metal or paper as long as it meets these requirements. Over time, forms of payment became more likely to be backed up by a centralized government source, and intermediaries like banks and brokerage firms were formed to connect consumers to that emerging financial system. But the backing of government and industry intermediaries is not actually necessary for the fundamental qualities of money to function.

The Promise and Problems of Digital Currencies

It follows that if money doesn't require a centralized source or a physical presence, there could be room for a digital currency, tracked by computer systems without the need for coins, paper money, banks, or even governments.

In fact, the idea of digital currency predates Satoshi Nakamoto's Bitcoin paper by almost thirty years. Some people argue the first real digital currency was born in 1981, when American Airlines and United Airlines began converting airline miles into points with real value.

Since then, there have been other variations on the idea of digital money. DigiCash, for example, founded in 1989, developed a secure electronic payment system for small transactions at a time before credit cards could be used on the nascent internet. Users took regular cash from their banks and bought digital codes that could be transferred and then converted back into cash. DigiCash wasn't a new currency, though, and it relied on bank participation, just like the old payment system.

By 1996, in the early days of the Web and e-commerce, the United States National Security Agency (NSA) published a paper that described how to create (or mint) electronic cash. In the same year, the Federal Reserve Bank of New York published a paper on ways to manage consumer payments over open computer networks rather than through the network applications that banks or other intermediaries operated.

Meanwhile, computer scientists and cryptographers attempted to create a peer-to-peer payment system. If it was possible to exchange messages, pictures, and music by email, why not cash?

The Double-Spend Solution

As the brains at the NSA, the Federal Reserve Bank, and Silicon Valley were thinking about electronic currencies, they struggled to solve the double-spend problem.

The double-spend problem is the risk of spending the same unit of currency twice. This risk is not present with paper money. Once you hand a bill over to pay, it belongs to someone else. If you write a bad check, the bank will slap you with a fee to try to deter you from doing it in the future; keep it up, and you could end up in prison.

As electronic transactions became more commonplace, these, too, required safeguards to avoid the double-spend problem. Under the Automated Clearing House (ACH) system, established in the US in 1972, and its global counterpart, the Society for Worldwide Interbank Financial Telecommunication (SWIFT), established in 1973, people could move money between banks around the world relatively quickly—but banks generally put a freeze on transfer balances until they were sure the transactions had cleared. This delay addressed the double-spend problem at the price of slowing down financial transactions.

Today, the electronic component of traditional banking has become quicker but works much the same way. You may notice that if you deposit a large sum of money at an ATM, not all of it will be immediately available to spend or withdraw.

But digital files are easy to replicate. If I send you a picture from my phone, I still have my version, and now you have a copy, instantly—a copy indistinguishable from my original. Obviously, that would not work for sending cash. If each transaction increased the number of coins available, the system's integrity would crumble.

It was difficult, then, to figure out how to manage digital money without a centralized authority tracking—and therefore delaying—transactions to ensure that no funds were spent more than once. Many people worked on the problem, and Satoshi Nakamoto finally arrived at the solution. The Bitcoin paper certainly drew on earlier developments, but this innovation—solving the double-spend problem—made it revolutionary.

One of the Bitcoin paper's essential contributions was presenting a solution to the double-spend problem.

Nakamoto solved this problem through a series of chain-linked transactions stored in a type of database called a blockchain. Blockchain incorporates computerized encryption or *cryptography* with a new way of validating those transactions, which I explore in the next chapter. The ideas in the Bitcoin paper presented a novel approach to replicating money's traditional functions. Bitcoin would be an all-digital currency without any physical notes or coins, existing as computer code running over the internet.

People like Tori's parents might struggle a little with this concept of money because computer code doesn't look like money. But it still acts like money—without requiring any of the conventions of the existing global financial system. Those conventions involve many different banks and companies with their own bookkeeping, linked together loosely and sometimes tenuously.

Instead of all these different users, accounts, and systems with various forms of verification, the blockchain system creates a single bookkeeping record shared by a network of computers, with the exact same data on each of the computers or nodes in the network. This single record is called a *distributed ledger*.

The Distributed Ledger

Let's back up a little and explain the origins of the distributed ledger, and what makes this idea distinctive from the old—indeed, ancient—way of doing things. Simply put, a *ledger* is a record of transactions. Ledgers have been around in different forms almost as long as writing itself. Indeed, many historians believe cuneiform, the ancient Middle Eastern form of writing, originated expressly in order to keep records. Figure 6 is a photograph of a proto-cuneiform tablet from Uruk, in what is today Iraq, from around 5,000 years ago. The pictures indicate the type of item and the holes represent the quantity.

fig. 6

Source: www.metmuseum.org
A proto-cuneiform tablet.

Ledgers enabled organizations of all kinds to keep track of money and other transactions. A store would use a ledger to track inventory and sales. A lender would use a ledger to record loans and payments. Banks used ledgers to track account activity, and customers tracked their own transactions in passbooks or check registers—tiny ledgers, but ledgers nonetheless. Having records allowed businesses to track revenue and expenses. Governments could use them to assess taxes. They created proof of ownership and activity. Ledgers were the records that tracked centuries of economic activity.

But when ledgers were kept in physical format, they could also be cumbersome. The records were often bound into large, heavy books that had to be carried from place to place, making them difficult to share. Any copies had to be reconciled against all the other copies, a tedious process.

Though office supply stores still sell ledger books, almost all major ledgers have been moved to computers. Spreadsheets and accounting applications have made keeping and sharing ledgers far easier, but software compatibility and security concerns can still complicate matters.

Blockchain, a distributed digital ledger that contains timestamped transactions, can be considered a next generation of online ledgers. "Distributed" means that it is spread among many users rather than centralized in a single location with governing authority.

Cryptocurrency is an application that runs on a blockchain. Because crypto rejects central oversight by design, it needs a way to ensure that people who don't know each other can depend on a transaction's validity. Blockchain solves that dilemma: it maintains the records of transactions, and any user can check a transaction's validity. It solves the double-spend problem while maintaining an authoritative, secure, and distributed account of transactions.

The Byzantine Generals Problem

Blockchain solves both the double-spend problem and a related issue, which is sometimes known in game theory as the Byzantine Generals problem. Imagine multiple generals in a Byzantine army who split up to attack an enemy from a variety of locations. The generals must communicate over distances to coordinate. But how can all the generals be sure that none of them are traitors who will send conflicting messages? Is there a way of being able to verify a message without trusting the messenger? Similarly, with a distributed ledger, there must be a way for the independent participants in the network to ensure that no participant will enter fraudulent transactions in the ledger—specifically, the blockchain database.

Cryptocurrency vs. Fiat Currency

We're all accustomed to using fiat currency in our daily lives, and cryptocurrency does represent some major departures from money as we've known it. Figure 7 summarizes some major differences between the two.

fig. 7

FIAT CURRENCY VS CRYPTOCURRENCY	
FIAT CURRENCY	**CRYPTOCURRENCY**
Can be physical (e.g., coins) or digital	Digital only
Digital transactions run through banking system	Digital transactions run through blockchain
Issued by governments	Issued by computers
Government can issue more currency	Each crypto has its own set of rules for creating new currency. For example, some have finite supply, while others have no upper limit on supply.

Why Does Cryptocurrency Have Value?

We know why government-backed currency has value: the government in question declares it (hence "fiat" currency), and citizens generally go along with it. So what gives cryptocurrency value without similar backing? The simplest answer to this question is that cryptocurrencies have value because people are willing to pay for them. Like other currencies that have been used throughout history, cryptos are a part of an intersubjective reality where widespread agreement on an asset's value permits it to be used for commerce. As with major fiat currencies, the agreement about the value of cryptocurrency is global in scale. For example, some may remain skeptical of Bitcoin's worth as a revolutionary technology or a long-term investment, but there's little disagreement with the notion that it possesses some value, in the sense that if you have some bitcoin, you can likely trade it in for goods, services, or other forms of currency.

In addition to the monetary functions enumerated in figure 5, there are other intrinsic attributes present in all forms of money that should be noted when assessing the value of cryptocurrencies.

» **Fungibility**: A unit of cryptocurrency (for example, one bitcoin) is interchangeable with another (for example, another bitcoin); there's no meaningful difference between them.

» **Divisibility**: Cryptocurrencies are all-digital. They may therefore be subdivided into smaller and smaller (or larger and larger) units, almost without limit. Divisibility is not only the hallmark of a viable currency, but it also helps cryptos continue to function amid severe price volatility.

» **Limited supply**: In the case of many cryptocurrencies, there is a finite supply (21 million in the case of Bitcoin). This scarcity and the assertion of deflationary pressure as demand goes up creates value. Notably, not all cryptos have this limitation.

» **Portability**: Cryptocurrency can be moved across the globe at reasonable cost.

» **Durability**: Cryptocurrencies are durable to the extent that their blockchains are secure and resistant to counterfeiting.

The aggregate effect of these attributes has allowed cryptocurrencies to assert their value in the global marketplace. In chapter 8, I discuss an additional set of factors that will help you assess the value of cryptocurrencies on a coin-by-coin basis.

Broadly speaking, cryptocurrency draws on both the history of money and digital innovations to create something new—a currency that could take money and the financial industry into the 21st century. So how does this work? In the next chapter, I give you a closer look at how crypto and blockchain technologies actually operate.

Chapter Recap

» Cryptocurrency and blockchain reflect a pattern of significant digital transformation, a core phenomenon of the Fourth Industrial Revolution.

» Bitcoin is the first cryptocurrency, introduced in 2009 following several prior attempts to create a digital currency.

» Bitcoin succeeds as a decentralized digital currency because it solves the double-spend problem.

» Cryptocurrency changes what we pay, how we pay, and how we keep records. It can be used as a traditional currency or an investment asset.

| 2 |

How Cryptocurrencies Work

Chapter Overview
>> Understanding centralized and peer-to-peer databases
>> Dissecting the blockchain
>> Introducing consensus mechanisms

If you're thinking of using or investing in cryptocurrency, it might help to understand something about how it works. True, this isn't absolutely necessary. It's easy to use a credit card without having any idea of what's happening under the hood when you do. That doesn't stop anyone from using a credit card. And, likewise, there are many user-friendly apps that can enable you to buy, trade, and sell crypto seamlessly.

But the situation isn't exactly comparable. Credit cards are a mature, established technology, and traditional banking, which goes back many centuries, even more so. The technology behind cryptocurrency is recent and innovative—even game-changing. Crypto goes beyond serving as a new form of money. It's also an investment vehicle, and it's never a good idea to make an investment in something you don't understand.

In this chapter, I go behind the scenes to explore the basics of how cryptocurrency works. I walk through the process: how these transaction records are managed, what makes the system innovative, and how these records remain accurate without a centralized system overlooking and checking each transaction.

Although Nakamoto never used the term in the Bitcoin paper, the core technology I discuss is called *blockchain*—a term I mentioned in chapter 1. But for many of you it remains a blurry, even confusing concept. This chapter should clear up that confusion.

Database Architecture

Blockchain can be considered a decentralized, peer-to-peer database. This design, which I explain in detail shortly, is different from the conventional databases that support most of the systems you use at home and at work.

Conventional Databases

In chapter 1, I discussed the technology of ledgers, which keep track of information, often financial in nature. Most ledgers are now digital and take the form of a database. Rather than being written on paper or papyrus, these ledgers are digitally accessible and built with any number of popular computer applications.

Tori's mother Lynn, a clinical psychologist, has a private therapy practice and keeps two related tables of client information in a database. The first table looks like figure 8:

fig. 8

PATIENT ID	LAST NAME	FIRST NAME	EMAIL	PHONE
1	Frick	Jeffrey	jfrick@example.com	760-555-9786
2	Messenger	Gil	gilm@example.com	805-555-4983
3	Buck	Ann	malibu5@example.com	310-555-9320

An example of a simple database table.

The second table, seen in figure 9, lists each client's payments along with payment dates. It is linked to the first by means of the ID number.

fig. 9

PATIENT ID	DATE	AMOUNT
1	2022-03-15	$200
2	2022-03-17	$150
3	2022-03-20	$100
2	2022-03-24	$150
3	2022-03-27	$100

Data from a relational database.

These two instances are examples of what's called relational tables. That means they are linked to one another, in this case by the patient ID number.

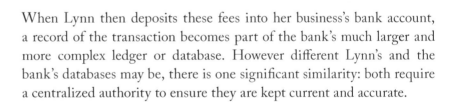

PATIENT ID	LAST NAME	FIRST NAME	EMAIL	PHONE
1	Frick	Jeffrey	jfrick@example.com	760-555-9786
2	Messenger	Gil	gilm@example.com	805-555-4983
3	Buck	Ann	malibu5@example.com	310-555-9320

PATIENT ID	DATE	AMOUNT
1	2022-03-15	$200
2	2022-03-17	$150
3	2022-03-20	$100
2	2022-03-24	$150
3	2022-03-27	$100

GRAPHIC

fig. 10

When Lynn then deposits these fees into her business's bank account, a record of the transaction becomes part of the bank's much larger and more complex ledger or database. However different Lynn's and the bank's databases may be, there is one significant similarity: both require a centralized authority to ensure they are kept current and accurate.

In the case of Lynn's database, there may be only one copy of the database, which is housed on her computer's hard drive. If the same database is uploaded to the cloud, she may be able to access it on her smartphone. Lynn protects access to the database with a password. She is the central authority overseeing and checking this database. Anyone else who accesses the database, such as her bookkeeper, can only do so if they have been provided access.

There is also a central authority supervising the bank's far larger and more complex database. Like most such databases, it has a layer of software that provides centralized control. This popular design has served the digital world well over several decades. Most of the world's databases, supported by technology giants such as Microsoft and Oracle, are designed this way.

In banks or other large organizations, such as those that Lynn's husband Peter and daughter Tori work for, there may be many different ways to access a database, but all are under the control of a central authority. The database resides on a central system called a server, and the computers that access the server are called clients (see figure 11). Clients can be desktops, laptops, smartphones, tablets, or other devices.

TRADITIONAL CLIENT-SERVER DATABASE ARCHITECTURE

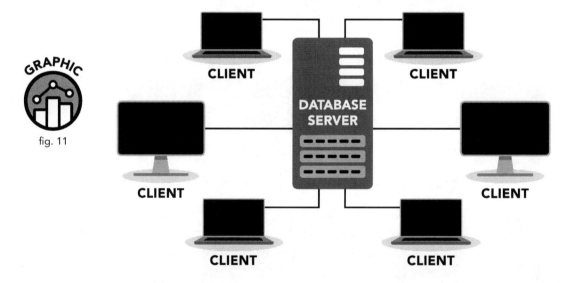

GRAPHIC

fig. 11

In this centralized architecture, most database management is conducted in one place: the server. The client device sends a request for data, called a query, to the database on the server, which then runs the query and returns a result to the client.

This client-server architecture is the dominant model for data management in most industries, including banking. But what makes this database architecture useful and powerful also makes it vulnerable. Anyone who has the right credentials can access a database. Customer login information can be stolen, or access can be hacked open. Payment information can also be pilfered, and malware—malicious software—can be installed that can cause real damage to business operations.

Centralized authority also means that controlling access is limited to the hands of a few and can be subject to bias and errors. It can create severe bottlenecks, too, if granting access rights is entirely manual and the capacity of administrators is constrained.

Peer-to-Peer Database Architecture

In this alternative architecture, databases can be distributed among several servers. One advantage of this design is that if one computer fails, copies of the database are available on other computers. All copies of the database are synchronized through a process called *replication*. This means that when changes occur on one copy, all the connected copies are updated. These distributed databases still act as a single, central server.

A peer-to-peer database structure takes the distributed setup a step further, by eliminating the administrative function. In this architecture, there is no centralized authority issuing permissions from a position of higher authority: power is *decentralized* and the databases are distributed to client computers. There is no server.

PEER-TO-PEER NETWORK

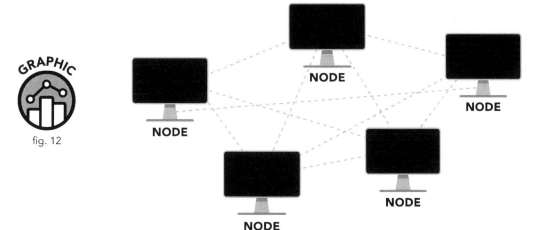
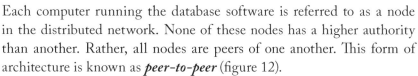

fig. 12

Each computer running the database software is referred to as a node in the distributed network. None of these nodes has a higher authority than another. Rather, all nodes are peers of one another. This form of architecture is known as *peer-to-peer* (figure 12).

In place of an administrative hierarchy, peer-to-peer architecture is governed by a set of rules in the software that must always be followed. What makes such a peer-to-peer network a viable means for financial transactions? The technology known as *blockchain*.

Though it's not essential for this study, you can listen to my brief summary on the differences between centralized, decentralized, and distributed computer networks in this short clip.

To watch the Quick Clip, use the camera on your mobile phone to scan the QR code or visit the link below.

or www.quickclips.io/crypto-1

SCAN ME   VISIT URL

Blockchain: A New Type of Database

So, what is this blockchain technology you've heard so much about? At its heart, a blockchain is a new type of database with a specific network architecture. It leverages the positive elements of a traditional database and reinvents other elements in order to overcome existing challenges. By redesigning these systems, blockchain technology creates a completely new platform for innovation.

Although it doesn't use the full word, only the term "block," the Bitcoin paper describes the blockchain concept. This version of blockchain was built when Bitcoin came into being. As the *New York Times* put it, "At a very basic level, blockchains are shared databases that store and verify information in a cryptographically secure way."[1]

The Blockchain Difference

The information stored in a cryptocurrency-based blockchain is a record of all monetary transactions that have occurred. No physical money is needed. (If this seems unusual or confusing, consider that far more fiat currency exists as records in centralized government, bank, and other databases than in the physical form of banknotes and coins. In other words, most conventional money only exists electronically.)

A blockchain database that contains all transactions is called a *full node*. These nodes, in addition to containing all data, deliver data to other nodes, and ensure that new blocks are valid.

This is the kind of detail that raises objections from Tori Forrest's father, Peter, a corporate lawyer with a legal mindset. If there's no central authority, Peter reasons, what's to prevent participants from claiming they have more crypto in their account than they actually do?

In so many words, Peter is bringing up both the double-spend and Byzantine Generals problems. The underlying question about double-spending is, how do we stop people from claiming to have more money than they actually do? And it boils down further: how can you trust the individuals in the network—whether they're Byzantine generals or Bitcoin investors—not to cheat?

Nakamoto's answer is that you don't. Blockchain queues up all the crypto transactions on its network, validates them, and then adds them to distributed copies of the ledger, without the need to personally trust any of the participants. It's the underlying process or code that ensures integrity. This is why blockchain is referred to as a ***trustless system***.

The Meaning of Blockchain

Before exploring the mechanism that allows you to trust in this trustless system, it may be illuminating to explain how blockchain was given its name. The term "block" might bring to mind an image of building blocks, but in this case, it refers to blocks of data. These data include updates to a running ledger, a documentation of transactions made. Transactions and other data are grouped into a distinct block that includes a linkage to the block that immediately preceded it, thereby forming a chain (figure 13).

A cryptocurrency's blockchain contains a record of all the transactions in that crypto since the time it was created. That is, when new transactions occur, a group of them are collected in what will, once they are validated, become the next block in the chain. Each new block is timestamped and cryptographically linked to the previous block via a process I explain in detail in chapter 3.

BLOCKCHAIN BASICS

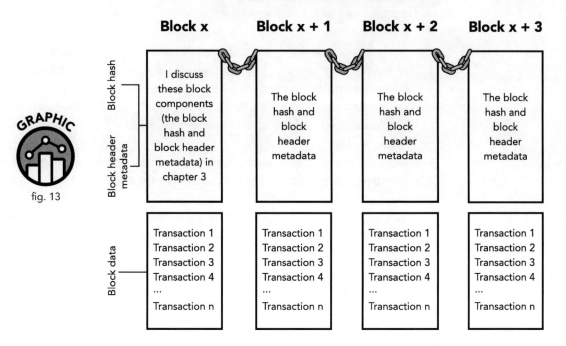

GRAPHIC

fig. 13

The Immutability of Blockchain

In a centralized database, the central authority can add, remove, update, or delete records. For instance, when Lynn Forrest gets a new patient, and she needs to add that patient to her database, she can easily do so. Similarly, if a patient leaves the practice, she can easily delete them from her database.

It's not possible to alter the data in a blockchain's previous blocks in this way. Blockchain is *immutable* because no one can change blocks once they have been validated and linked into the chain. This is what's known as an "append-only" data structure. So how are blocks validated in the first place?

Validating Transactions through Consensus Mechanisms

The blockchain design in the Bitcoin paper emerged as a way to enable a viable cryptocurrency by solving the double-spend problem. The fundamental issue here was trust. The magic of blockchain is that it ensures trust in transactions without a centralized authority vetting and approving them. Or, rather, it bypasses the need for trust.

Blockchain does this through what's known as a consensus mechanism. Establishing consensus—agreement by all parties in a transaction—is a nontrivial problem, as anyone who's tried to get a group of people to agree on where to go for lunch knows. The type of consensus applicable here does not rely on people; rather, it's entirely software-driven.

Tori Forrest has convinced her family to invest in cryptocurrency on a trial basis. As an inducement, she has offered to give her father, mother, and brother each a starting stake of a hundred units of a cryptocurrency called Cowrie. (Like the Forrest family, Cowrie is fictional; no need to research whether it might be a good investment!) She initiates these transactions on her computer, in order to send 100 cowries from her account to each of her three family members.

This is only the beginning of the transaction, which the consensus mechanism must now validate. There are several steps that take place to protect from the double-spend problem. Together they comprise the ***consensus mechanism*** that ensures these transactions are valid and permissible. The most common type of consensus mechanism is called ***proof-of-work***, which was originally developed to validate Bitcoin transactions and is outlined in Nakamoto's white paper.

Tori's transactions are first sent to a holding area called the ***memory pool*** or ***mempool***, where they await assignment to a potential new block in the blockchain. Before they are added to the blockchain, they must be validated through the consensus mechanism. In this instance, Cowrie uses proof-of-work.

Proof-of-work involves nodes competing in a mathematical contest that awards the winner—the node that first solves a complex equation—some free crypto. These nodes are those that choose to participate in proof-of-work simply for the potential reward. Generally, the node with the highest computing performance will succeed in the contest and win the reward. The winning solution to the contest is confirmed by the other nodes in the network, thus reaching consensus. In chapter 3, I walk through this process at a more technical level.

Considerable computing power—and in turn, electrical power—is expended in trying to win the reward. This is the "work" in proof-of-work. It's proof that the necessary effort was expended to approve the new transactions in the block. The considerable work involved in validation is also a highly effective disincentive to bad behavior, such as attempts to validate false transactions. It's literally not worth the very considerable effort to try to game the system.

DETOUR

The Longest Chain. Blocks are appended to the blockchain one by one. It's possible, however, that two mining nodes might solve and begin circulating different blocks at the same time. When this happens, the blockchain temporarily creates a new chain. Blocks begin to be added to both the main chain and the new chain, which is unsustainable and must be resolved.

The solution to this dilemma is known as "the longest chain." If another block is appended to block A's chain first, then block A and its subsequent blocks are considered part of the blockchain. If another block is appended to block B's chain first, then block B and its subsequent blocks are considered part of the blockchain. The longest chain gets priority because of the assumption that miners have devoted more energy into that set of blocks and thus it is most likely to be the valid chain.

DETOUR

The Risk of a 51% Attack. Under the longest-chain rule, it could still be possible for a malicious miner or group of miners to subvert the system and create fraudulent transactions. They would need to control over half the system's hash rate (computing power), which would give them the ability to produce blocks faster than anyone else. This would allow them to outpace any other longest chain.

This threat is known as a 51% attack, or majority attack. Because they would be able to rewrite the blockchain's history, such an attacker could reverse transactions, double-spending crypto they had previously spent.

However, a 51% attack, while theoretically feasible, is not economically advantageous. Attackers would need to invest billions of dollars to acquire that much hashing power, and the potential gain would be comparatively small. On reflection, any rational miner would reject the attempt. And it would be most unlikely that an irrational miner could buy the kind of power such an attack would require.

Crypto advocate Tori Forrest is determined to educate her family about this new technology. She opens up accounts on an exchange for her father, mother, and brother and then sends each of them 100 cowries. The process, simplified here, takes the following steps:

1. Using her *crypto wallet*, which I discuss shortly, Tori specifies the amounts and destination addresses for the cowries she wants to send.

2. She submits the request to the Cowrie blockchain.

3. Her request is queued up for processing on the cowrie blockchain.

4. Miners place her request and other pending requests into a block and compete to validate the transactions by performing a complex mathematical calculation. I discuss mining again in this chapter, and in varying degrees of depth throughout this text.

5. Relatively quickly, one miner wins the validation competition and then broadcasts the solution to the network.

6. Once the solution is confirmed by the network, this new block of transactions, including Tori's request, is added to the cowrie blockchain.

7. Her father, mother, and brother now each have 100 cowries assigned to them, and Tori has 300 cowries less assigned to her. The process is complete.

Public and Private Keys

I want to zero in for the moment on one specific transaction. Let's take Tori Forrest's gift of 100 cowries to her brother Alan. How does she send that amount of crypto to him, and how does he receive it? The answer is through a paired set of *public* and *private* keys.

To understand what this means, think of Alan's account in terms of physical mail. A public key—a unique series of letters and numbers—is a lot like a mailbox address at a residence or business. In the physical world, if you want to send something to someone's mailbox you need the street address of the building. Similarly, public keys are the address you would use to send someone cryptocurrency.

If a public key is analogous to a physical mailbox address, then a private key is akin to the physical key to opening a locked mailbox. Only the owner has the key, so only the owner can access what's been put inside. In other words, Tori or anyone else who knows Alan's public key can assign crypto to him, the way you could send someone a letter or a package. But only Alan can use the crypto that's been granted to him.

So, to recap: Tori sends the cowries to Alan by signing the cowries with her private key (similar to opening up her account and making a withdrawal) and then using Alan's public key as the new address for the cowries. Once the block is mined, the cowries are associated with Alan.

Unlike the public key, the private key must remain a secret. One way of considering the private key is as the equivalent of a password. However, unlike a password, a private key does not involve or rely on a central authority. That's also why a private key can't be retrieved if it's lost. Once it's gone, it's gone for good, along with your access to your crypto recorded on a blockchain. This has happened on many occasions, so taking care with your private key is of utmost importance.

Public and private keys are cryptographically linked. First, a private key is assigned by some authority or randomly generated using any number of software tools. Many of these tools are free and can be found easily online. Then a public key is created from the private key using one of a number of complex cryptographic algorithms—a popular choice is called elliptic curve cryptography—making it essentially impossible to derive the private key from the public one.

Your Wallet

Should you decide to participate in cryptocurrency, your keys are stored in what's called a *crypto wallet*, or just *wallet* for short. These wallets don't store the cryptocurrency themselves. Each crypto transaction is recorded in the cryptocurrency's blockchain. What's in your wallet are the private keys that prove your ownership of your crypto.

There are several types of wallets. You could decide to write your keys down on a piece of paper—on what's called a "paper wallet." After all, keys are just a series of letters and numbers. But if you lost the piece of paper, you would no longer have access to crypto associated with those keys—as some people who have lost or forgotten their private keys have discovered.

Intuitively, electronic wallets are more reliable than paper ones. There are two kinds: hardware and software. A hardware wallet is a physical device such as a thumb drive. Encryption and passcodes can protect access to the device. If the wallet is lost, depending on the type of device, the vendor can sometimes recover the keys and other information stored in it. You can see in figure 14 what a typical hardware wallet looks like.

A software wallet, on the other hand, is an application you access via your computer or laptop, or an app for your smartphone, as shown in figure 15.

Hardware Crypto Wallet by Ledger, named among the "Top 10 Cryptocurrency Wallets …
in 2023" by Analytics Insight. The wallet can connect to your computer via a USB cable.

A software wallet.

During cryptocurrency's beginnings, users were responsible for generating keys and keeping track of their holdings. These days, crypto users generally rely on their wallets and third-party *cryptocurrency exchanges* to handle the creation and storage of their keys. I discuss exchanges at length in chapter 8. Figure 16 summarizes the full process of Tori providing 100 cowries to Alan.

CRYPTOCURRENCY TRANSACTION PROCESS
Tori sends 100 cowries to Alan

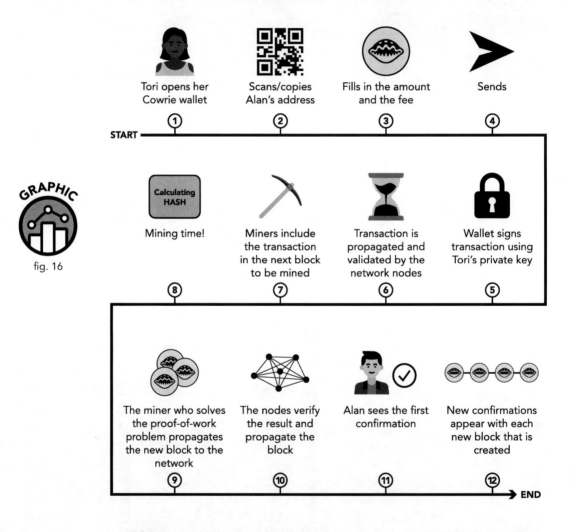

fig. 16

START

1. Tori opens her Cowrie wallet
2. Scans/copies Alan's address
3. Fills in the amount and the fee
4. Sends

8. Mining time!
7. Miners include the transaction in the next block to be mined
6. Transaction is propagated and validated by the network nodes
5. Wallet signs transaction using Tori's private key

9. The miner who solves the proof-of-work problem propagates the new block to the network
10. The nodes verify the result and propagate the block
11. Alan sees the first confirmation
12. New confirmations appear with each new block that is created

END

If this seems like a lot of work just to send some crypto to family members, remember that conventional bank transfers, while familiar, are also quite complicated. If you've ever set up a direct deposit, you have some idea of what I mean; it requires an account number, a routing number, and sometimes verifying micro-transactions to make sure the account information is correct.

Mining for Crypto

The nodes that choose to do the work in the problem-solving contests used to validate blocks are called *miners*, meant to evoke miners of gold and other precious metals. Gold can be mined only with a considerable amount of physical work; similarly, proof-of-work requires significant computing power.

Miners are nodes in the network; in other words, they're computers, not people.

Why do miners bother to do this work? Or, more accurately, why do individuals or companies bother to invest in extremely expensive, high-powered mining computers? It's because they are rewarded for their efforts with the network's cryptocurrency, as well as with fees that accompany the transactions in the block they are mining. Depending on the cryptocurrency involved, some of these rewards can be quite substantial.

In chapter 3, I discuss the details of the contest miners participate in as part of the proof-of-work consensus mechanism. It's the most complex of the cryptocurrency processes and deserves special attention.

Without using the word "blockchain," the 2008 Bitcoin paper described decentralization and proof-of-work as integral to a whole new way of verifying transactions in a distributed ledger without a central authority—which is why so many are comfortable describing Nakamoto's white paper as a work of genius, despite the overuse of that word.

There is one catch to this game-changer. The extremely powerful computing systems that provide the "work" in proof-of-work use a lot of electric power—which means that, when all is said and done, the proof-of-work system may have unintended, negative effects on the real-world environment. I explore this problem in greater detail in Chapter 11.

Because it's so effective, proof-of-work remains, at least for now, a widely used crypto consensus mechanism. It's the one Bitcoin uses, for example. And it's the consensus mechanism that Cowrie, the crypto that the Forrest family is investing in, uses as well.

When Alan Forrest learns Cowrie cryptocurrency runs on proof-of-work, he impatiently asks his sister Tori why she couldn't have given them crypto that runs on an alternate consensus mechanism. In fact, there are several other consensus mechanisms aside from proof-of-work, such as proof-of-authority and proof-of-activity. The second most popular after proof-of-work is called proof-of-stake, which I discuss in chapter 5. If you're interested, several of these other consensus mechanisms are listed and discussed in appendix II.

Chapter Recap

» Traditional databases run on centralized networks.

» Bitcoin and other cryptocurrencies run on decentralized, peer-to-peer networks.

» New transactions create new blocks, which can only be appended to the blockchain if they're validated.

» Consensus mechanisms, the most common of which is proof-of-work, perform this validation.

» A public key is derived from its paired private key by a cryptographic process.

» The keys that unlock your cryptocurrency are stored in a "crypto wallet" or "wallet."

» Proof-of-work miners validate new blocks by participating in a mathematical contest.

| 3 |

The Role of Cryptography

Chapter Overview
- » Exploring cryptography
- » Hashing explained
- » Blockchain linkage and immutability
- » Winning the game of nonces

The words *cryptocurrency* and *crypto* have become part of everyday language. But most people use the words without knowing what they mean. Examining their roots and origins can offer a better understanding of cryptocurrency as a concept.

The word cryptocurrency is derived from ***cryptography***, a related term with Greek origin that roughly translates to "secret writing."

In this chapter, I walk you through how cryptography enables cryptocurrency to work.

Cryptography 101: Secret Writing

Though the Bitcoin white paper introduced the concept, the word "cryptocurrency" does not appear in the document. Instead, the paper says, "What is needed is an electronic payment system based on cryptographic proof instead of trust, allowing any two willing parties to transact directly with each other without the need for a trusted third party." The word "cryptography" is itself derived from two ancient Greek words: *kryptos* meaning "hidden" or "secret," and *graphein* meaning "to write." Hence the definition "secret writing." Writing in a secret code is called ***encryption*** and deciphering that code is ***decryption***, these are terms you may recognize from their uses related to computers.

The term *cryptocurrency* is shorthand for what Nakamoto was describing: a *crypto*graphically-enabled electronic payment system becomes *cryptocurrency*.

Substitution Codes

Cryptography may summon images of spies, espionage, and communicating in a secret code that enemies can't understand. The codes can also be called *cryptograms* or *ciphers*. Only those with access to the key that unlocks the cryptographic code are able to decipher or decrypt secret messages written in it. Codebreaking is deciphering a code whose key you don't have access to and need to figure out.

There are any number of ways to create cryptograms or ciphers. Some, like those referred to as *substitution ciphers*, are relatively straightforward. For instance, you could substitute the next letter in the alphabet for the actual letter: *a* becomes *b*, *b* becomes *c*, and so on. In this cipher, the word "cipher" becomes "djqifs." Or you could substitute the letter that comes three letters afterward, in which case "cipher" would be written "flskhu." This would be an easy code to crack.

More complex substitution ciphers can be more difficult to decrypt. There is a cryptogram featured in master-of-suspense Edgar Allan Poe's story "The Gold-Bug," written in 1843, which describes the location of hidden treasure. Poe is said to have invented detective fiction. While he didn't invent cryptography and code-breaking, he did help to popularize it. The message in "The Gold-Bug" looks like figure 17:

fig.17

53‡‡†305))6*;4826)4‡.)4‡);806*;48†8¶60))85;1‡)
;:‡*8†83(88)5*†;46(;88*96*?;8)*‡(;485);5*†2:*‡(;4
956*2(5*——4)8¶8*;4069285);)6†8)4‡‡;1(‡9;48081;
8:8‡1;48†85;4)485†528806*81(‡9;48;(88;4(‡?34;48
)4‡;161;:188;‡?;

Cryptogram in Poe's "The Gold-Bug."

fig. 18

LETTER	a	b	c	d	e	f	g	h	i	l	m	n	o	p	r	s	t	u	v	y
SYMBOL	5	2	-	†	8	1	3	4	6	)	9	*	‡	.	(	)	;	?	¶	:

Figure 18 shows the key to deciphering or decrypting the message, with each letter corresponding to the symbol or number that replaces it. As you can see, *a* is coded as 5, *b* is translated to 2, and so on.

The deciphered message reads:

A good glass in the bishop's hostel in the devil's seat
forty-one degrees and thirteen minutes northeast and by north
main branch seventh limb east side
shoot from the left eye of the death's-head
a bee line from the tree through the shot fifty feet out.

Hashing

In a world where security is of the utmost importance, substitution ciphers can no longer do the job they were originally intended to do. For example, they can often be broken by *brute force attacks*: trying every possibility in turn, usually with the help of a computer.

A particularly useful method of creating more secure ciphers is called hashing. A **hash** is a one-way cryptographic method that takes an input and produces an output that is almost impossible to decipher. This means that hackers and other bad actors who might intercept a message en route to its intended destination or access it in a database will be unable to make sense of it.

Hashes are created by computer algorithms containing complex mathematics. The hashing process takes an input of any length and transforms it into a garbled-looking output. The new output has a fixed length.

Hashing Algorithms

So how do these complicated hashing algorithms actually work? If all you want to know about the use of cryptography in cryptocurrency is *what* the cryptographic process is, you're all set: it's a way of encoding data that is effectively impossible for a person to decipher. If you want to know more about what's involved with this process, this section goes into greater detail.

Some hashing algorithms are designated as SHA-1, SHA-2 and so on, where SHA stands, quite logically, for "Secure Hash Algorithm." Bitcoin uses a version of SHA-2, which is also known as SHA-256. Many cryptocurrencies employ SHA-256, though some use other algorithms.

The 256 in SHA-256 designates the number of bits—short for binary digits, which can either be 0 or 1—in the hash. The hash output is initially a series of 256 bits: 1s and 0s in different combinations. Each set of four bits represents one of 16 characters in the hexadecimal numbering system, which uses the numbers 0 through 9 and the first six letters of the alphabet (A, B, C, D, E, F). The following table, figure 19, shows how binary bits convert to hexadecimal characters.

fig. 19

BINARY	HEXADECIMAL
0000	0
0001	1
0010	2
0011	3
0100	4
0101	5
0110	6
0111	7
1000	8
1001	9
1010	A
1011	B
1100	C
1101	D
1110	E
1111	F

This conversion allows the SHA-256 hash to be reduced to 64 characters without losing any meaning, while improving performance efficiency in computing, which is highly valued.

In short, the process goes like this: an input of any length is hashed to produce a 256-bit string of 0s and 1s. That string of 0s and 1s is converted to hexadecimal, resulting in a 64-character code. You can see examples of the initial input and final output in figure 20.

fig. 20

INPUT	OUTPUT (HASH)
hi	8f434346648f6b96df89dda901c5176b10a6d83961dd3c1ac88b59b2dc327aa4
100 cowries	e1cd2fc7749fd7b9b577fd6166a05c042a29520d83fe7a223e190b9857bc6ccb
101 cowries	4e2439b663ef22a341e8d8f13d9f1b3aaddc55c51005bfa270342456b8e58601

Notice that the hash outputs for each input are completely different; the only constant is that they are always 64 characters. The inputs "100 cowries" and "101 cowries" are very similar, but their outputs are completely distinct. For a given input, the output will always be the same series of hexadecimal characters. There isn't an easily identifiable pattern that marks them as similar; they're as different from each other as "100 cowries" is different from the unrelated greeting of "hi." The hash for a specific input will always be the same, but it will not be identifiable based on any other inputs. In other words, you couldn't take the hash of "101 cowries" and decrypt it (arriving at "101 cowries"), even if you knew the output for "100 cowries". This is what separates hashing from less sophisticated methods of cryptography such as substitution codes.

Hashing and Blockchains

Hashing an input to create a new fixed-length output is a complicated process mathematically, but it's particularly important to understand what it does, rather than how it works, because it has multiple applications within a system of cryptocurrency. It is used in the linking of blocks on the blockchain *and* in the process of mining for new crypto.

The Role of Hashing in Linking Blocks

Recalling figure 13 from chapter 2, you may have noticed that the links from one block to the next are forged along a specific block component known as the **block headers**. Think of the body of a block as containing the transactions themselves—the data. The block header contains information *about* those transactions—the metadata. You may be familiar with metadata in the context of other digital files. One common example is music: If you have a digital file of a song, the song itself is the data. The metadata is any attached information *about* the song: the artist, album, year of release, and so on.

I'm going to point you to an image here (figure 21) that will diagram the basic anatomy of a block and specify some major components.

THE ANATOMY OF A BLOCK

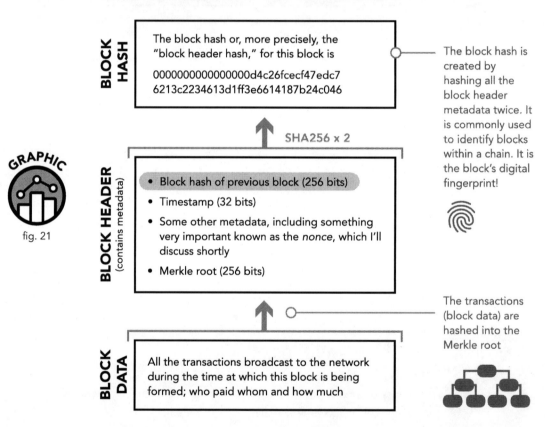

GRAPHIC

fig. 21

BLOCK HASH

The block hash or, more precisely, the "block header hash," for this block is

0000000000000000d4c26fcecf47edc7 6213c2234613d1ff3e6614187b24c046

The block hash is created by hashing all the block header metadata twice. It is commonly used to identify blocks within a chain. It is the block's digital fingerprint!

SHA256 x 2

BLOCK HEADER (contains metadata)

- Block hash of previous block (256 bits)
- Timestamp (32 bits)
- Some other metadata, including something very important known as the *nonce*, which I'll discuss shortly
- Merkle root (256 bits)

The transactions (block data) are hashed into the Merkle root

BLOCK DATA

All the transactions broadcast to the network during the time at which this block is being formed; who paid whom and how much

In a blockchain, each block's header includes the previous block's block header hash (block hash). The block header also includes additional metadata, such as the timestamp and something called a Merkle root. A **Merkle root** is itself a hash of all the block's transactions and is used to speed up transaction verification. Put simply, the header for each block contains encrypted information about the transactions it contains *and* encrypted information about the previous block in the chain. Attempts to fraudulently alter the contents of blocks that already possess a validated block hash (i.e., a block that has been mined) will generate a wholly separate chain, one on which proof-of-work consensus has not been built. The altered block will in turn corrupt the block hashes that come after it, even if all of the accurate transaction data is maintained; the chain will be hopelessly out of sync with the network consensus. Simply put, attempts to defraud the blockchain do nothing but pave a long road to nowhere. The exception to this would be a fraudulent blockchain that somehow became more heavily validated than the authentic chain. This is the *51% attack* that I discussed in chapter 2.

In its elegance the blockchain architecture permits a clear, singular, and practically incorruptible link from block to block (see figure 22).

fig. 22

THE ANATOMY OF THE BLOCKCHAIN

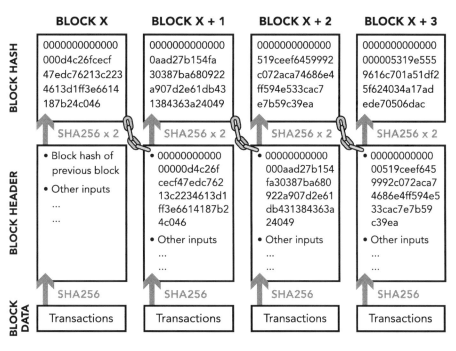

Because of hashing, each new block is cryptographically bound to the previous block; it's therefore not possible to interfere with the data they contain.

NOTE

To keep it simple, think back to the idea of a digital music file. Imagine metadata on a song file that indicates its position on an album or an established playlist. The block header contains similar information, establishing where in the blockchain it belongs. (The major difference is that metadata on a music file can usually be edited easily. The blockchain cannot.)

Hashing and the Proof-of-Work Crypto Mining Competition

Hashing again comes into play in the process of mining for new crypto. I touched on mining and proof-of-work in the previous chapter, and I told you I'd be breaking it down in greater detail here. What follows is a walk-through of the process that takes place when the creation of a new block gets underway. At this point, the previous block has been created, and the block hash has been successfully generated. So, what happens as the next block is mined and added to the chain?

» **Phase 1**: Transactions are broadcast to the network, coming in from all across the world. They are destined to be memorialized and permanently archived in our new block, but for now they are stored in a digital holding area called the *memory pool* as they await assignment to a block. They will eventually be hashed into the *Merkle root*, one of the data inputs used to form the current block's block hash.

» **Phase 2**: The blockchain system then generates what's known as the *target hash* (sometimes referred to as simply "the target"). Here's where the miners come in. They are going to compete to generate a hash whose value must be equal to or less than the value of the target. How do they do this? By guessing at a number. That's right, miners compete to identify a suitable value for an additional datum known as a *nonce*, which, when added to the block header, will result in a hash that satisfies the target (figure 23).

DETOUR

The Difficulty Target. As seen in figure 23, this is a 32-bit number generated by the system, which determines how difficult it will be for miners to successfully find a suitable nonce. The system is configured to use the difficulty target for governance purposes. Bitcoin, for instance, per Nakamoto's design, wants an average mining rate of ten minutes per block. If blocks are being mined too fast, the value of the difficulty target will be lowered, so the system will generate target hashes that are tougher to solve (like a limbo bar, a lower value of the difficulty target is actually more difficult). Similarly, if blocks are taking too long to mine, then the system will increase the value of the difficulty target, making mining easier.

THE ANATOMY OF A BLOCK IN PROGRESS

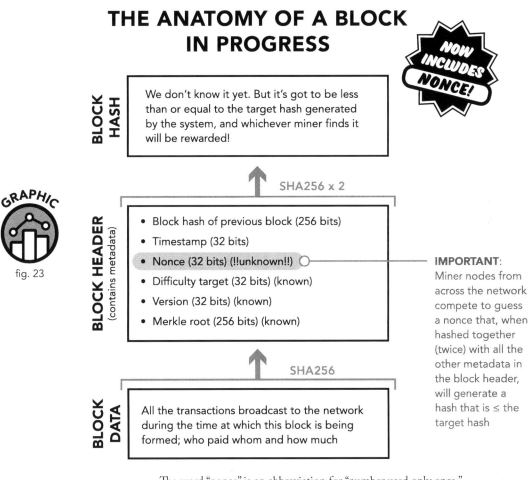

NOW INCLUDES NONCE!

BLOCK HASH

We don't know it yet. But it's got to be less than or equal to the target hash generated by the system, and whichever miner finds it will be rewarded!

SHA256 x 2

BLOCK HEADER (contains metadata)

- Block hash of previous block (256 bits)
- Timestamp (32 bits)
- Nonce (32 bits) (!!unknown!!)
- Difficulty target (32 bits) (known)
- Version (32 bits) (known)
- Merkle root (256 bits) (known)

IMPORTANT: Miner nodes from across the network compete to guess a nonce that, when hashed together (twice) with all the other metadata in the block header, will generate a hash that is ≤ the target hash

SHA256

BLOCK DATA

All the transactions broadcast to the network during the time at which this block is being formed; who paid whom and how much

GRAPHIC

fig. 23

The word "nonce" is an abbreviation for "number used only once."

DETOUR

The Version. This datum in the block header is merely the current version number for the blockchain software/protocol. It's used to track upgrades.

» **Phase 3**: Miners continue to guess in the competition to find the winning nonce. Figure 24 shows a miner's basic execution of this guessing game.

GRAPHIC

fig. 24

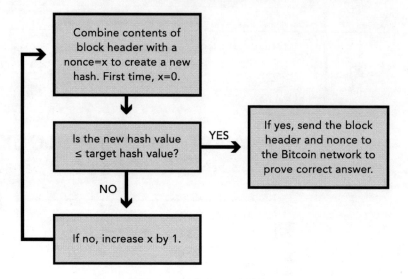

It seems simple enough, but this process is done on a massive scale. Across the globe, the estimated 50,000 nodes on the Bitcoin network make about 190 quintillion guesses per second.[1]

» **Phase 4**: When a miner supplies a nonce that results in a new block header hash value that is less than or equal to the target hash value, they present the winning nonce to the network, which collectively verifies it, to prove they expended work—hence proof-of-work.

» **The Epilogue**: Here is a step-by-step account of what happens after the nonce is discovered:

- Once the correct hash, incorporating the nonce, is discovered, the new block is mined.
- The newly mined block is then broadcast through the network.
- The other miner nodes in the network, utilizing the winner's nonce, confirm that the solution is correct.
- If the solution is correct, the new block is appended to the blockchain and the winning miner node is rewarded with crypto.
- The hash resulting from the winning nonce becomes the new block hash.
- The new block is then reproduced on every full node in the network.

REMEMBER

Once a new block is added to the blockchain, the transactions in the block are *immutable*. That means they can't be altered or changed.

A miner is a computer that performs the computations in proof-of-work.

If you'd like a brief recap on the topic of the nonce—what it is and what it does—then check out this short video clip.

To watch the Quick Clip, use the camera on your mobile phone to scan the QR code or visit the link below.

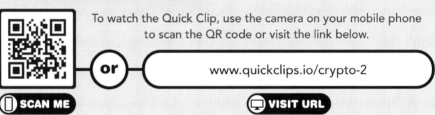

or www.quickclips.io/crypto-2

SCAN ME   **VISIT URL**

I want to emphasize again that finding the nonce is no easy task. One reason is that the target hash begins with a certain number of so-called "leading zeroes." The more zeroes at the beginning, the greater the difficulty of arriving at a hash that's less than or equal to the target. All in all, the chances of a Bitcoin miner coming up with the correct nonce on the first try is one in 66 billion trillion. This is why extremely high-powered computers that utilize considerable electric power are used to mine cryptocurrency. Some miners are capable of testing up to a hundred trillion nonces a second. The solution is ultimately reached by brute force.

I hope you enjoyed getting a closer look under the hood of blockchain. In part 2, *The Cryptocurrency Universe*, I ask you to step out of the service shop and into the showroom as we examine cryptocurrencies like Bitcoin, Ethereum, and others in detail.

Chapter Recap

» The word "cryptocurrency" derives from "cryptography," which means "secret writing."

» Cryptocurrency relies on a type of cryptography known as "hashing."

» Hashing is integral to establishing new blocks for the blockchain and to the mining process.

THE CRYPTOCURRENCY UNIVERSE

| 4 |

Bitcoin

Chapter Overview
- » Origins of Bitcoin
- » How Bitcoin is used
- » Forks and why they matter
- » Bitcoin pros and cons

The technological architecture of cryptocurrency described in part 1 of this book is intended as an explanation of how crypto works in general, but it is based most directly on the world's most popular and best-known crypto, Bitcoin. Some people will even use "Bitcoin" and "cryptocurrency" interchangeably, and given Bitcoin's dominance, that's understandable. Though there were attempts at a viable digital currency prior to Nakamoto's paper or Bitcoin, neither cryptocurrency nor blockchain as we know them would exist in quite the same way without Bitcoin. Think of it like Kleenex or Vaseline; brand names so well-known that they became synonymous with products like tissue and petroleum jelly, respectively.

As of 2023, Bitcoin is the most important cryptocurrency in existence. As of this writing, its value accounts for 40% of the value of the entire crypto market; Ethereum (discussed in chapter 5) is the closest runner-up at 20%, leaving more than 19,000 other cryptos to comprise the remainder of the market. Remarkably, nearly a quarter of these other cryptos were derived from the code that powers the Bitcoin network. In this chapter, I drill down into the current story and future prospects of this iconic coin.

What Is Bitcoin?

Bitcoin is the digital asset built on the rails of Satoshi Nakamoto's envisioned distributed ledger that we now refer to as blockchain technology. The name Bitcoin is derived from its singular component part—the "bit." Bits are binary digits, 1s and 0s, the basic units of information used to power the digital revolution.

Like other cryptos, and unlike fiat currencies, Bitcoin has no physical form apart from artistic representations (figure 25). It is merely the unit of account used to define transactions that occur on the Bitcoin network. The **Bitcoin network** is the worldwide collection of nodes, such as laptops, smartphones, and server computers, that run the Bitcoin client software. The software connects the node to a peer-to-peer (admin-free) distributed ledger (discussed in chapter 2) on which all Bitcoin transactions are logged, verified, and organized into cryptographically linked and chronologically ordered blocks.

fig. 25

Bitcoin has a recognizable logo that appears on the internet,
but it doesn't appear on any actual physical currency.

The prevailing style conventions hold that when referring to the crypto itself—the units of currency—bitcoin is spelled with a lowercase "b," whereas the capital "B" is used when referring to the larger Bitcoin network. Units of the currency can also use the abbreviation "BTC," where "50 bitcoins" can be written as "50 BTC."

The Bitcoin client software is **open source**, which means that anyone may inspect the code, modify their own version, or distribute it. Anyone may also, of course, download the software and host a node using their own computing resources, though you are not required to host a node in order to invest in and use Bitcoin. As of this writing, minimum system requirements for hosting a node include 350GB of disk space and the ability to download 500MB of data per day.[1] For reference, there are some laptops that only include 350GB of disk space total, and 500MB is roughly the equivalent of the data downloaded to stream music for 10 hours.

Ownership of Bitcoin or any other crypto is defined by ownership of your private key and a blockchain's recording of the amount of crypto associated with your public key.

Some users prefer to host their own full node because, for example, they want to have the ability to broadcast transactions directly to the Bitcoin network without using an intermediary such as an exchange. Moreover, they desire exclusive and unmediated control over their own private keys.

MY TAKE

A Bitcoin user who hosts a full node may be motivated by security. If you broadcast your transactions directly to the network (without going through an exchange) then you, in theory, minimize the exposure of your private keys hosted on a platform that you don't control, thereby reducing the risk of the keys being lost or stolen.

The Origins of Bitcoin

In a way, the birth of Bitcoin as cryptocurrency's flagship asset is the result of a perfect storm; it was the right innovation at the right time. As described in chapter 1, the Bitcoin network was conceived of and born in the midst of the Great Recession, which lasted from 2007 to 2009, a time when trust in traditional financial institutions was at an extraordinary low. But timing alone did not account for Bitcoin's breakthrough. Other key factors included Bitcoin's solution to the double-spend problem (discussed in chapter 1), its elegant application of the distributed ledger concept, and the open-source nature of its software. Some of Bitcoin's significant inaugural milestones are depicted in figure 26.

A RECAP OF THE BITCOIN LAUNCH TIMELINE

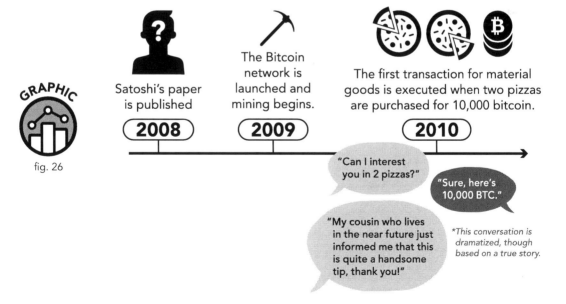

GRAPHIC

fig. 26

Satoshi's paper is published

2008

The Bitcoin network is launched and mining begins.

2009

The first transaction for material goods is executed when two pizzas are purchased for 10,000 bitcoin.

2010

"Can I interest you in 2 pizzas?"

"Sure, here's 10,000 BTC."

"My cousin who lives in the near future just informed me that this is quite a handsome tip, thank you!"

This conversation is dramatized, though based on a true story.

Blockchain emerged as the backend technology to enable Bitcoin. The blockchain concept, as articulated in the white paper, introduced other key elemental concepts into the perfect storm, such as the concept of immutability (see chapter 2).

Here's a quick run-through of some of the other key events that precipitated and assisted Bitcoin's rise to fame.[2]

» **August 18, 2008**: While the Bitcoin white paper was still two and a half months away from being released, the domain bitcoin.org is registered. The registering service used is called anonymousspeech.com, and, as the name implies, it was a service that emphasized privacy, allowing customers to register domains without having to list their names on any public records such as ICANN (the Internet Corporation for Assigned Names and Numbers).

Bitcoin.org remains a key resource for Bitcoin enthusiasts. As of this writing, it is one of the sites where the Bitcoin client software, "Bitcoin Core," may be downloaded.

» **October 31, 2008**: The famous white paper penned by the pseudonymous Satoshi Nakamoto makes its debut on a cryptography-themed mailing list hosted by metzdowd.com.

» **January 3, 2009**: Bitcoin's first block, known as the genesis block, is created containing 50 bitcoins.[3] These bitcoins are thought to be unspendable due to an anomaly in the computer code governing the blockchain. Bitcoin's actual spendable "money supply" began to accumulate with the mining of successive blocks that awarded winning miners with bitcoins they could actually spend (more on mining in chapter 11).

The winning miner's bitcoin allotment or block reward decreases every few years via an ongoing process called halving, whereby the new award amount is half of its previous value. While 50 BTC was the initial block reward value, it became 25 BTC after the first halving and 12.5 BTC after that. Halving occurs after every 210,000 blocks are added, which takes about four years. At the time of this writing the block reward is 6.25 BTC. Given the significant value of BTC, even 6.25 BTC is a handsome sum. But, as you'll learn in greater detail in chapter 11,

The software dictates that, since Bitcoin's inception, only 21 million bitcoins will ever be available to be mined. At the time of this writing the number of bitcoins already mined was just under 19 million. Due to *halving*, however, it is projected to take until the year 2140 for the remaining 2 million BTC to be awarded.[4]

» **January 9, 2009**: The first version of the Bitcoin software is released. Anyone may download, run, view, and suggest modifications to the open-source code.

» **February 6, 2010**: A prototype for a Bitcoin exchange is created by a forum user on a website called bitcointalk.org. The user, "dwdollar," seeks other forum members to test his prototype. Later that year, "The Bitcoin Market" is launched, allowing speculators to trade their fiat currency for bitcoins. One of the important benefits of having a working exchange is that it provides a means by which to value Bitcoin in terms of US dollars. The Bitcoin Market sought to treat Bitcoin as a commodity and to answer a very important question: how much are people willing to pay for ownership of a cryptocurrency? Cryptocurrency exchanges are covered in more depth in chapter 8.

» **May 22, 2010**: Known in the Bitcoin community as "Pizza Day," 5/22/10 is the day that Bitcoin is officially used as an instrument of commerce. A forum user on bitcointalk.org offered 10,000 BTC to anyone who could procure two pizzas for him. Someone took him up on it and arranged for the pizzas to be delivered. The 10,000 BTC that person received in compensation is now worth hundreds of millions of US dollars. Those were some mighty expensive pizzas!

» **Aug 15, 2010**: A vulnerability in the Bitcoin software is discovered and exploited by a hacker who creates a transaction awarding him with 184 billion bitcoins (well in excess of the 21 million cap that is built into the protocol). Once the breach is discovered, the greater Bitcoin community creates a "fork" in the blockchain to exclude the fraudulent transaction. I discuss forks later on in this chapter.

> » **February 9, 2011:** The value of one bitcoin reaches parity with the US dollar per the 1:1 exchange rate defined on a popular exchange called Mt. Gox. (See figure 27 for a bigger look at its price over the long term.)

NOTE

The Mt. Gox exchange went on to gain notoriety as the site of the biggest hack/heist in the history of cryptocurrency. Taking advantage of lax security around private keys, hackers were able to steal over 800,000 bitcoins (mostly from customers, and some from the company itself); that's around 7% of all bitcoins in existence at that time. At the time of this writing, an updated, comprehensive listing of cryptocurrency exchange hacks can be found at the following URL: www.hedgewithcrypto.com/cryptocurrency-exchange-hacks.

BITCOIN'S PRICE OVER THE LONG TERM

GRAPHIC

fig. 27

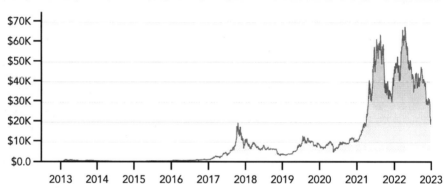

Bitcoin has come a long way since it was at 1:1 parity with the US dollar. Its price history is one of astounding growth but is marked with equally astounding volatility.

DETOUR

The Forrest Family: Using Bitcoin

Mr. Peter Forrest, our fictitious family's patriarch and principal breadwinner, is now 20 years into his career in corporate law, and he has seen enough. Major reputable financial institutions are rolling out cryptocurrency investment products. A handful of associates at his own law firm have already taken the plunge and made significant investments, mostly in Bitcoin—though a few have taken modest positions in other cryptocurrencies as well. Meanwhile, the small gift of cowries from his daughter Tori has done more than just hold its value; it has appreciated significantly. The FOMO (fear of missing out) is becoming too great to ignore. It's time, he thinks, to make a real investment, and Bitcoin seems a logical place to begin. At the next family dinner, Mr. Forrest shows up and brings with him an open mind.

"So, Alan, this crypto thing, it all began with Bitcoin, right? I'm thinking it's time for me to make a move into this stuff," Peter says.

"Hey!" says Alan with mock gratitude. "You've finally seen the light! I thought the day would never come."

"Well, I'm a big Peter Lynch fan. You know him? He's a famous investor—and I don't just like him because he's got a great first name. He's also got great ideas. One thing he says is that you have to know what you own and know why you own it. So if I'm going to invest in Bitcoin," Peter continues, "I need to know a little more about what I'm getting into and why."

Alan's sister Tori interjects. "Dad, Alan's still just in high school. He's never managed a portfolio or made a contribution to an IRA, or sold a bond in the aftermarket. He's not going to be able to explain to you why you should move 5% of your retirement assets into Bitcoin at the expense of your favorite mutual fund."

"I'm not asking Alan for investment advice," Peter clarifies. "I'm just asking him to describe Bitcoin. I want to know what it is. What's so funny?" Peter has noticed Alan beginning to laugh.

"I'm just thinking of Satoshi," says Alan, "wherever and whoever they may be, seeing what's become of that vision for Bitcoin. I'm sure it was never supposed to be like this."

"Like what?" Peter presses his son.

"Honestly, Dad?" says Alan. "I don't think Bitcoin was supposed to be something we'd be talking about as an investment option, like stocks or real estate."

The Intent of Bitcoin vs. the Reality

Alan is right. Nakamoto's original intent was not to create a new investment asset but a viable, electronic peer-to-peer payment method. The users of this new payment system would be wholly anonymous, and it would function without the need to trust any higher authorities, such as banks or governments, which we may infer that Nakamoto had deemed unworthy of trust.

There was a purity and perhaps even a naiveté to the earlier visions of Bitcoin and how it would function in society. The initial purveyors—the same crowd that was buying pizzas for 10,000 BTC—could not have foreseen the extraordinary price appreciation of BTC that was to come and the ensuing effect on how the technology would be used. Early adopters were enthused not only about the privacy and anonymous secure transactions; they were also interested in Bitcoin's ability to facilitate *micro-transactions*.

So, what are micro-transactions and their significance for Bitcoin?

Using available US fiat currency, the lowest unit one may transact with is one cent, using the penny. As a currency, Bitcoin allows for even smaller units of exchange, down to what's currently thought of as the smallest denomination of Bitcoin (and perhaps the smallest denomination of any currency in existence), the *satoshi*—one hundred-millionth of a bitcoin, or .00000001 BTC. Micro-transactions have futuristic implications, particularly in the world of video gaming, virtual reality, and even on social apps, as they allow for the semblance of a real economy to take form and function within virtual spaces. Micro-transactions can make these kinds of economies highly accessible, transcending some socioeconomic, demographic, and even global economic boundaries.

Related to participatory democratization, the earlier conceptions of the Bitcoin network, beginning with what's described in Nakamoto's paper, envisioned a far-flung network of computers contributing modest increments of processing power from around the globe. It's possible that Nakamoto would be appalled by the trend toward centralized mining hubs with warehouses full of computer servers gobbling up energy and leaving a carbon footprint that, in aggregate, is equivalent to that of a small country.[5]

Furthermore, Bitcoin's signature advantage of user privacy has become diluted over time as law enforcement, tax authorities, and others have sought means to penetrate Bitcoin's veil of privacy. Take the example of an infamous application of Bitcoin as an anonymous payment system: the online market Silk Road. This dark-web site, specializing in illegal drugs and other illicit items, launched in 2011 and only accepted payment in Bitcoin. And just as Bitcoin's anonymity had attracted the attention of criminal enterprises, it also attracted the attention of the US government, which shut down Silk Road in October 2013.

Silk Road would not be the last marketplace to criminally exploit Bitcoin's privacy. As time went on, Bitcoin would acquire an unwanted reputation as the online criminal's currency of choice. The rise of Bitcoin and other cryptos has paralleled a rise in ransomware attacks, whereby criminals gain leverage over individuals or businesses and extort them for crypto. For instance, hackers may lock up critical computer files at a hospital and demand ransom in Bitcoin.[6] Such criminal activity has created an incentive for the FBI and other law enforcement authorities to create techniques designed to penetrate user anonymity on the Bitcoin network and on other blockchains. In June of 2021, the US Department of Justice (which oversees the FBI) recovered a large amount of extorted funds in the form of 63.7 bitcoins,[7] equivalent to over a million dollars. In September of the same year, the Biden administration imposed sanctions on a cryptocurrency exchange for enabling extortion and illegal payments.[8]

What might it be like from the investigative end, attempting to pierce Bitcoin's veil of privacy? A Bitcoin user's public keys are, after all, public (I discuss keys in chapter 3), and so are the transactions themselves. So how hard would it be to "unmask" blockchain participants? Such an investigation might begin by aggregating data on known Bitcoin transaction participants. This may come by way of computers seized by the FBI, or by blockchain participants acknowledging their use of Bitcoin for various purposes. Data may also be subpoenaed from cryptocurrency exchanges that contain account records linking personal data to public key addresses. Once a handful of noteworthy public key holders are unmasked, contextual evidence may be used to further refine the data.

Where was the suspect on the date of a given transaction? Were there any associated shipping records servicing the suspect's address during a given time period, and do any of the shipping entities use a known public key for transactions? It's reasonable to assume more of these tactics will develop over time.

Due in part to its extraordinary appreciation in value, as well as its subsequent adoption by institutional financial powers, Bitcoin is now widely regarded as a significant investment asset. The price of 1 BTC rose from $0.08 in 2010 to more than $68,000 in 2021, an utter phenomenon of an investment for those who were willing to "hold on for dear life" throughout its intensely volatile periods. In fact, the term *hodling*, originally derived from the misspelling of "holding" on a popular Bitcoin forum, has become synonymous with buying and holding BTC, a practice I address in more detail in chapter 10.

For now, what's important to note is that no one could have predicted BTC's price surge. Further, the emerging contemporary attitude toward BTC as an investment asset represents a stark departure from its original conception as a novel payment utility that presented a compelling alternative to fiat currency.

QUICK CLIP

Check out my short video here as I give my perspective on whether crypto, and Bitcoin in particular, is best thought of as an alternative form of money or merely a new type of investment.

To watch the Quick Clip, use the camera on your mobile phone to scan the QR code or visit the link below.

or

www.quickclips.io/crypto-3

SCAN ME

VISIT URL

Bitcoin as a Hedge Against Inflation?

Much has been made about the prospect of BTC as a hedge against inflation, but the evidence isn't yet fully formed. *Inflation* is the ongoing loss of a currency's purchasing power—the reason why the costs of goods and services are higher today than they were last year, and much higher today than they were fifty years ago. Inflation is caused by a multitude of factors, but it's generally rooted in circulating too much money with too few goods and services to placate the demand for the same. An asset is said to be a hedge against inflation when it can be relied on to retain its purchasing power as fiat currencies lose theirs.

One of the popular narratives about Bitcoin as a hedge against inflation is based on the fact that, like gold, Bitcoin has a fixed supply, and its regular creation and distribution is computationally managed—it cannot be manipulated to suit market conditions. Compare this computational management to the centralized management of fiat currencies. For decades governments have printed more money than consumers actually need, with currency inflation as the natural by-product. When inflation progresses too quickly, the US Federal Reserve can raise interest rates on borrowers, leading to less money in circulation and thereby reducing inflation. It is the absence of such controls that set Bitcoin and other cryptos apart from fiat currencies.

Only 21 million bitcoins will ever be mined; supposedly, this lends the asset an innate stability—might it thus be a true hedge against inflation?—and yet, the asset is not especially stable! Based on historical data, it's quite volatile: BTC plummeted in value by 80% in December of 2017. It fell by 50% in March of 2020, and by 53% in May of 2021. An asset that whips around in value in response to the whims of the marketplace cannot be said to have stable, reliable, and predictable purchasing power.

Hard and Soft Forks

The proponents of Bitcoin's initial promise did not give up their ideals. In August of 2017, a new cryptocurrency called Bitcoin Cash (BCH) was created with everyday transactions in mind. This new crypto would use larger blocks than BTC. Larger blocks meant more transactions and faster processing time. The idea was that with everyone's wallets full of BCH, widespread crypto transactions could be used regularly. It would be used for filling up your gas tank or buying your morning cup of coffee. This could all happen with BCH, heralding the arrival of crypto as commonplace—crypto as it was originally intended!

BCH was made possible by a *fork* (specifically a *hard fork*, which I explain shortly). **Forks** are formed when a sizable group of users agree upon new parameters for an existing blockchain, creating a new branch that is based on, but now distinct from, the original. A new blockchain can fork off of the old one, like a side road, and become the official ledger of record for a new cryptocurrency.

Bitcoin Cash (BCH) presents us with a convenient example, as it was the first of several Bitcoin forks.

THE BITCOIN CASH FORK

GRAPHIC

fig. 28

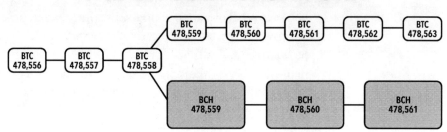

As you can see from figure 28, the fork occurred after the 478,558th Bitcoin block was mined (which took place on August 1, 2017). The BCH blocks, though not drawn to exact scale, are indeed larger than the Bitcoin blocks. It was in fact this very issue of block size that inspired the BCH fork: a community of Bitcoin users believed that bigger blocks were the solution to Bitcoin's long transaction times and expensive fees. Because each Bitcoin block is only 1 megabyte in size, it can only hold a certain number of transactions. A user may initiate a transaction and have to wait for several blocks to be mined before the transaction is added to a block. This takes time, and, as the proponents of the BCH fork argued, a cryptocurrency would need faster transaction times to truly compete with fiat currency in everyday commerce.

This well-intentioned subcommunity within Bitcoin decided they would adopt a set of new protocols to allow for blocks that were more than double the size of Bitcoin's 1MB. A new network was born, and BCH became a separate cryptocurrency from Bitcoin.

The BCH fork was an example of a *hard fork*, where the parameters of the software that powers the network aren't just tweaked but substantively revised to a point where entrants to the new blockchain are fully walled off from the participants still using the old blockchain. The result of a hard fork is two separate blockchains wholly distinct from one another.

A *soft fork*, on the other hand, is where protocols are changed by a group of network proponents, but the resulting update allows for backward compatibility—that is, the ability for a new technology to utilize tech that came before it (think of a high-definition Blu-ray player, which can also play standard-definition DVDs). So, even the network proponents who don't adopt the update are still able to participate alongside those who did. There is no chain split, as there is in a hard fork.

One of the interesting things about a hard fork is that it essentially mints a new coin by splitting off an old blockchain into a new one. The result is that a holder of a certain number of cryptos on the old chain will automatically own that many cryptos on the new chain. When BTC hard forked into BCH, all the BTC owners with recorded holdings as of block 478,558 retained their allotment of BTC *and* were awarded an equal allotment of BCH.

Underscoring the importance of Bitcoin in the cryptocurrency universe, there are over one hundred hard forks that emanate out of the BTC blockchain. These forks are of varying degrees of significance and are anywhere from dormant, to in development, to fully operational. Figure 29 is a listing of 45 Bitcoin forks that, according to forkdrop.io, are up and running.

fig. 29

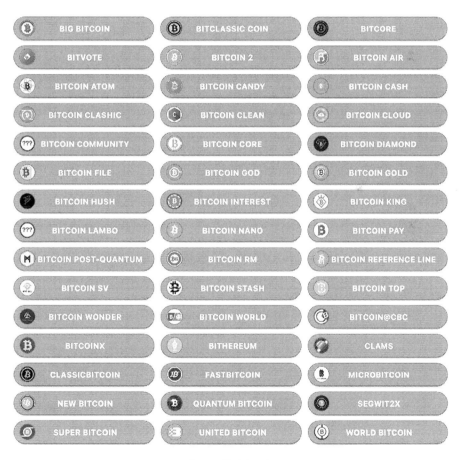

Source: Forkdrop.io

New forks can also be made on a blockchain that's already been forked off another blockchain. A little over a year after the Bitcoin Cash fork, BCH was itself forked and a new blockchain was created to support a crypto called Bitcoin SV or BSV (it's listed in figure 29; this list includes both direct forks like BCH and subsequent forks). The SV stands for Satoshi's Vision, advertising that the community responsible for the fork is adamant about staying true to the original intent of Bitcoin, going so far as to claim that Bitcoin SV should be regarded as the "real" Bitcoin. This claim is based in part on Bitcoin SV's adoption of the earliest Bitcoin design protocol, version 0.1.

As you might infer, the success of a given fork depends in large part in the ability of the fork's proponents to convince the public at large that the new crypto has value. Despite noble efforts and well-articulated arguments, none of the many BTC forks have been able to supplant the original Bitcoin. None have even come close.

Why Does Bitcoin Still Dominate?

So why did the attempts to dethrone Bitcoin tend to come up short? And what is the larger lesson regarding how cryptocurrencies are valued? Answering this question recalls my part 1 discussion on the nature of money. Much of money's value is not innate, but rather asserted. Bitcoin continues to dominate among cryptocurrencies because it has been able to garner the most widespread awareness, usage, and institutional support. BCH and BSV may offer faster transaction times and comport better with the ideas laid out in the original white paper, but they have yet to capture the imagination of the broader public in the same way that Bitcoin has. Because so many Bitcoin owners use the crypto as an investment—a vehicle for storing value as opposed to making everyday transactions—it should come as no surprise that BCH, BSV, and other forked coins have not been as widely noticed by the growing mainstream of crypto investors. Bigger blocks and faster transaction times are not necessarily of interest to that crowd. And even within the world of crypto enthusiasts, there's no shortage of Bitcoin loyalists willing to go to bat for the original version. Here are some of the main advantages you will commonly hear articulated by BTC diehards:

Might Makes Right

It's plain and simple—and historically validated at that: in any system of trading throughout history, you will find that whatever currency is most easily tradeable and enjoys widespread adoption will accrue value, whether it be cowrie shells, tulips, or cattle.

Bitcoin's widespread adoption by both users and financial institutions has made the coin the flagship cryptocurrency, the natural first point of entry for newcomers to the space.

You Don't Need a Hard Fork to Solve a Problem

Outside resources, such as SegWit and the Lightning Network, have had success in speeding up transaction time on the Bitcoin network. *SegWit* is a soft fork and shorthand for "Segregated Witness." It reduces the size of the transactions stored in a given 1MB block. It does this by storing certain digital signature records ("witness" records) in a segregated space outside the block, allowing the freed-up space to be used to store more transactions. This increases throughput and speeds up transactions.

The *Lightning Network* is an invention designed to be used alongside Bitcoin. It is essentially a second layer network (called layer 2) that provides a separate space for Bitcoin or other transactions to be brokered. The idea is that you can log your transactions faster on the separate Lightning Network rather than on the main (called layer 1) Bitcoin blockchain, and at any time you can "cash out," so to speak, and have your amalgamated transaction records relayed to the main blockchain, thereby making them official. The bloggers at Coinbase cleverly liken the Lightning Network to a high-occupancy vehicle (HOV) lane diverting privileged traffic off the main thoroughfare and accelerating commute times for all parties.[9]

DETOUR

The "layering" of blockchains is a response to what's known as the *blockchain trilemma*, the notion that a single blockchain network cannot possess security, scalability, and decentralization all at once. The evolutions of both Bitcoin and Ethereum are testament to the truth of this trilemma, as each of these cryptos has favored decentralization and security at the cost of incurring massive scalability problems. Whenever you hear about a "layer 2" solution, such as the Lightning Network, it is generally in reference to a separate blockchain that works in conjunction with the first layer to help boost the neglected component of the trilemma in order to provide a more balanced, higher quality overall experience for the users of a given blockchain-based network.

Is the Bitcoin Design Unbeatable?

While I believe strongly in the vast and yet untapped potential for more and better innovation in the field of blockchain and cryptocurrency, some among the Bitcoin faithful will argue that its core design is so strong that it leaves competitors without viable inroads.

Satoshi ... left no design space for a superior technology to [intervene] and out-compete Bitcoin ... you can't get more divisible, durable, recognizable, portable, or scarce than Bitcoin.[10]

—ROBERT BREEDLOVE

Bitcoin evangelist and influencer

I don't believe Bitcoin is permanently enshrined as the leading cryptocurrency. For one thing, the environmental impact of the proof-of-work consensus mechanism will continue to face criticism. Furthermore, at the core of this technology, and the culture surrounding it, is antipathy toward any semblance of monopoly. The playing field is wide open for new ideas and new players. The dynamics of a highly innovative marketplace suggest that future entrants could displace Bitcoin, as has happened with other dominant market players throughout history.

Advantages and Challenges of Bitcoin

The advantages of Bitcoin as a currency and its advantages as an investment are interlinked—as are its challenges in both areas. So, if you are contemplating Bitcoin as a store-of-value asset, you should understand the value that this technology adds to the real-world currency marketplace. As a prospective investor, you need to evaluate whether that claim is based on realism or idealism. In this section, I offer an analysis of the value propositions offered by Bitcoin, along with some challenges—and caveats for both.

Advantages of Bitcoin

1. **There is value in removing the intermediaries**: Bitcoin's proponents celebrate the user's autonomy, or independence—that is, users have complete control over their own currency. No bank or government is going to impose its fees, or print more bills (and thereby dilute the value of the currency). Moreover, the lack of an intermediary

offers more privacy. Users are not required to trust any distinct third party to confirm their transactions, as the network protocol can execute a "trustless" confirmation.

- **OK, but**: The Bitcoin network does collect small fees to compensate miners for their work of validating transactions (this compensation is separate from their *block reward*), and the fees imposed by exchanges where Bitcoin is converted to fiat currencies or other cryptos can be hefty. And, as discussed previously in this chapter, the true anonymity of Bitcoin transactions is not absolute.

2. **There is value in the ease of cross-border transactions**: If you've ever sent US dollars or some other fiat currency across borders, then you're familiar with the substantial fees imposed on international payments. Bitcoin puts an end to all this cross-border drama. The blockchain doesn't care what country you live in. Bitcoin is Bitcoin, a true universal currency!

- **OK, but**: There are only so many goods and services you can buy with Bitcoin. Though you can use it for purchases from a diverse set of retailers, most don't accept it.

NOTE Auxiliary services such as Bitrefill and BlockCard provide (for a cost) workaround solutions for consumers wanting to buy stuff with BTC or with other cryptocurrencies even when merchants do not accept crypto payments.

3. **There is value in the irreversibility of Bitcoin transactions**: Blockchain technology is immutable; once a transaction is added to a block there's no way to cancel it, short of having the recipient refund the BTC in a new transaction. This is an advantage for merchants who struggle with credit card payments being "charged back" by the customer. Some merchants even incentivize Bitcoin payments for this reason, offering them a discount on products if they pay with Bitcoin.

- **OK, but**: The wonders of irreversible transactions might not seem quite so utopian to a Bitcoin user who makes an address mistake and inadvertently sends the bitcoins to the wrong entity.

There are mechanisms used by the Bitcoin software to sniff out typos and prevent transactions from being initiated erroneously. Nevertheless, even the most veteran Bitcoin users have at times been known to send funds to the wrong address or to send the wrong amount of funds.

4. **There is value in the convenience of Bitcoin:** You can set up a Bitcoin wallet a lot faster than you can set up a new bank account. Transactions, even if they take a full 20 minutes or so to finalize, are faster and cheaper than other common channels for moving money such as ACH and wire transfers.

   • **OK, but:** The elephant in the room here is the inconvenience of actually using Bitcoin to pay for stuff in normal day-to-day transactions. In the short term it's still more convenient to use cash or a credit card (rather than Bitcoin) when paying your water bill or filling up your gas tank.

5. **There is value in Bitcoin as a solution for the world's unbanked:** All you need to transact with Bitcoin is a private and public key pair. You don't need to undergo any credit or background checks, and Bitcoin isn't going to charge for not maintaining a minimum balance. Your Bitcoin wallet doesn't care if you overdrew your last twelve checking accounts and then skipped town. As of a few years ago, 1.7 billion adults are unbanked worldwide.[11] Think about what that means: though many among the unbanked have no money to speak of at all, there are others who regularly hold cash but have no mechanism for securing it beyond their physical person. With Bitcoin, the only barrier to entry is ownership of a computer or a smartphone, and smartphone ownership is very prevalent even among the world's poor.[12] It's just as Satoshi Nakamoto dreamed: global equity sailing in from on high on the wings of Bitcoin. I discuss this further in chapter 12, where I get further into the world of DeFi—decentralized finance.

   • **OK, but:** We keep coming back to this pesky little detail. If I'm going to trouble myself to acquire and hold bitcoins, then I need to be able to spend them.

As the official Bitcoin website of record, Bitcoin.org, still proclaims: "Bitcoin is still experimental" and "nobody can predict Bitcoin's future."

If you're contemplating a serious investment in Bitcoin, I advise keeping a close eye on its ongoing implementation throughout the normal channels of commerce. Absent real, ongoing, and expanding demonstrations of utility, the price of Bitcoin will be driven by nothing other than the volatile whims of the market.

Right now, given crypto's extreme volatility, you might consider a popular adage: "Only invest what you are prepared to lose."

Challenges of Bitcoin

Bitcoin brought blockchain and its technological potential into the public consciousness. Increasing numbers of enterprises are finding ways to apply blockchain technology. According to a recent PricewaterhouseCoopers survey of 600 executives, 84% of respondents have a blockchain initiative underway and 15% have a fully live operational blockchain being run out of their organization.[13]

What does that tell us as prospective investors in Bitcoin? To me, it suggests the technology that powers Bitcoin is going to be around for a while. It is impossible to know this for sure, however, and serious Bitcoin investors would do themselves a great disservice by failing to acknowledge and understand the specific challenges that stand in the way of more widespread use of Bitcoin.

1. **Volatility**: Some say that the volatility of Bitcoin in and of itself prevents it from gaining widespread acceptance as a true currency. How do you use Bitcoin to budget for monthly expenses when the value may explode or implode at the drop of a hat (or a tweet from Elon Musk)? For perspective, the exchange rate between the US dollar and the euro changes by less than 1% daily, and less than 3% monthly. Bitcoin's value changes by 1% to 3% daily. Over the course of a month, that can add up to some pretty wild swings that impede its ability to serve as a reliable store of value.[14]

   - **OK, but**: It's a promising new technology that's still growing and adapting; the volatility may just be a necessary part of that process. Moreover, the ongoing acceptance and integration of Bitcoin by major financial institutions (which includes growing numbers of mainstream financial advisors recommending Bitcoin as a standard portfolio component) should create more stability for the asset as time goes on.

2. **Transaction throughput**: Given the limited capacity of a block in the Bitcoin blockchain and the more-or-less fixed speed at which new blocks are added, there are inevitable data traffic jams that have the potential to slow down Bitcoin transaction times. The Bitcoin protocol tries to process any given transaction within about 10 minutes, but 1) that's not especially fast, and 2) 10 minutes is the goal but not always the result. The challenge of transaction throughput is compounded and complicated further by another factor: the solicitation and collection of extra fees from Bitcoin users to expedite their placement in the queue and provide faster transaction times to the highest bidder. This activity represents a departure from the democratic peer-to-peer playing field envisioned by Satoshi Nakamoto.

   - **OK, but**: Add-on utilities such as the Lightning Network and SegWit can be stacked on top of the Bitcoin protocol to speed up transaction time.

For perspective, the centralized Visa credit card payment processing network has a TPS (transactions per second) rate of 45,000. Bitcoin's TPS is 3.[15]

3. **Reputation for criminal activity**: It's no secret that Bitcoin, especially in the early days, was tainted by its association with criminality. The promise of anonymity attracts those wanting to launder money or to buy or sell illicit goods or services.

   - **OK, but**: As noted earlier, law enforcement doesn't throw up its hands and accept defeat just because a criminal uses Bitcoin. Keep in mind that the transactions themselves are public record even if the transactors are, by default, anonymous. And furthermore, a few bad actors shouldn't reflect poorly on an investment with so many legitimate uses, including freedom from banks and government manipulation.

In addition to those named here, there are other challenges to Bitcoin and cryptos in general, including their environmental impact, tax implications, and vulnerability to theft, all of which I discuss in this book.

₿ BITCOIN AT A GLANCE

Value History (per unit):

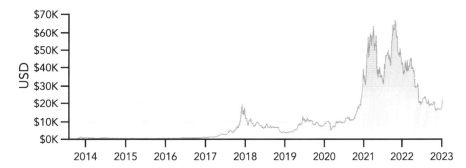

fig. 30

BRIEF HISTORY:

Introduced by Satoshi Nakamoto in 2008 as a decentralized peer-to-peer currency that could function without intermediaries like banks, Bitcoin's novelty in conception and design has allowed it to retain status as the flagship cryptocurrency

KEY CHARACTERISTICS:

- Dominant cryptocurrency
- Appreciation in value has captured world's attention
- Uses proof-of-work consensus mechanism
- Has finite supply of 21 million bitcoins

KNOWN ISSUES:

- Popularity/restricted block size can make its network busy and its transaction times long
- Mining coins requires a major expenditure of energy and accompanying carbon footprint
- Volatility impedes original goal of becoming a widely used currency

Source: www.coinmarketcap.com

The Future of Bitcoin

The Bitcoin faithful are eager to refer to the crypto's famous supply cutoff of 21 million units. There will never be any more than 21 million bitcoins in circulation, barring some dramatic alteration to the protocol. This hard cutoff is what makes Bitcoin scarce, finite, and similar in nature to gold. As I mentioned earlier, given that a new block is mined every 10 minutes and that block rewards (currently at 6.25 BTC per block mined) will continue to be cut in half roughly every four years, it can be inferred that all remaining BTC will be mined and in circulation by around 2140. After that, blocks can still be added, but miners will be incentivized entirely from transaction fees, which, in the current age of mining, make up less than 10% of miner compensation.[16]

Depending on protocol adjustments and the market value of BTC, the transition to smaller, and eventually nonexistent, block rewards could be smooth. Meanwhile, there is more than a century to go before the block rewards are taken fully off the table. Until then, block rewards can continue to incentivize the network participation on which all Bitcoin commerce depends.

The more immediate and relevant future concerns for prospective Bitcoin users and investors are political, social, and economic in nature. As such, they're not easily predicted. Another financial collapse could raise the demand for Bitcoin as more people flee into hard assets, digital included. A massive security breach at an exchange could result in the theft of thousands of bitcoins, spooking the market and driving down the price. Governments may adopt Bitcoin as legal tender, as El Salvador did in 2021, or they may elect to sponsor their own cryptocurrencies.

Chapter Recap

» Bitcoin changed the financial landscape by ushering in the era of cryptocurrency.

» Bitcoin has flourished in large part due to its solving of the double-spend problem, its application of the distributed database concept, and its use of open-source software.

» The present-day applications of Bitcoin as an investment asset represent a stark departure from its originally conceived vision as a peer-to-peer payment utility with potential for widespread use.

» A "fork" on a blockchain is formed when a group of users agrees to abide by a new set of parameters different from those defined in the existing blockchain. A "hard fork" creates a whole new and separate chain, whereas a soft fork can coexist with its parent blockchain.

» Despite an array of significant challenges and an uncertain future, Bitcoin's first-mover advantage has led it to dominate among cryptocurrencies.

| 5 |
Ethereum

Chapter Overview
  » Origins of Ethereum
  » How Ethereum is used
  » Smart contracts, dapps, and the Ethereum Virtual Machine (EVM)
  » Ethereum vs. Bitcoin

Back in the 1960s and 1970s, car rental company Avis was consistently in second position behind industry leader Hertz. Avis's advertisers came up with a brilliant slogan that turned this problem into an advantage: "We try harder."

fig. 31

Source: www.gettinsaltyapparel.com

Car rental company Avis campaigned on its second-place status for decades with a slogan that became one of the most famous in advertising history. Today, both Avis and its rival Hertz have been overtaken by Enterprise.

Today, you could see Bitcoin and Ethereum as the Hertz and Avis of cryptocurrency. But Ethereum's advocates, like would-be entrepreneur Tori Forrest, would argue that it does indeed try harder. Bitcoin established its blockchain as a method for creating and sustaining a cryptocurrency. Ethereum has both followed Bitcoin's example and extended the uses of blockchain beyond the narrowly defined crypto space. In this chapter, I discuss Ethereum's distinctive and compelling features.

What Is Ethereum?

According to the definition on the home page of the Ethereum.org site:

> *Ethereum is the community-run technology powering the cryptocurrency ether (ETH) and thousands of decentralized applications.*
>
> – ETHEREUM WEBSITE

So, Ethereum is both a cryptocurrency, referred to as ether (ETH), and a technology that can power decentralized apps (dapps). I discuss dapps later. But first, what is Ethereum's origin story?

The Birth of Ethereum

Satoshi Nakamoto's 2008 white paper "Bitcoin: A Peer-to-Peer Electronic Cash System," described the creation of cryptocurrency in general and Bitcoin in particular. Arguably the second most important crypto white paper, clearly inspired by the Bitcoin paper, is Vitalik Buterin's "A Next Generation Smart Contract & Decentralized Application Platform," released in 2013. This white paper proposed the creation of not only a distributed ledger to support a cryptocurrency, but the technology to build distributed applications.

Access the white papers for both Bitcoin and Ethereum in the Crypto Research and Analysis Library at clydebankmedia.com/crypto-assets.

Another notable difference between Nakamoto and Buterin is that Buterin's identity is not a secret. He was born in Russia in 1994 and moved with his family to Canada at age six. Remarkably, he was only nineteen when he wrote the paper that moved blockchain beyond crypto.

Buterin is a programmer and, prior to Ethereum, was one of the founders of *Bitcoin Magazine*. He is also a cofounder of the Ethereum Foundation, the decentralized (appropriately!) organization established to create the Ethereum blockchain and issue ether, among other good works. Although Buterin is arguably the most significant, there are seven other Ethereum Foundation cofounders: Anthony Di Iorio, Charles Hoskinson, Mihai Alisie, Amir Chetrit, Joseph Lubin, Gavin Wood, and Jeffrey Wilcke.

A July and August 2014 crowdfunding initiative, which raised US$18 million, financed the Ethereum blockchain's early development. It officially launched a year later, in July 2015. As with Bitcoin, the time that elapsed between proposing and executing the system was compressed. And as with Bitcoin, both the increase in value and the volatility have been notable.

ETHEREUM AT A GLANCE

Value History (per unit):

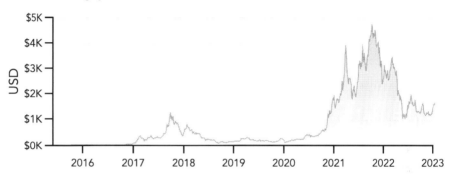

fig. 32

KEY CHARACTERISTICS:

- Ether cryptocurrency is second only to Bitcoin in market size
- Basis of smart contracts
- Ethereum 2.0 upgrade launched in September 2022

KNOWN ISSUES:

- Low number of transactions/second (being addressed in v. 2.0)
- Consistent second-place status

Source: www.coinmarketcap.com

Why the names "ether" and "Ethereum"? While surfing the web, Buterin came across the term "ether" and adapted it into the name "Ethereum," of which he said: "I immediately realized that I liked it better than all of the other alternatives that I had seen; I suppose it was the fact that [it] sounded nice and it had the word "ether," referring to the hypothetical invisible medium that permeates the universe and allows light to travel."

In fact, the term *ether* (sometimes spelled "aether") goes back to antiquity, being the fifth element—referred to in the film of the same name—that draws together and binds the four basic elements of earth, water, air, and fire (figure 33). It was considered the "quintessential" element (*quint* meaning "five").

fig. 33

EARTH   **AIR**   **WATER**   **FIRE**   **ETHER**

Using Ethereum

Ethereum can, of course, be used to complete transactions involving ether, its native cryptocurrency. But Buterin's white paper also focuses on blockchain applications.

The white paper's fundamental innovation, as its title indicates, is support for a feature called a *smart contract*—an agreement in computer code that automatically executes once certain conditions are met. The purpose is to simply remove middlemen from, business and trade of all kinds. Unalterable records of these transactions are stored on Ethereum's blockchain, circumventing many of the disputes so common in the normal course of business.

Smart Contracts

Smart contracts are another technological element of blockchain, particularly on the Ethereum network, describing autonomous and transparent agreements that can't be altered. Though the blockchain tech that enables it is relatively new, computer scientist Nick Szabo proposed both the term *smart contract* and the concept as early as 1993.

Like almost everything crypto, the name creates debate: are "smart contracts" really "smart" or not? Are they even contracts? Attorneys might argue that they are not because they aren't necessarily built on legally enforceable principles. Even Buterin feels that a more technical term such as "persistent scripts" would have been preferable.[1]

There has been a good deal of speculation that Nick Szabo really is the person behind Satoshi Nakamoto. I can neither affirm nor deny this assertion, and Szabo himself certainly hasn't.

It could be said that any Bitcoin or other cryptocurrency transaction occurs as part of a very limited and restricted form of a smart contract. If Tori Forrest sends her brother Alan a thousandth of a bitcoin, the code will only make the transfer if these terms are met:

1. Tori has that much Bitcoin in her account and
2. Alan has a valid Bitcoin address to which the money can be transferred.

The difference between Ethereum and Bitcoin is that Ethereum provides a platform on which smart contracts of all kinds can be developed and executed, with much wider applicability than financial transactions restricted to a specific cryptocurrency. A smart contract can be seen simply as computer code that runs on the Ethereum blockchain, as well as other blockchains, such as Tezos, that have adopted Buterin's strategy.

An Example of a Smart Contract

When Peter and Lynn Forrest bought their house twenty years ago, the transaction was highly mediated. Real estate agents, banks, and escrow companies were involved in both the sale and the transfer of title from the seller to the buyers. Some US states also require lawyers to become involved in such transactions.

BUYING A HOUSE ON ETHEREUM

fig. 34

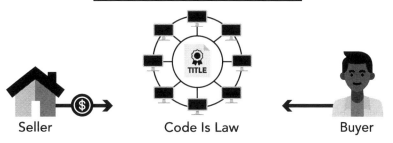

A smart-contract sale eliminates the need for such intermediaries. It's a transaction mediated by a blockchain, rather than third parties.

How is this possible? The governing principle here is "code is law," meaning a smart contract's code, not some outside regulation or arbitrator, determines what occurs on the blockchain network.

In this example, the system's underlying code determines what needs to be done to meet the conditions of the home sale. Because that code is on a blockchain, it is unalterable.

Once the transaction has been approved and title transferred, the action cannot be undone. The terms and execution of the contract, like all blockchain code, are "trustless, autonomous, decentralized, and transparent," none of which is true in a traditional real estate transaction.

What is meant by "code is law"? The requirements that validate a smart contract transaction are expressed in its underlying programming rather than a law book.

The Vending Machine Example

A vending-machine analogy is often used to explain how smart contracts work.

VENDING MACHINE
Analogy to a Smart Contract

fig. 35

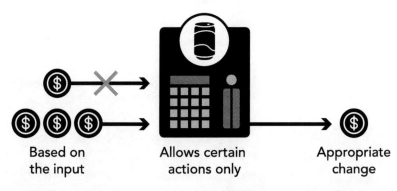

| Based on the input | Allows certain actions only | Appropriate change |

A vending machine is set up to deliver a specific result when certain conditions are met, as illustrated in figure 35. If you feed the machine only $2 worth of change, but the drink costs $2.50, the machine won't dispense the product. It will only do so when you insert an amount equal to or greater than $2.50. If you insert $2.50, it will dispense a can with your soft drink. If you insert $3, it will dispense the soft drink and fifty cents in change. No intermediary is required to enforce this arrangement between human and vending machine. We may not think of vending machines as "smart" technology, but smart contracts work in largely the same way.

EVM: The Ethereum Virtual Machine

Smart contracts are replicated and processed on all the computers in the Ethereum network, without central supervision. The vision set forth in the Ethereum white paper is for the creation of a decentralized worldwide computer.

Ethereum was created to provide a platform for running smart contracts. The network consists of nodes all running the same blockchain software. All the nodes in the network work together and in many important ways act as a single computer, providing substantial processing power, executing the same sets of instructions. That's why it's given the name Ethereum Virtual Machine, or EVM.

Indeed, the Ethereum Foundation website's definition of Ethereum places smart contracts at the center of the EVM technology:

Ethereum is software running on a network of computers that ensures that data and small computer programs called smart contracts are replicated and processed on all the computers on the network, without a central coordinator. The vision is to create an unstoppable censorship-resistant self-sustaining decentralized world computer.

- ETHEREUM FOUNDATION

Specifically, the EVM calculates or computes its smart contracts' logic without relying on a central server.

Solidity: Ethereum's Programming Language

In 2014, Gavin Wood, one of the Ethereum Foundation's cofounders, proposed the creation of a full-fledged computer language for building smart contracts, called Solidity. Solidity is *Turing-complete*, a reference to Alan Turing, one of the founders of modern computing.

A Turing-complete language means a general-purpose computer language that can simulate the computational aspects of any other real-world, general-purpose computer language, such as C++ or Java. Turing-complete systems are able to run any possible computation, including the most complex types, such as those found in blockchain. The general-purpose computer language that Solidity is most often compared to is JavaScript, one of the most common computer languages used today. The Ethereum Virtual Machine (EVM) is essentially the computer on which Solidity runs.

A critical underlying difference between Ethereum and Bitcoin is the computer language in which they are programmed. Bitcoin is written in a language called Script, which, unlike Solidity, is intentionally not Turing-complete. This is a specific choice to prevent computational loops—pieces of code executed repeatedly under certain conditions—from consuming too many resources. Although you might say that technically Bitcoin is a smart contract, Script—the language it is written in—cannot spell out certain fundamental conditions. This creates efficiency but imposes limitations in comparison to Ethereum.

Solidity can be used to build full-fledged programs, called dapps—applications that perform multiple functions. The term dapp is short for "decentralized application" and refers to an application run on a blockchain-based distributed network. A dapp would be needed, for example, to run the decentralized real estate brokerage service described earlier in the chapter. Theoretically, any kind of computer application could be built and run on the EVM.

As of 2022, 2.4 million people were using dapps daily[2] and over half of those dapps are housed on the Ethereum blockchain. Advocates argue that these applications' decentralized approach has major security benefits: because dapps are irreversible and unmodifiable, they are far less subject to third-party hacking and manipulation. This also makes dapps a good fit for the DeFi space, where many of them have been created. DeFi, which I discuss in much greater length in chapter 12, is the term for financial services delivered using blockchain technology, primarily Ethereum. With DeFi, you can earn interest, borrow, lend, buy insurance, and trade derivatives and assets—the functions that banks conventionally take on—without paperwork or third-party intervention. There are now several billion dollars of assets in the DeFi sector, and this is the aspect of blockchain that Tori Forrest finds so compelling.

DAOs

The concept of the DAO—decentralized autonomous organization—takes dapps a step further. A DAO is an organizational structure where members agree to abide by certain rules codified into smart contracts. The underlying, radical concept here is that a decentralized organization, such as a business, will run on peer-to-peer rather than hierarchical, centralized, command-and-control principles.

Smart contracts are a DAO's building blocks. In a DAO, trust is encoded in the blockchain software rather than invested in the system's human participants. DAOs are set up to allow all those affiliated with the organization direct input into decision-making. They are nonhierarchical; users become members by buying the DAO's cryptocurrency. All members have voting rights commensurate with the amount of the DAO's crypto they own. This promotes the transparency that centralized business and government organizations often say they aspire to but rarely achieve.

As of mid-2022, the dedicated website deepdao.io was tracking 4,833 DAOs.[3] Examples include the decentralized crypto exchange Uniswap, launched in September 2020, which became the largest DAO less than two years later, and Dash, a decentralized payment system notable for the speed of its transactions.

Although still in the early stages, Vitalik's vision of a decentralized world computer seems to be an idea whose time has come. This is the foundation for a decentralized internet known as Web3, which I introduced in chapter 1.

Gas

Aside from being the quintessential "fifth element," ether is also a gas used as a surgical anesthetic from the mid-nineteenth century to the early 1960s. One of the most famous of T. S. Eliot's lines, from "The Love Song of J. Alfred Prufrock," describes the evening as "spread out along the sky/Like a patient etherized upon a table."

In a somewhat convoluted pun, Ethereum also uses the term gas to refer to the fees, paid in its ETH cryptocurrency, that fuel transactions of all kinds on the network. Gas is what keeps the network running. As Cryptopedia puts it, Ethereum was created as a "dynamic Swiss-army knife kind of protocol with a broad range of practical applications and a native currency, ether (ETH), and gas, that serves to fuel the network."

With few exceptions, transactions that occur on the Ethereum network, including those involving dapps, require a fee paid in gas to be executed. Gas costs are usually denoted in *gwei*, a denomination equal to a billionth of an ether. In general, the more complex the smart contract, based on the number of computational steps and the amount of memory used, the higher the gas fee required.

As with any fee, there have been numerous complaints about the cost of gas on the Ethereum network. Some of this was associated with proof-of-work validation fees, which no longer apply since the launch of Ethereum 2.0 in September 2022 moved the Ethereum blockchain from proof-of-work to proof-of-stake validation (see below).

Another issue has been the relative slowness of the system, especially during busy periods. Extra gas payments known as "tips" can be paid to accelerate processing time, leading to further complaints about excessive fees. The Ethereum 2.0 upgrade is also meant to address this issue.

Here is the formula for calculating a gas fee: total fee = gas limit * (base fee + tip), where the gas limit is the maximum amount of gas you're willing to use for the transaction, the base fee is the system-calculated cost per unit of gas, and the tip is any extra amount you are willing to pay to expedite the transaction.

For example, if I want to send you 1 ETH, the average amount of gas needed for this transaction is 23,000 units. I would set that as my gas limit. The base fee, or price per unit of gas at the time, is 150 gwei. However, I want to get the crypto to you faster, so I add a tip of 20 gwei per unit to the transaction.

Plugging these figures into the formula yields the following: 23,000 units * (150 gwei + 20 gwei). The total fee to send you 1 ETH would be 3,910,000 gwei, or 0.00391 ETH. This means that I would send 1.00391 ETH to the Ethereum blockchain and you would receive 1 ETH to go buy some cool non-fungible tokens/NFTs (I discuss NFTs in chapter 7).

Ethereum vs. Bitcoin

Bitcoin inspired Vitalik Buterin to propose Ethereum and cofound the Ethereum Foundation. However, the differences between the two systems, including Ethereum's support of smart contracts, dapps, and the EVM "world computer," are now as significant as their similarities.

Some other differences between the two:

» There is a cap on how many bitcoins can be created: 21 million. There is no such limit on the amount of ether that can be created in total, although only 18 million ETH can be mined annually.

» Blocks in the Bitcoin blockchain are validated approximately every ten minutes. Ethereum blocks are validated about every twelve seconds.

Another, arguably more significant, difference between the two systems is that Ethereum has moved to a proof-of-stake (PoS) validation of its transactions, while Bitcoin remains firmly rooted in the proof-of-work (PoW) protocol. Although Ethereum was originally proof-of-work, Ethereum 2.0 converted the system to proof-of-stake. The cryptos Cardano and Tezos, discussed in chapter 6, also use proof-of-stake.

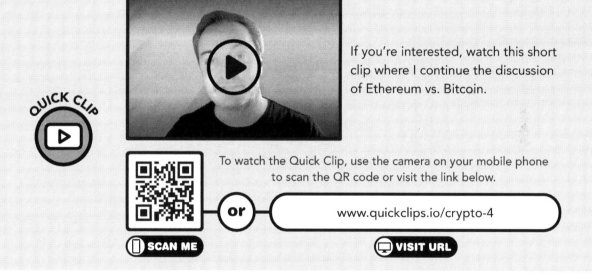

QUICK CLIP

If you're interested, watch this short clip where I continue the discussion of Ethereum vs. Bitcoin.

To watch the Quick Clip, use the camera on your mobile phone to scan the QR code or visit the link below.

or

www.quickclips.io/crypto-4

SCAN ME

VISIT URL

Proof-of-Stake

Proof-of-work, which I discussed in chapter 2, is an energy-intensive process that has come under intense criticism for the potential environmental impact of all the power it consumes. *Proof-of-stake*, its advocates assert, is both more energy-efficient and far less complex. On the other hand, the dependability of the proof-of-stake system is currently less established than that of proof-of-work.

How does proof-of-stake operate? In a proof-of-stake model, each node in the network has the opportunity to make itself a validating node—a node entitled to validate a block of transactions—by staking some or all of its crypto. You pledge a number of your coins to be used to verify transactions. The coins can't be spent while being staked but can be unstaked when you want to trade them.

When a transaction block is ready to be processed, an algorithm running on the network randomly selects which node will perform the actual validation. The more crypto you have staked, the more likely it is that your node will be chosen. If the block is validated and added to the blockchain, the validator node receives a reward. Fraudulent miners are disincentivized because their staked crypto is forfeited for such criminal behavior. Of course, this also creates a barrier to entry; just as it now requires significant computing power to participate in proof-of-work validation, it requires a certain amount of crypto to earn rewards through proof-of-stake.

So Why Isn't Ethereum #1?

You now know how Ethereum, the number two cryptocurrency network, tries harder. It has considerably expanded the capabilities of blockchain through smart contracts, the EVM, dapps, and DAOs. What's more, it's taken to heart the criticisms made of proof-of-work on environmental grounds and has moved to proof-of-stake.

So, with all these virtues, why does Ethereum still have only half of Bitcoin's market capitalization?

Any answers to this question remain speculative. Bitcoin, after all, had a five-year lead over Ethereum when the latter was launched. Within the general population, Bitcoin is most closely associated with the cryptocurrency movement. Ethereum's advocates believe that it is the superior system, one that builds upon and beyond Bitcoin's strengths. They might argue that Bitcoin's ongoing dominance is much like the conflict between the two early videotape technologies, VHS and Betamax, in which the technically inferior VHS won out over the superior Betamax. But the analogy is hardly exact, and for now, Bitcoin and Ethereum continue to coexist, along with a universe of alternative cryptocurrencies that I discuss in chapter 6.

Chapter Recap

» In 2013, Vitalik Buterin and his colleagues proposed Ethereum as both a cryptocurrency and a means of programming and executing blockchain-based computer code.

» This code is known as a smart contract, which is run on a computer consisting of the nodes in the blockchain system, also called the Ethereum Virtual Machine or EVM.

» Smart contracts can be used to create decentralized applications (dapps) used in a variety of contexts today, quite prominently in decentralized finance or DeFi.

» Ethereum's cryptocurrency is known as ether (ETH) and is used both as a medium of exchange in itself and to pay for the gas, the fee for powering smart contracts.

| 6 |
Altcoins

Despite the relative infancy of the cryptocurrency ecosystem, there's already a high number of diverse offerings. While big players Bitcoin and Ethereum make up a combined 60% of the market, as of this writing in early 2023, there are nearly 20,000 other independent circulating cryptocurrencies. Many of the newer cryptos are forked out of Bitcoin or run on the Ethereum blockchain, and some cryptos are designed to mimic more traditional currencies such as the US dollar and the euro (or to reflect the value of more traditional assets such as gold), while others have more specific uses.

In this chapter, I provide an overview of the various directions that cryptocurrency has taken since its invention and discuss the underlying concepts that power some of the lesser-known cryptos. This may help you make more informed investment decisions.

What Are Altcoins?

Altcoins, short for alternative coins, is a term used to refer to any cryptos that are not Bitcoin. It's a very broad label, one that encapsulates thousands of crypto assets. Some use a blockchain that is designed for additional applications beyond tracking crypto payments. Some have different consensus mechanisms other than proof-of-work (see appendix II for a list of alternative consensus mechanisms). Some even began as jokes but turned into legitimate cryptocurrencies.

fig. 36

"Dogecoin," based on the Doge internet meme, began as a joke aimed at satirizing crypto speculation. Within two weeks it had a total market value of $8 million.[1]

Popular Altcoins

When an asset climbs in value from $0.08 to $68,000 in just a few years, people take notice. The desire to replicate the success of Bitcoin is inevitable, as is the creative inspiration some people have taken from Bitcoin. Of course, not all altcoins meet with equal success. Keeping in mind the many variables in play, here are some altcoins I currently find most representative of today's market.

Altcoins are continually jockeying for position. New players regularly emerge, and old ones disappear. I've prepared a Crypto Research and Analysis link library to help you stay up-to-the-minute on all the latest action in the cryptocurrency universe, including the latest on altcoins. Access this and the rest of your digital assets at go.quickstartguides.com/crypto.

As you might imagine, what's popular in the altcoin universe is subject to change over time. The cryptos featured in this chapter (both in figure 37 and in the sections that follow) were significant players at the time of this writing. But other coins, such as Litecoin, Iota, Dash, Zcash, and Bitcoin Cash (discussed in chapter 4) are all worth watching. In the volatile world of cryptocurrencies, any given bit player could emerge as a powerhouse in a very short amount of time.

MAJOR CRYPTOCURRENCIES
As of February 3, 2023

GRAPHIC

fig. 37

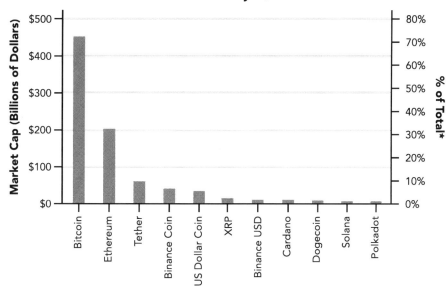

*% market cap relative only to the major cryptocurrencies listed here

Source: www.coinmarketcap.com

NOTE

At several points throughout this chapter and others I refer to a given crypto's market capitalization or "market cap." This measurement is commonly used to describe the total value of a given asset, like a business, by multiplying its share value by the total number of outstanding shares. With cryptocurrencies, the market cap refers to the total units of currency in circulation multiplied by its value per unit. As of this writing, all of the cryptos featured in the sections below are among the top ten in global market cap.[2]

Indeed, there are thousands of altcoins in the ecosystem, all waiting patiently to either break through or die. I discuss trading and investing in cryptocurrencies in more depth in part 3; this chapter highlights some significant altcoins in the current market. For each altcoin, I ask two questions—questions that I suggest you ask yourself when exploring any future altcoins not covered here:

» What do you perceive as the underlying basis for a given coin's success?
» Will you be able to recognize these elements in lesser-known coins?

XRP

XRP presents a model of an investable cryptocurrency whose primary purpose is to help solve a particular problem in commerce. XRP (figure 38) is the product of Ripple Labs, a for-profit enterprise that serves the financial services industry. The mission of Ripple Labs and its crypto is to facilitate an international funds transfer protocol (a process for moving money across borders) that is faster and cheaper than other available services.

XRP AT A GLANCE

Value History (per unit):

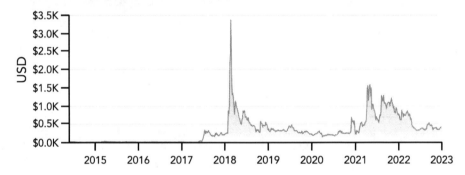

fig. 38

BRIEF HISTORY:

Created in June 2012 by developers David Schwartz, Jed McCaleb, and Arthur Britto, who sought to create a cryptocurrency that could achieve trust in the main ledger without mining

KEY CHARACTERISTICS:

- Native digital asset tracked on the RippleNet
- Provides a method for expediting cross-border transfers
- Allows for fast transaction times (<5 seconds) and high throughput (15,000 transactions per second)
- Infinitesimally small costs for transactions
- Does not require mining, therefore no massive energy consumption
- Consistently within the top ten of all crpytos in terms of total market capitalization

KNOWN ISSUES:

- More centralized—institutional influence is significant
- Arguably less secure—the UNL consensus mechanism is theoretically easier to defraud than proof-of-work or others
- Under scrutiny by SEC, claiming that it should be treated as a security, not cryptocurrency

Source: www.coinmarketcap.com

The RippleNet, as it's known, is a network of payment providers, banks, and other financial institutions that all use a reliable messaging and real-time clearing and settlement protocol to facilitate cross-border transactions at a reasonable speed and cost. This network includes over 300 institutions across 40 countries.

To accomplish this mission, RippleNet relies on both blockchain technology and its native blockchain-based asset, the cryptocurrency XRP. XRP transactions process, on average, in under five seconds.[3] Compare this to a traditional cross-border money transfer, which can take several days to settle, or even Bitcoin, which requires, on average, ten minutes to transact. Ripple's costs to transact are also exceedingly low at .00001 XRP (well under a penny at current valuations for the crypto).

RippleNet's innovations in the area of cross-border money transfers are a compelling example of how blockchain technology can be used in novel ways that go beyond cryptocurrency.

The founders of RippleNet believe in an emerging phenomenon known as "the internet of value," a network through which valuable digital assets can and should flow just as easily as information flows through the conventional internet. Similar to the abbreviation "HTTP" for "hypertext transfer protocol," RippleNet can be referred to with the abbreviation RTXP, which stands for "Ripple Transaction Protocol." Ripple Labs prides itself on bringing its XRP cryptocurrency to market alongside a clear use case.

But are there any drawbacks to this novel approach to cryptocurrency?

Among cryptocurrency's most ardent enthusiasts you'll find a slew of detractors who can't stomach the idea of a cryptocurrency appearing to be controlled by a private company. Why? The RippleNet blockchain doesn't rely on proof-of-work, proof-of-stake, or any of the other common consensus mechanisms. Instead, XRP transactions are confirmed by a collection of selected validators. Anyone can be a validator, but—unlike with Bitcoin—there is no real financial reward structure in place for them, just the respect of the community. Moreover, on the RippleNet blockchain not all nodes are treated equally. Participants select which validators they prefer to use in the form of a "Unique Node List" (UNL). Recommended UNLs are published by a small group of entities, including Ripple Labs itself. This creates the impression that Ripple Labs has undue influence when it comes to choosing the referees for the game. XRP proponents are quick to point out that RippleNet is open source, and that the freedom of participants to choose alternative UNLs disincentivizes Ripple Labs from recommending or conspiring with bad actors. The related, more thematic problem for XRP is that these unique verification processes, along with its more institutional foundations, have led to some debate over whether the currency is truly decentralized—which, as you likely know by now, is a major sticking point within the crypto community.

NOTE

To be fair, XRP isn't the only crypto forced to weather accusations that it's not sufficiently decentralized. Big players Bitcoin and Ethereum have also come under scrutiny for the outsized influence of big mining operations that not only consume massive amounts of energy (not a significant problem with XRP) but also secure and control a staggering amount of the crypto itself.

Solana

Anatoly Yakovenko, a Ukrainian-born engineer, created Solana in 2017 after experiencing a late-night eureka moment: what if the passage of time itself could be integrated into the data structure of a blockchain and used to order transactions and other events? In November of that year, Yakovenko published the Solana white paper, which introduced a concept called *proof-of-history*.

Solana uses a hybridized consensus mechanism that combines proof-of-stake (validators in lieu of miners) with its signature protocol, proof-of-history. Proof-of-history attaches a cryptographic timestamp to all transactions submitted to a block. These timestamps are readily verified by the network. Adding the timestamps requires an added degree of processing power but results in higher throughput. Whereas other blockchains, namely Ethereum and Bitcoin, require more spacing out of blocks to ensure the orderly sequencing of transactions, the transactions on the Solana network can be sequenced rapidly.

According to the Solana white paper, its design has the theoretical potential to process a staggering 710,000 transactions per second (TPS). Even though its real-world workload is closer to 3,000 TPS, it is considered to be among the very fastest of blockchains in existence; Ethereum's average TPS is 10, for example.[4] The potential downside is that due to that aforementioned workload, network outages may be more frequent than with some other blockchains.

⊜ SOLANA AT A GLANCE

Value History (per unit):

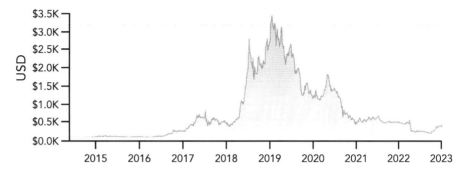

fig. 39

BRIEF HISTORY:

Created in 2017 by Anatoly Yakovenko, a former software engineer aiming at creating a new blockchain that could scale at a global level while maintaining very fast throughput capabilities

KEY CHARACTERISTICS:

- Applies "proof-of-history" tool that allows for reliable cryptographic verification of timestamps, thereby unencumbering the blockchain and allowing faster throughput (a capacity of up to 710,000 transactions per second)
- Among the fastest of all blockchains in existence

KNOWN ISSUES:

- Known for frequent network outages and episodes of throttled back or failed performance

Source: www.coinmarketcap.com

Cardano

In the fall of 2017, the Cardano blockchain platform and its native asset, the cryptocurrency known as ADA, was founded by Charles Hoskinson, also one of the cofounders of Ethereum. The coin debuted on the crypto-tracking sites with a market cap of $600 million and by year's end was worth upwards of $10 billion.[5]

The names associated with Cardano are not without significance. "Cardano" itself is an homage to the mathematician Gerolamo Cardano, and ADA is named for the famous early 19th century computing maven, Ada Lovelace.

Cardano's blockchain is comprised of two layers: the Cardano Settlement Layer (CSL) and the Cardano Computational Layer (CCL). The CSL is the crypto ledger, tracking and administering the transfers of ADA. The CCL is used to execute smart contracts (for an explanation of smart contracts, see chapter 5). This two-layer approach is a reaction to Ethereum's single-layer blockchain and its perceived weakness in scalability. Similar in theory to Solana, the Cardano blockchain was designed to speed up processing time in direct response to higher demand, a counter to the scalability problems of Bitcoin and Ethereum. Scalability was the first of three common cryptocurrency challenges that Cardano was designed to solve, and the two-layer blockchain solution (devoting exclusive access to one layer for transaction processing) was fundamental in establishing Cardano's scalability advantage.

The second challenge was *interoperability*, the ability of a blockchain to handle other crypto assets and decentralized applications (dapps). Cardano uses *cross-chain bridges* to accomplish this. These "bridges" are protocols that permit blockchains to interface with one another, allowing for the transfer of crypto assets, smart contract instructions, and miscellaneous data from one chain to another. For example, you could use the bridge to deploy blockchain-secured digital assets on a dapp maintained on a separate blockchain.

The third challenge was sustainability. Cardano boasts on its website that it's four million times as energy efficient as Bitcoin. At the core of this claim is Cardano's use of a proof-of-stake consensus mechanism rather than a proof-of-work consensus mechanism.

Cardano's unique proof-of-stake protocol is known as Ouroboros, and according to its 2019 white paper, it's more than just a standard-issue energy-efficient proof-of-stake protocol. It also boasts "security properties ... similar to those achieved by the Bitcoin blockchain protocol," a best-of-both-worlds approach to getting data logged and verified on the blockchain.[6]

Within the context of Cardano and many cryptos, sustainability has meaning beyond the environment. It also refers to the ability of the crypto to propagate itself and evolve. Given that cryptos are (or at least strive to be) decentralized, a sustainable design must be put in place to ensure that the technology surrounding the crypto will survive and thrive over time. A key ingredient of Cardano's success was its all-systems-go approach to building a strong community of interested participants. The Cardano community has developed an enviable reputation for producing a large body of high-quality, peer-reviewed research and white papers—great signs of a commitment to a *sustainable* crypto.

CARDANO AT A GLANCE

Value History (per unit):

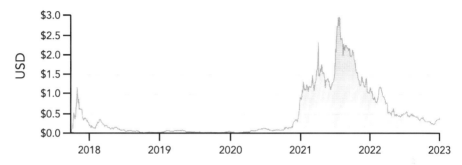

fig. 40

BRIEF HISTORY:
Founded in 2015 by Ethereum cofounder Charles Hoskinson but not launched until 2017, Cardano became the largest cryptocurrency (by market cap) to use a proof-of-stake blockchain

KEY CHARACTERISTICS:
- Facilitates transactions of its native cryptocurrency, ADA, as well as other cryptos using "bridges"
- Uses a two-layer blockchain with a "settlement layer" for transactions and a "computational layer" for dapps and other projects
- Utilizes Ouroboros, a unique proof-of-stake protocol

KNOWN ISSUES:
- Network congestion has led to choppy rollout of some dapps
- Regulatory uncertainty has caused Cardano to be delisted on at least one major exchange

Source: www.coinmarketcap.com

Binance Coin

Before becoming a force unto itself—a regular entrant among the top ten cryptos in existence according to *market capitalization*—the Binance Coin (BNB) was initially a utility token to be used on the Binance cryptocurrency exchange to pay for transaction fees and other services at a discount. The Binance exchange (figure 41), as of this writing, is a popular crypto exchange service where almost every crypto in existence trades at the highest available volumes. It is the largest of all crypto markets.

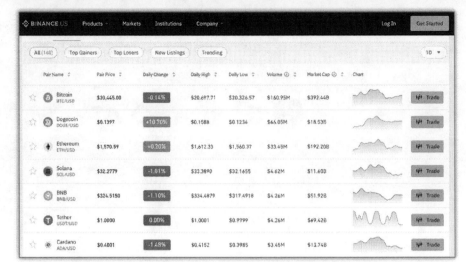

fig. 41

A screencap of the Binance cryptocurrency exchange (binance.com).

When the Binance exchange launched in 2017, it raised $15 million from investors, who received BNB coins with an initial value of 10 cents. At its peak in 2021, a BNB coin was worth almost $700.

The BNB Beacon Chain: BNB initially ran according to the ERC-20 protocol (discussed further in chapter 7) on the Ethereum blockchain before being moved to its own blockchain known as the Binance Chain. Now rebranded as the "BNB Beacon Chain" or "Beacon Chain," this blockchain does a lot more than merely track the movement of BNB. Binance offers a decentralized exchange known as "Binance DEX." Core elements of this exchange service are recorded, updated, and verified on Beacon Chain. Data on account balance info, fees paid, and available trading pairs can all be found on this ledger. I discuss decentralized exchanges in more depth in chapter 12. Binance runs another blockchain known as the "BNB Smart Chain" (BSC) that runs alongside the BNB Beacon Chain. BSC enables smart contracts and is EVM-compatible, meaning it can run Ethereum-based applications.

Due to the success of Binance, its founder, Changpeng Zhao, known as "CZ," is one of the wealthiest players in the crypto ecosystem, among only a handful of crypto billionaires. A Chinese-Canadian coder, CZ spent his early career building high-frequency trading systems for Wall Street's elite-level day traders.

Since its inception, Binance has proved itself a whale in the crypto space, gobbling up (that is, buying out) key crypto-related properties such as the now infamous crypto exchange FTX, the website coinmarketcap.com, and the company Swipe.io, which administers its own native crypto token, SXP.

fig. 42

BNB QUARTERLY BURN DATA				
DATE	BNB TOTAL SUPPLY	BNB BURN	BURN %	TOTAL ($)
2017-10-18	200,000,827	986,000	0.4930	1,311,380
2018-01-15	199,014,827	1,821,586	0.9153	35,630,222
2018-04-15	197,193,241	2,220,314	1.1260	29,996,442
2018-07-18	194,972,927	2,528,767	1.2970	29,991,177
2018-10-17	192,444,160	1,643,986	0.8543	16,998,815
2019-01-16	190,800,174	1,623,818	0.8511	9,401,906
2019-04-16	189,176,356	829,888	0.4295	15,601,894
2019-07-12	188,346,468	808,888	0.4295	23,797,485
2019-10-17	187,537,580	2,061,888	1.0995	36,701,606
2020-01-18	185,475,692	2,216,888	1.1952	38,795,540
2020-04-18	183,258,804	3,373,988	1.8411	52,465,513
2020-07-18	179,884,816	3,477,388	1.9331	60,506,551
2020-10-17	176,407,428	2,253,888	1.2777	67,999,801
2021-01-19	174,533,652	3,619,888	2.0786	165,790,870
2021-04-16	170,533,652	1,099,888	0.6450	595,314,380
2021-07-18	169,433,764	1,296,728	0.7653	393,673,654
2021-07-18	168,137,036	1,335,888	0.7945	639,462,868

Binance uses *burning* as a mechanism to forestall excessive inflation in the supply of BNB. ***Burning*** refers to a transaction made on a blockchain that deletes units of crypto. This is done by sending the crypto to a *burner* address, one that can receive crypto but not send it. In the case of BNB, Binance routinely buys back a portion of BNB and burns it (figure 42). In theory, this limits supply, boosts demand, and protects the value of a coin. According to the initial Binance white paper, the company committed to an ongoing quarterly burn of 20% of its quarterly profits. It made good on that promise for several years, but the burning strategy has recently been modified to an auto-burn approach that burns coins in response to a variety of variables, such as the current BNB price and the volume of activity on the Binance Smart Chain.[8]

Figure 42 shows the quarterly burn quantities recorded on the blockchain through 2021, prior to the adoption of auto-burn. Note that the value of the coins burned in terms of their worth in US dollars reaches the tens and hundreds of millions!

BNB AT A GLANCE

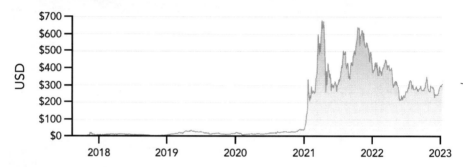

Value History (per unit):

fig. 43

BRIEF HISTORY:

BNB began in July 2017 as a utility token to aid and incentivize activity on the Binance cryptocurrencey exchange. It has since become a premier cryptocurrency asset with its own blockchain, consistently in the top ten of all cryptos in terms of market cap.

KEY CHARACTERISTICS:

- Usage has expanded from paying transaction fees on the Binance exchange to include payments for more everyday items such as travel booking and entertainment
- Runs on the Beacon Chain (formerly the Binance Chain), one of two blockchains in the Binance ecosystem (the other being the BNB Smart Chain)

KNOWN ISSUES:

- Heavy regulatory scrutiny due to the size of the Binance exchange[9]
- Being the largest crypto exchange in the world, it tends to attract the attention of regulators
- Large amount of BNB (possibly up to 80%) is held by the Binance exchange itself, centralizing the currency's ownership[10]

Source: www.coinmarketcap.com

Is coin-burning a mechanism for price manipulation—that is, burning coins intentionally to artificially increase the price? To be clear, the well-regimented and transparent burnings of Binance Coin do not represent this kind of fraud. But if you're going to navigate the world of altcoins, then you should know that there are other groups and individuals out there that will burn off the coins they're promoting in order to hack their way to a higher price point in the short term. This is bad and fraudulent; if you get wind of this type of activity, run the other way.

Polkadot

Why have one blockchain or even two, when you could have one hundred? Founded by Ethereum cofounder and creator of Solidity (discussed in chapter 5) Dr. Gavin Wood, the Polkadot blockchain protocol expanded the scope of what's possible within a blockchain ecosystem.

Wood, who holds a PhD in music visualization, envisioned Polkadot as a kind of Tolkienesque blockchain to connect all chains—one chain to rule them all, that sort of thing. The notion of interoperability and bridges (see the previous discussion on Cardano) appears again here and in a highly ambitious form, as Polkadot seeks to be the internet of blockchains, providing cross-chain interoperability between blockchains of all varieties, which in turn enables interoperability between dapps as well as oracles. *Oracles* enable information to be fed into smart contracts from non-blockchain-based systems and for the output of smart contracts to feed back out to non-blockchain-based systems.

The hub of the Polkadot network, its "core layer," is the relay chain. The relay chain is the glue that holds the rest of the ecosystem together, the one ring—or, um, Polkadot—to rule them all. It is the overseer of all network transactions. The secondary layer of the network is the hundred or so *parachains* that are leased at public auction for use in blockchain-based projects. Such projects might include the development of dapps or the creation of a DAO (discussed in chapter 5). The parachains can be leased for up to 96 weeks. In this way, Polkadot operates a bit like an art studio co-op or a small business incubation center.

The native currency token of the Polkadot universe is the DOT. While DOTs can be traded and speculated on like any other cryptocurrency, they are also applied in special capacities to assist the functioning of the Polkadot ecosystem. For example, DOTs are used to vote on governance decisions facing the network. In this way they assume the role of "governance tokens," a tool for the creation of decentralized governance over an enterprise, a concept I discuss in more depth in chapter 12 on DeFi.

A developer proposes that Polkadot increase its transaction fees. This proposal polarizes the community, so it is put to a vote. The weight of a given vote is determined by a) the quantity of DOT tokens held by the voter and b) the duration of time for which the tokens are locked up. This "locking up" of tokens while voting is similar to the process of staking tokens in order to validate blocks.

⚫ POLKADOT AT A GLANCE

Value History (per unit):

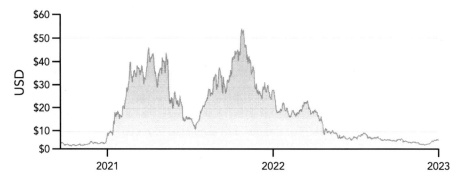

fig. 44

BRIEF HISTORY:

Founded in 2016 by Ethereum cofounder Dr. Gavin Wood, Polkadot is overseen by the Web3 Foundation and Parity Technologies, both founded by Wood

KEY CHARACTERISTICS:

- Interoperability-friendly architecture, with a base blockchain that serves and coordinates a multitude of secondary "parachains," resulting in high flexibility and diversity of use
- Upgrades made to the protocol with democratic voting system, without the need to create a fork

KNOWN ISSUES:

- Limited parachain slots, preventing the testing and development of some projects, especially smaller ones
- Competitive environment pitting Polkadot against Cardano and Ethereum, both of which have loyal developers and user bases[11]

Source: www.coinmarketcap.com

DOTs are also used to reward the minting of new blocks. Polkadot uses a proof-of-stake consensus mechanism for minting new coins that is similar to what is now used in Ethereum 2.0. Polkadot's spin on proof-of-stake is known as "nominated proof-of-stake" (NPoS) and relies on two distinct parties to accomplish the work of minting new blocks, nominators and validators. Nominators, as the name implies, make nominations from among a pool of validators. Their role is to select the most trustworthy of the lot, those least likely to act in bad faith. The validators in turn mint new blocks on the Polkadot relay chain and on all of the parachains.

In addition to nominators and validators there are a handful of other bit players that have roles and titles within the Polkadot ecosystem, including "collators" who help various parachains remain in good standing with the relay chain, and "fishermen" who monitor the relay chain and are rewarded for sniffing out bad behavior. This abundance of roles and blockchains makes the Polkadot protocol stand out as the most dynamically diverse addition to the canon of major altcoins.

Other Categories of Coins

In general, as an investor, the name of the game with altcoins is to find a good one that's undervalued, stock up, and cash out when you believe the time is right. In this section I discuss a few novel approaches to the altcoin game. I also walk you through some highly practical and somewhat less speculative altcoin applications.

Meme Coins

Meme coins are cryptos that were developed in the spirit of tongue-in-cheek homage to a given cultural touchstone (a meme). For example, the best-known meme coin, Dogecoin (figure 36), was invented in 2013 by two software engineers looking to poke fun at how easy it was for anyone to create a cryptocurrency about virtually anything. They chose to devote their crypto to the popular "doge" meme featuring a cuddly Shiba Inu dog—and despite its intentionally silly origins, it caught on.

To give you a sense of how comically arbitrary the meme coin market can be, look no further than the release of the Shiba Inu coin in 2020. It was fashioned as the "Doge Killer" and has acquired a cult following of devotees willing to sticker their cars and even tattoo their bodies with the likeness of the Shiba Inu icon.

To be clear, the creation of a cryptocurrency as an inside joke doesn't necessarily render it worthless. After all, if people accept a currency as payment, then it has value. In that sense, meme coins becoming genuinely valuable is not much different from the idea of fiat currency. That said, while some meme coins may catch on, there are many more that don't, and they currently don't make up a substantial part of the crypto ecosystem.

Shitcoins

As the creators of Dogecoin proved with an unexpected degree of success, anyone can create a cryptocurrency using some basic software. Maybe someone will want to buy some; who knows? It is this arbitrary quality that brought the term "shitcoin" into the dialect, referring to a crypto created with no discernible purpose, plan, or value proposition. (It also relates to the practice of "shitposting"—posting something strange or vexing on the internet as a joke.) The term shitcoin is often applied with a broad brush and as a pejorative to cast aspersion on any fledgling altcoin or on altcoins in general (some refer to all coins other than BTC or ETH as the "shitcoins").

Stablecoins

Stablecoins are cryptos that are pegged to the value of an established fiat currency or non-digital asset like gold. They are designed to enable crypto users to enjoy blockchain-based, peer-to-peer payments without having to weather the extreme volatility that is common in the cryptocurrency marketplace.

One of the initial use cases for stablecoins was to provide a smoother exit for altcoin investors. In the earlier days of the cryptocurrency phenomenon, traders who wished to extract their profits from a winning altcoin investment would first need to convert their altcoins into Bitcoin. This intermediary conversion exposed traders to another volatile asset (Bitcoin) and created frustration, especially when profits on altcoins became diminished before the Bitcoin could be liquidated into a more stable fiat currency. To add insult to injury, the Bitcoin intermediary conversion also meant paying another separate fee. Stablecoins provided traders with a clean exit into a fiat-like coin that would preserve their profits.

As time went on and altcoin markets became more liquid across the board, stablecoins remained useful for investors and traders who simply had no interest at all in converting back to fiat currency but were content to bank their gains in stablecoins and trust that the value of their profits would be preserved. Meanwhile, they'd avoid the costs and overhead of having to cash out in fiat.

There are three principal types of stablecoins[12]:
- » Fiat-collateralized
- » Crypto-collateralized
- » Non-collateralized

See figure 45 for a breakdown:

fig. 45

TYPES OF STABLECOIN COLLATERAL AND EXAMPLE COINS			
COLLATERAL TYPE	DOES IT REQUIRE TRUST?	EXAMPLE COINS	
Fiat	Yes, a central entity must be trusted to hold the required cash reserves.	USDC	Tether
Crypto	No, collateral assets (cryptos) are verifiable, as they are locked into the blockchain and can be publicly confirmed. However, due to the volatility of crypto, crypto-collateralized stablecoins should be over-collateralized, by a ratio of at least 2:1.	Dai	USTC
None	Yes, but more so because these non-collateralized stablecoins are at highest risk for entering a "death spiral," where a compounding wave of sell-offs causes the coin to become less valuable than the fiat currency to which it's pegged. On some occasions, the crypto may be driven all the way down to zero. After all, what's the worth of a stablecoin if it's not stable?	Zero Collateral Dai (ZAI)	Empty Set Dollar

In addition to the questions of collateralization, there are other challenges for stablecoins. Perhaps the most significant are regulatory in nature. Any asset brought to market that poses even a semblance of guaranteed value is apt to attract the attention of regulators. Many coin issuers across the wider cryptocurrency ecosystem would like nothing better than to avoid such scrutiny. The United States Treasury Department has been researching ways to regulate what it deems a "sizable" and "growing" stablecoin market. Their concerns are that an inability to maintain the value of these coins could lead to destabilizing runs on the currencies, cascades of "fire sales" that could spread from one coin to another after one or more coins fails to maintain its value. They are also concerned about the concentration of economic power in the payments sector by businesses that operate stablecoins.[13]

There's another question about stablecoins: will they remain *independently* viable? It's already known that the Federal Reserve Bank and the National Security Agency were looking into creating cryptocurrencies in the 1990s. There's no reason that the Federal Reserve Bank, the Bank of China, or another central bank couldn't create its own government-sponsored blockchain currency. If that happens, then the demand for other stablecoins could be negatively affected. They could be seen as an unnecessary middle ground between crypto that's untethered from any type of fiat currency and crypto that's government-backed like more traditional fiat currencies.

CityCoins

CityCoins are city-specific cryptos that are utilized as a funding mechanism with the objective of building prosperity and increased cultural participation within a given city. CityCoins are built on an open-source crypto protocol known as Stacks (with an associated token known as "STX"). Stacks is known for its ability to execute smart contracts that can be finalized and secured on the Bitcoin blockchain. It is this functionality that allows Stacks to power the CityCoins infrastructure. Here's how it works: STX miners forward some amount of STX (from their mining reward) into a smart contract and are rewarded, per the dictates of the contract, by a certain quantity of new CityCoin tokens. Take MiamiCoin as an example. Per the contract, 70% of STX mining reward x is sent to existing owners of MiamiCoin (this is part of their incentive for holding the coin), while the remaining 30% of x is sent to the City of Miami. The STX can be converted to Bitcoin or US dollars whenever the city wishes to do so.

The CityCoins project (citycoins.co) is really no more than an infrastructure that anyone can develop on behalf of any given city. You will need approval from the city's mayor or some equivalent authority who can claim the city wallet. You will also need a minimum of 20 individuals to send STX tokens to the smart contract that will activate the mining process.

The infrastructure for CityCoins has not been further refined. But the basic incentive structure for creating, holding, and trading these tokens has proven its ability to generate a significant quantity of new wealth for the treasury of at least one major US city: in 2021 Miami made seven million US dollars thanks to CityCoins,[14] though the subsequent 2022 drop in value of Bitcoin reduced these gains considerably.

With continued innovation and creative energy, it's possible to envision a robust utility for these tokens. Imagine if CityCoins could be used as substitute payment for mass transit or for paying for arena concert tickets. It seems cities could be strongly incentivized to create CityCoins spending opportunities for their citizens. The more spendable the coin, the higher its demand. The higher the demand, the more STX miners will participate in the CityCoins smart contract, which directly generates revenue for the city itself.

Create Your Own Altcoin

Would you like to create your own cryptocurrency … or at least know how to create one? There are a surprising number of options for doing so. One of the reasons that so many altcoins exist is that they're relatively easy to create.

There are several ways to create cryptocurrency:

1. **Open source**: Bitcoin, for example, is built on open-source software, which you can download, use, and modify as you like, to create your own crypto. You can download the code from GitHub, among many other repositories. Modifying the code, however, requires programming skills.

2. **Using a third-party service**: WalletBuilders, one of the many such services that have sprung up as interest in crypto has soared, claims, "We make blockchain technology available for everyone. Create your own coin with our coin wizard without any knowledge of programming."

3. **Hard-forking**: An existing open-source blockchain can be hard-forked. This involves creating a new blockchain, as well as its altcoin, from an existing one. Hard-forking occurs when there is a fundamental change to a blockchain's underlying protocol. If you change the rules in this way, there is a permanent divergence from the earlier version of the blockchain, as shown in figure 46.

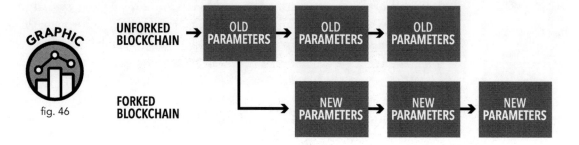

GRAPHIC

fig. 46

UNFORKED BLOCKCHAIN → OLD PARAMETERS → OLD PARAMETERS → OLD PARAMETERS

FORKED BLOCKCHAIN → NEW PARAMETERS → NEW PARAMETERS → NEW PARAMETERS

Adding a new rule to the code essentially creates a fork in the blockchain: one path follows the new blockchain, and the other path continues to follow the old blockchain. In the process, a new cryptocurrency or altcoin is created. There are several examples of this happening on the Bitcoin blockchain, including Bitcoin Cash, which became the eleventh-largest cryptocurrency in 2021, and Bitcoin Gold.

4. **Use Ethereum**: Using the Ethereum network to create what's known as an "ERC-20 token" is perhaps the most common way new altcoins are created. You will find countless tokens throughout the crypto-verse, including several of the most prominent, that are powered by Ethereum. I discuss the ERC-20 standard and its implications in more depth in chapter 7.

Why New Crypto?

With so many cryptocurrencies available, why create a new one? You may be so intrigued by crypto and blockchain that you simply want to go deeper and check under the hood. There's nothing like doing something for yourself if you want to understand it better. Part of what's interesting here is the chance to create a crypto with a monetary policy that you yourself design.

Don't forget that creating a new altcoin often involves creating a new blockchain. Perhaps you're interested in creating a cryptocurrency to support a specific functionality. For example, Polkadot facilitates interoperability among different blockchains, and the XRP altcoin supports the settlement of financial transactions in real time. There are many business use cases to which creating a new crypto could be applied.

The Future of Altcoins: Opportunities and Challenges

With nearly 20,000 coins in the market, the altcoin scene right now is very much the Wild West. The frenzy is driven in part by the enormous amount of growth that has been observed in this space. Back in 2021, the crypto market as a whole grew from $965 billion and hit highs of $2.6 trillion.[15] Altcoins, making up roughly 40% of the entire crypto market, grew by a staggering 550% over this same period.[16] The sheer magnitude of the money in play makes this phenomenon impossible to ignore.

As with the California gold rush of the 19th century, not everyone will get rich under these conditions. Some are going to show up ill-prepared; others will arrive too late on the scene, holding their pickaxes and gold pans and looking foolish when they try to mine a barren landscape. In addition to having a little bit of luck and good timing, the successful altcoin proprietor will have solid management and leadership skills, as well as sound capital backing to sustain themselves through the bearish periods.

To me, the most inspiring opportunity in the altcoin realm is the wide-open spaces still left for innovation. From my brief tour of some major altcoins, you can likely envision how new coins boasting new innovations and advantages will likely continue to arrive in the marketplace. Major players in the space will continue to serve up fresh ideas to the greater community of investors, speculators, and developers, and the market will reward those who excel at bringing the benefits of blockchain and cryptocurrency back to the end user.

As for the challenges facing altcoins, they are not trivial. Altcoin pioneers must navigate a terrain riddled with risk and volatility. Those risks have a variety of sources. Fraudsters and bad actors, as well as ill-informed players, all pose substantial risks to the well-intentioned altcoin investor, speculator, or entrepreneur. There's also a lack of overarching standards and regulations for cryptocurrencies. When regulation does hit the industry, it may come suddenly, increasing the volatility of an already-volatile market.

The absence of widespread interoperability is another challenge. Few exchanges maintain a market for a wide variety of altcoins, which means that owners of the crypto could have a hard time cashing out. Finally, not everyone will take the time needed to fully understand this new technology and its implications the way that you have. If less-informed parties do end up making investments, those decisions could be driven by impulse, creating a boom-and-bust cycle rather than opportunities for long-term growth. Just remember the questions I posed throughout this chapter: what is the basis for a coin's success, and will you be able to recognize these elements in lesser-known upstarts?

Chapter Recap

» The nearly 20,000 altcoins in the market today represent a variety of blockchains, consensus mechanisms, and essential functions.

» The altcoins that have made gains in a market where Bitcoin has seen such staggering growth are driven by innovators who deliver maximum value to their end users.

» Some altcoins have practical applications, such as CityCoins, which are used to raise revenues for cities, and stablecoins, which are pegged to the value of a fiat currency. Other altcoins don't even offer a pretense of functionality, yet some of these have nonetheless exploded in value.

» While the playing field for new altcoin development and expanded applications of existing altcoins remains ripe for innovation, there are a myriad of challenges that altcoin entrepreneurs and investors should be well aware of, including fraud, lack of regulation, lack of interoperability, and ill-informed investors who drive boom-and-bust cycles.

| 7 |

Tokens

So far, I've been focusing on the details of cryptocurrencies. But crypto coins are not the only crypto assets that can be enabled by blockchains. Blockchains can serve as platforms for an entire universe of functionality, based on what are known as *tokens*. Aside from coins, tokens are where a lot of the emergent and innovative action is happening.

Tokens have been around since the early days of crypto. A later development in this space is the non-fungible token, or NFT. But what makes a token non-fungible or fungible? And how does a token differ from a cryptocurrency coin such as a bitcoin, ether, or the many proliferating altcoins? I answer these questions and more in this chapter.

A Token of What?

I like to think of a *token* as a simple stand-in for a physical or digital object. That's the broad definition: something that stands in for, or can be exchanged for, something else. For example, the voucher you get in the mail that entitles you to two entrees for the price of one at a local restaurant, or a winning lottery ticket.

You may have encountered metal, coin-like tokens at old-fashioned video arcades, where some games require tokens rather than quarters or dollars. Tokens were also used for admission to the New York City subway for much of its history and are still in use in many subways around the world. In these systems, you buy tokens at the booth and then feed them into the turnstile for admission to the underground train system. In New York's system, tokens were phased out in favor of a magnetic digital card (figure 47) around the turn of the 21st century; now, the magnetic cards are in the process of being phased out in favor of contactless phone and credit card payments, which are already accepted at all stations.

fig. 47

Subway token   Magnetic digital card

Regardless of the mechanics of the transaction, the New York subway still essentially uses a token system. The metal subway-admission tokens are now electronically registered on a card that you swipe or tap on a card reader, which then lets you into the subway system. The first token is physical and analog; the second is electronic and digital. Both types serve the same function.

So, while some may associate the word "token" with a metal, coin-like object, a token can represent anything of value. It can represent either digital or real-world assets. In the world of crypto, tokenization transforms real-world assets into digital tokens on a blockchain, enabling an easier exchange and transfer of assets.

Tokens vs. Coins

Just as arcade tokens or subway tokens can resemble coins and function in their place, it's easy to confuse a crypto token and a crypto coin. What's the difference between, say, ether, and a token that runs on the Ethereum blockchain? Understandably, a lot of people think of coins and tokens as synonymous.. I'll clear the confusion up now.

It's true that crypto coins and tokens have many attributes in common. Both represent a store of value, and both run on blockchains. However, crypto coins, such as bitcoin and ether, are basically digital versions of money, the equivalent of cash. Tokens, on the other hand, aren't money as we usually think of it. Instead, they represent assets—things that can be bought.

In other words, while crypto coins are a form of money, crypto tokens represent something that can be assigned a price and that money can buy. Like subway or arcade tokens, crypto tokens are tokens *of* or *for* something. Tokens can hold value and be exchanged, and because cryptocurrencies are digital, you could create a token that stands for a crypto coin, or a specific number of crypto coins (sort of like those all-purpose gift cards stored on credit cards). But tokens can also be used to represent physical and digital assets, such as goods and services.

There are other notable differences between crypto coins and tokens. One is the architecture that supports them. Crypto coins have their own dedicated blockchains, such as Bitcoin and Ethereum. Tokens are built on top of smart contract-powered blockchains, such as Ethereum.

The dapps that run on Ethereum use tokens for a wide variety of functions, including the delivery of products or services. For example, Ethereum's Basic Attention Token (BAT) dapp is designed to disrupt the digital advertising industry, making it easier to pay publishers. BAT token-holders can use the platform to buy a variety of advertising services.

The creation of digital coins involves building a new, dedicated blockchain. While this has been simplified by the ability to copy the Bitcoin source code, creating tokens is even easier: anyone with a computer and a good or service to tokenize can do it. There is no need to create and build a new blockchain. The software to create these tokens is readily available.

Figure 48 is a simple summary of these contrasting characteristics:

fig. 48

COIN	TOKEN
An independent digital asset that acts as an alternative to traditional or fiat currency.	Generally created to be used in conjunction with an application.
Native to its own blockchain with its own protocol.	Created on top of an existing blockchain.

Fungible vs. Non-Fungible Tokens

Tokens come in two varieties: fungible and non-fungible. You might reasonably ask what on earth that means, because "fungible" isn't a word that often appears in everyday conversation. It doesn't exactly come tripping off the tongue.

Merriam-Webster's first definition of *fungible* sounds complex: "being something (such as money or a commodity) of such a nature that one part or quantity may be replaced by another equal part or quantity in paying a debt or settling an account." Its second, more compact definition is clearer and simpler: "capable of mutual substitution; interchangeable."

Fiat currency, for example, is fungible. If you have a $20 bill, I can exchange another $20 bill with you, and neither of us will be richer or poorer; we'll both be the same as we started. The same is true of cryptocurrency: your Bitcoin is worth the same as, and is interchangeable with, any other Bitcoin.

Other fungible assets include precious metals like gold, commodities like oil, and financial instruments like bonds. All things being equal, one ounce of 24-carat gold is interchangeable with any other ounce.

Non-fungible items, by contrast, are not interchangeable. This is true even if the items are similar in many respects.

For example, there are two houses built at the same time as part of a suburban housing tract. They have the same floor plan and square footage. They may even be painted the same color. However, one house was necessarily built in a different location than the second, possibly making it more or less desirable—say with a view of the nearby mountains. Or imagine that one house may have been meticulously maintained, while the other has become more run-down over time. As similar as they may be, the houses aren't interchangeably the same, which means their values can also vary.

Works of art are another example of non-fungible assets. A painting by even a talented amateur artist is hardly interchangeable with a work by Picasso that's considered a masterpiece. Even two paintings by the same artist, painted in the same style and with similar subject matter, are non-fungible. They can be similar to one another but have many different qualities that affect their value either upward or downward.

Fungible Tokens: Security, Utility, and Governance

There are four main types of fungible crypto token: security, utility, governance, and transactional.

1. **Security tokens**: Security tokens can be used to represent ownership of an asset that already has value, such as real estate, a car, or corporate stock. Someone could own a token that represents a 5% share of a private jet, for instance. This token is fungible, because your ownership of 5% of the jet is interchangeable with anyone else's 5% ownership. A new altcoin venture might, for example, issue investors security tokens equivalent to company stock.

2. **Utility tokens**: Utility tokens give users access to a future product or service. For example, a start-up can issue utility tokens to investors in order to raise money. Later, those investors can redeem the tokens to use the start-up's services or products. Anyone who invests a certain amount of money in the start-up will receive the exact same interchangeable services if the start-up becomes a viable enterprise. An example of a utility token might be tokens issued by a gaming company as in-game currency. (More on gaming tokens below.)

   As an analog, airline, hotel, and other reward-points systems are examples of utility tokens. They have value but only within their own ecosystems. When you fly Southwest Airlines, you can accrue or redeem reward points, but you can't redeem them for a trip on Delta Airlines.

3. **Governance tokens**: Governance tokens are becoming more prominent as DeFi (decentralized finance) and DAO (decentralized autonomous organization) initiatives continue to explore the potential of blockchain technology. They represent ownership in a decentralized protocol and provide token holders with certain governance rights that influence that protocol's direction. In other words, you can think of them as tokens of voting rights on a blockchain. Those with governance tokens will be able to vote, for instance, on whether a proposed change to a blockchain is to be put into practice. I discuss governance tokens at greater length in chapter 12 on DeFi.

4. **Transactional tokens**: As the name suggests, transactional tokens

can be exchanged for goods and services. These tokens often function like traditional currencies but are also used in industry and supply chains that see the benefit in record-keeping that combines smart-contract flexibility with blockchain immutability. A shipping company could, for instance, use transactional tokens to keep records of its international commerce so as to minimize product loss. The tokens have no function outside of their native enterprise or industry.

ICO: Initial Coin Offering

Fungible tokens have often been used to help fund crypto start-ups. In crypto's early days, utility tokens in particular were often issued in what were called *initial coin offerings*, or ICOs.

ICOs, sometimes known as "crowdsales," are a vehicle that crypto start-ups use to raise the funds needed to launch. They are roughly the equivalent of a public company's initial public offering or IPO. One significant difference is that ICOs aren't regulated by the US SEC (United States Securities and Exchange Commission), as IPOs are.

Typically, a new crypto's white paper serves as the ICO's prospectus. Investments are made with a previously existing cryptocurrency, such as Bitcoin, in exchange for the tokens. There have been some notably successful ICOs. Ethereum's ICO took place in 2014 and raised $18 million in forty-two days.[1] The original investors, who purchased utility tokens using Bitcoin, have earned back their investment many, many times over.

Unfortunately, without regulations by the SEC, ICOs became a popular vehicle for fraudulent schemes. It wasn't until 2020, for example, that the US Department of Justice instituted a wire and security fraud indictment of the founders of PlexCoin, a worthless token that three years before had raised $8 million that they then absconded with.

Peter Forrest's objections to his daughter Tori's interest in crypto are largely based on the news stories about such frauds. He points out that one study concluded that up to 80% of the ICOs offered in 2017 were scams. On the other hand, the amount lost in these scams was only 11% of the amount invested in legitimate ICOs: $1.34 billion was invested in scams as opposed to $11.0 billion in up-and-up offerings.[2]

But why are ICOs unregulated in the first place? Remember that Satoshi Nakamoto conceived of cryptocurrency as a peer-to-peer monetary system without the need for intermediaries or any oversight. This means that ICOs exist in an unregulated environment. Founders of ICOs argue that the tokens they issue are not meant as a speculative investment but rather as a means of accessing the goods and services in their platforms.

How accurate is this characterization? While slow on the uptake in crypto's early days, the SEC eventually turned its eye to the crypto market. It generally determined that so-called utility tokens were in fact securities—negotiable financial assets that have some kind of value, like stocks or bonds.

The SEC has a standard definition of what a security is, as well as a test that can determine if an offering is in fact a security, governable by SEC regulations, or not. In response to a 1946 case involving the sale of tracts of citrus groves then leased back to the seller, the W. J. Howey Co., the Supreme Court established the Howey test's criteria to determine whether an investment transaction has occurred.

Under the Howey test, an investment contract involves the following[3]:

1. An investment of money in an enterprise
2. An expectation of profit from the investment
3. Profit derived from the efforts of others

Using this test, the SEC has the power to declare an ICO to be a security—an investment—even though those initiating the ICO declare it a utility token. When identified as a security, it becomes subject to regulation, making the ICO process far more complex and expensive. An ICO declared a security therefore becomes a less attractive means of funding a start-up. Once popular, ICOs are now rarely used.

STO: Security Token Offering

Security token offerings (STOs) were created in 2018 and became a safer alternative to ICOs. An STO, which issues security tokens rather than utility tokens, must comply with the security laws administered by the authorities in the jurisdiction in which they are issued. In the United States, this authority is the SEC.

These strictures demonstrate the ongoing tension between crypto's fundamental impulse toward decentralization and the centralized governmental authorities whose job it is to protect the public from the kinds of ICO scams that proliferated around 2017. STOs were created to provide investors with a better regulated and more transparent fundraising vehicle.

The Difference Between an STO and a Traditional IPO

The fundamental difference is that an STO involves a blockchain, while an IPO (initial public offering) does not. In an IPO, an investor buys regulated stocks representing the assets, while in an STO, the investor buys tokens representing digital assets. This makes an STO a less cumbersome and considerably more cost-effective process than an IPO, albeit a more heavily regulated one than an ICO.

This distinction has numerous implications. One way of looking at this is that an IPO is an analog process and an STO is a digital one. The stocks and other securities that an IPO generates must be offered on a registered stock exchange. Security tokens don't have to surmount this hurdle.

Non-Fungible Tokens (NFTs)

In the late 2010s, a new type of token, the non-fungible token or *NFT*, exploded in popularity. *Non-fungible* means that these tokens represent unique assets that can't be substituted for one another, such as works of art. They are *not* interchangeable.

NFTs have been created to represent digital art as well as things like photos, collectibles, sports memorabilia, virtual real estate, and items within games. NFTs can be used not only by collectors but in any industry that wants to confidently authenticate assets or products, whether digital or non-digital.

Enabling digital assets such as images to be certified as unique has been a tough problem to solve, because the design of most digital files makes them easy to copy. However, blockchain and smart contracts have built the conditions for an emerging, thriving marketplace for digital assets. This is achieved by creating a certificate in the form of a token and storing it on a blockchain. The token can be traded as the equivalent of a physical certificate of authenticity passing ownership of the token from one person to another.

The first major NFT initiative was CryptoKitties, an Ethereum-based game that enables users to buy, sell, collect, and breed virtual or digital cats (figure 49). The game created such a sensation with its 2017 launch that it threatened to overwhelm the Ethereum network.

An array of CryptoKitties.

When selling digital items, a creator now has the option to assign one or more as unique versions of the digital asset. Each asset can then be issued a unique NFT that contains authenticity data. Unlike a tangible painting or print signed by the artist, the NFT is then stored on a blockchain as a tamper-proof, immutable transaction. However, someone who possesses an NFT generally doesn't own the item represented. Rather, they've been assigned an instance of the item with a unique digital signature.

The world of collectibles transposed to the digital realm has become the subject of debate. Many argue it's as valid to collect a digital art piece with the artist's digital signature as, say, a signed baseball card or a signed print of a painting. Detractors see a superficial and temporary marketplace that naive enthusiasm is overinflating. Time will tell which perspective ultimately wins out.

One of the fastest-growing categories of NFTs is what's known as *gaming tokens*. These represent gaming assets like weapons, costumes, and skills. These tokens are also an immutable, provable source of ownership. In other words, you or your avatar own the NFT gaming token, not the gaming system or blockchain. So it's you who will benefit should the asset increase in value. Some gaming tokens also enable token holders to participate in the project's governance.

Ethereum Token Standards: ERC-20, ERC-721, and ERC-1155

As of early 2023, much of tokenization takes place on Ethereum. This make sense, as a token is generally a representation of a transaction governed by a smart contract. Other NFT options, such as Solana, are emerging, but Ethereum's relative maturity and support capabilities have established it as the primary platform.

Various sets of guidelines for the creation of tokens come from Ethereum's process for development and improvement of its platform, known as "Ethereum Request for Comments," or ERCs for short. ERCs are numbered consecutively, with certain new protocols proving particularly significant.

ERC-20

Perhaps the most fundamental of these is ERC-20, which provides a list of rules for smart contracts that implement fungible tokens. Think of ERC-20 as a set of guidelines that any new token created in the Ethereum network must adhere to. Tokens that follow the ERC-20 protocol are fundamentally interoperable with one another. For example, the standard enables the transfer of tokens from one account to another.

ERC-721

In 2018, Ethereum programmers created a dedicated NFT standard called ERC-721. It provides functionalities to transfer NFTs from one account to another and to get the current token balance of an account, a token's owner, and the total supply of the token available on the network. Because NFTs are typically managed on a growing ecosystem of third-party solutions, ERC-721 implements an application programming interface (API) between these other applications and the smart-contract-driven tokens on Ethereum. ERC-721 connects those applications with the Ethereum blockchain's token store.

ERC-1155

ERC-1155, a more sophisticated standard that allows for issuing multiple tokens at the same time, is becoming popular and may overtake ERC-721 in the future. The ERC-1155 protocol covers the creation of both fungible and non-fungible tokens. In other words, an ERC-1155 token can do the same functions as a fungible ERC-20 and a non-fungible/ NFT ERC-721 token. Ethereum maintains that ERC-1155 improves on the functionality and efficiency of both ERC-20 and ERC-721.

Real Estate Tokenization

For many, the value that NFTs represent can feel somewhat abstract. On the other hand, nothing is more real and concrete than real estate: property and buildings.

Until recently, it would have been impossible for someone as young and of relatively limited means as Alan Forrest to think of investing in real estate. Yet his sister Tori shows him it's now possible for him to do so using a blockchain-based solution.

Rather than having to buy a property outright for an untenable sum, Alan could purchase, through a blockchain-based broker, one or more tokens representing fractional ownership in a property for a fraction of the total price. For example, in the case of an apartment building, if Alan used his savings to buy a 5% share of the property, he could expect to receive 5% of its rental income until he decides to sell.

Alan eventually figures out that this would still be a stretch for him—a 5% share of the property is still too high a barrier of entry. But in the course of these discussions, his parents Peter and Lynn become intrigued. They've often considered investing in real estate, but prices have gone through the roof. Not only does tokenization make partial purchases far more viable, but blockchain-based exchanges considerably reduce the legal complexities and costs of these transactions.

Lynn and Peter decide to conduct an experiment and take the leap by purchasing 10% of a fourplex. They soon begin receiving small but significant passive income from rent on the four units. If the experiment continues to work out, they might consider another such investment.

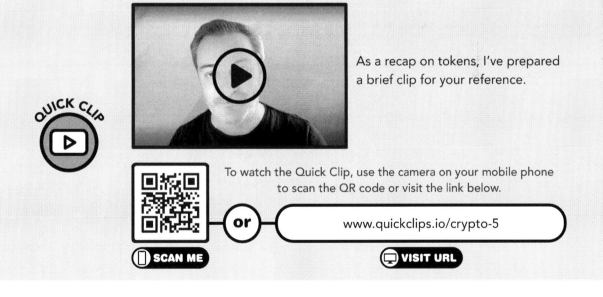

As a recap on tokens, I've prepared a brief clip for your reference.

To watch the Quick Clip, use the camera on your mobile phone to scan the QR code or visit the link below.

or   www.quickclips.io/crypto-5

SCAN ME   VISIT URL

Creating, Publishing, and Selling Your Own NFTs

So where do these NFTs actually come from? Here's a step-by-step guide on how to create, publish, and sell your own NFTs using the popular OpenSea (www.opensea.io) platform. The process outlined is for the purpose of turning your own digital photo into an NFT, which can then be sold.

Before you get started, you should note that publishing an NFT on OpenSea requires the use of a wallet and some cryptocurrency. At step 2, you'll see a list of supported wallets. You may want to refer to chapter 2, where I discuss wallets. Also note that along the way, you'll need to pay some fees. See, for example, chapter 5 for an explanation of gas fees required in the Ethereum blockchain.

> » **Step 1**: Go to https://opensea.io/ If it's your first time visiting OpenSea as an NFT creator, you'll need to click on Profile on the home screen and follow the steps to establish your account (figure 50).

fig. 50

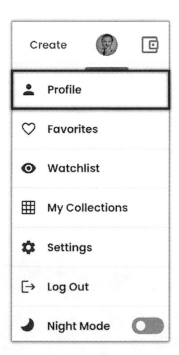

> » **Step 2**: Whether you are setting up your account for the first time, or you are ready to create a new NFT, you will be prompted to connect your wallet. Select your wallet from the list (many more are listed under Show More Options). Connecting your wallet is

the equivalent of logging into the system. You'll notice that there are a number of times during the process when your wallet will be required. This is for payment and authentication requirements (figure 51).

fig. 51

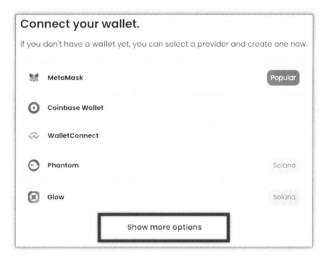

Connect your wallet.

If you don't have a wallet yet, you can select a provider and create one now.

MetaMask   Popular

Coinbase Wallet

WalletConnect

Phantom   Solana

Glow   Solana

Show more options

» **Step 3**: I use the popular MetaMask wallet, so I am presented with this screen (figure 52). You'll get a prompt for your wallet once you select or create it.

fig. 52

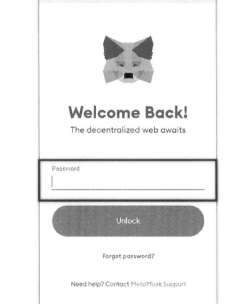

MetaMask Notification   —   □   ×

Welcome Back!
The decentralized web awaits

Password

Unlock

Forgot password?

Need help? Contact MetaMask Support

» **Step 4:** When you're ready to create your NFT, click on Create on the menu (figure 53).

| Explore | Stats | Resources | Create |

» **Step 5:** You're now prompted to create your NFT. Here you will upload and describe your digital asset (figure 54). In this example step-by-step guide, I am creating an NFT for a picture of an iceberg I took on a recent visit to Alaska.

Create New Item

* Required fields

Image, Video, Audio, or 3D Model *

File types supported: JPG, PNG, GIF, SVG, MP4, WEBM, MP3, WAV, OGG, GLB, GLTF, Max size: 100 MB

Name *

Item name

» **Step 6:** During creation of your NFT, you can select from a number of options. Most of these are discretionary, and if you don't enter them now, you can come back and edit them any time you wish (figure 55).

» **Step 7:** Continue to complete the details for your NFT. You may want to mint this NFT more than once so that there are several unique versions available for sale. In addition, while Ethereum is by far the most popular blockchain to use for NFTs, you may have a reason to sell your NFT on one of the others listed under the blockchain dropdown box (figure 56).

fig. 55

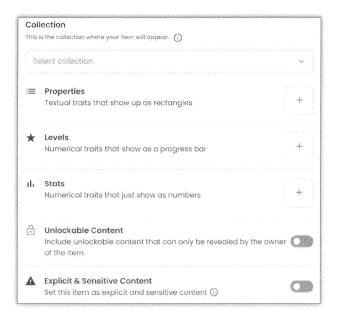

fig. 56

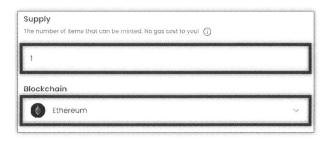

» **Step 8**: Once you click on Create, your NFT details will be recorded and stored (figure 57). While it will be viewable by users of OpenSea, it's not yet available for sale. That will happen in the next steps.

» **Step 9**: Unless you want to edit your NFT record at this point, you can now click on Sell to complete the process and make it available for sale (figure 58).

» **Step 10**: Before making it available for sale, you have to make some decisions about how you want to sell your NFT. You can either list it at a fixed price and sell it to anyone who pays the requested amount, or you can auction and sell to the highest bidder. After entering all the relevant details, click on "Complete Listing" (figure 59).

fig. 57

fig. 58

fig. 59

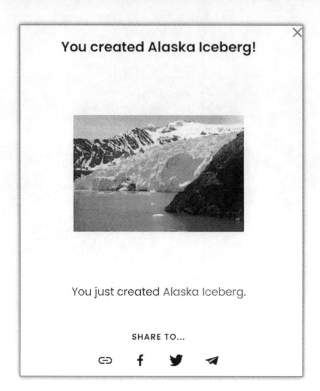

» **Step 11**: A summary of your listing will appear, and you will be prompted to sign the NFT with your wallet to approve the listing (figure 60). Once you've signed it, your NFT will be queued up and processed as a tradeable NFT. Note that on OpenSea—at the time of writing—the first NFT you create requires some gas if it is being published on the Ethereum platform, but subsequent NFTs don't require more gas.

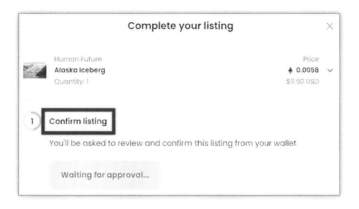

fig. 60

» **Step 12**: You'll next receive confirmation of your listing (figure 61). It's now available for sale!

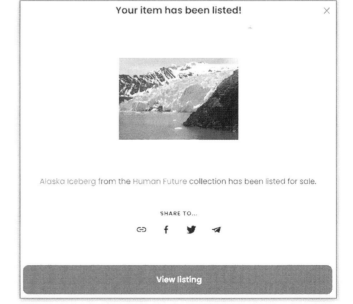

fig. 61

Tokenomics: A Brief Introduction

At the beginning of the chapter, I distinguished tokens from cryptocurrency. It can still be easy to confuse the two, especially because all crypto assets are also essentially tokens. In everyday English, "token" is a relatively common, and sometimes slippery, term. One important crypto and blockchain term retains this ambiguity: *tokenomics*, a portmanteau (a word made up of parts of two or more other words) of "token" and "economics." This makes tokenomics sound like a study of tokens in particular. But it's actually a catchall that covers everything that makes a cryptocurrency valuable (or not). For example, it addresses questions such as what is the crypto's supply? How is it issued or mined? What can it be used for?

Until recently, only a government's central bank was authorized to issue currency. Then along came cryptocurrency. Tokenomics takes what central banks call monetary policy and describes it for cryptocurrencies and tokens. This includes issuing (mining or minting) and distributing a blockchain's cryptocurrency, as well as governance of the underlying decentralized system.

Tokenomics involves the psychological and behavioral factors that affect the short- and long-term viability of a crypto's ecosystem. Something's value is, at least in part, determined by what that value is perceived to be. Many other factors, such as cultural trends, influence these perceptions in depth. This is a subject studied in great depth by disciplines like behavioral economics and socioeconomics.

If you're considering whether or not to buy a crypto asset, understanding its tokenomics is a very useful first step. How we value or assign a cost to something is a complex topic studied by marketers, philosophers, and economists.

I explore tokenomics further in the context of part 3's discussion on buying, selling, trading, and investing in cryptocurrency and related assets.

Tokens: Advantages, Challenges, and the Future

The blockchain community is just beginning to explore the many possible uses of tokens. Accordingly, some efforts and experiments will succeed and others will fail.

Security tokens remain a viable, regulated method of raising funds for new crypto initiatives. Fungible tokens constitute a practicable means of representing whole or partial ownership of real assets of all types. However, there's certainly plenty of debate today about the value of NFTs. Critics maintain that the value of NFTs is essentially a house of cards, representing a temporary, superficial marketplace that may suddenly collapse.

Others, though, maintain that NFTs represent a viable new asset class that is finally rewarding digital creators who have been exploited for far too long. Some are even more bullish, believing that in the long term, NFTs may represent a completely new and important business model for trading goods and services.

Perhaps one of the most compelling uses of NFTs is their role as a financial instrument. NFTs are beginning to be used in the emerging DeFi arena for use in staking pools, governance, and loan collateralization. DeFi is a blockchain- and smart-contracts-based set of financial services that are outside of traditional financial intermediaries such as banks and brokerages. I discuss DeFi in detail in chapter 12.

The bulk of NFTs are based on the Ethereum platform, which seems stable and has strong long-term prospects. But other new, Ethereum-like blockchains that are minting NFTs may not have such staying power. What will happen to any NFTs that are stored on an unsuccessful blockchain if it goes away? Unfortunately, they may go away, too.

Those who choose to engage early must recognize the risks and behave accordingly. There is a lot to gain, but also a lot to lose. NFTs are in that category where the risk is extremely high, but the potential upside is significant.

Reasonable people can disagree, which is what the members of the Forrest family continue to do. Tori continues to firmly believe that the upside justifies the potential downside: reward is always tied to risk.

Chapter Recap

» A token represents something and can be exchanged for something else.

» Unlike crypto coins, tokens aren't money. Instead, they represent assets—things that can be bought.

» Tokenization transforms real-world assets into digital tokens on a blockchain, enabling an easier exchange and transfer of assets.

» Crypto coins have their own dedicated blockchains, such as Bitcoin or Ethereum. Tokens, on the other hand, are built on top of blockchains powered by smart contracts, like Ethereum.

» Tokens come in two varieties: fungible and non-fungible.

» There are four main types of fungible crypto token: security, utility, governance, and transactional tokens.

» Fungible tokens have often been used to help fund crypto start-ups. In crypto's early days, utility tokens in particular were often issued in what were called initial coin offerings or ICOs.

» Non-fungible tokens represent unique assets that can't be substituted for one another, such as works of art. They are not interchangeable.

» Someone who possesses an NFT generally doesn't own the item represented. Rather, they've been assigned an instance of the item with a unique digital signature.

PART III

CRYPTOCURRENCY IN ACTION

| 8 |
Buying and Selling Cryptocurrency

In the early days of cryptocurrencies, they weren't all that easy to acquire. Technology enthusiasts were among the few willing to engage in a process which used to require some fairly complex steps, a significant amount of risk, and awareness of the relatively few pathways available to initiate the exchange. When the Bitcoin software was released in January of 2009, there were only two avenues available to obtain Bitcoin: you could either mine it yourself, or you could find another crypto enthusiast and negotiate a transfer.[1] It was this latter method that brought about the famous pizza purchase of 2010. You can find that story in chapter 4.

These days, access to cryptocurrency is democratized and has been largely simplified. Cryptocurrency exchanges have popped up in droves, while established financial brands such as PayPal, Goldman Sachs, Robinhood, Ally Bank and others have made it simple to purchase selected cryptocurrencies on their platforms. In this chapter I discuss some of the tools and resources available for buying and selling cryptocurrency and NFTs. I also walk you through the fundamentals of crypto valuation, a process we continue to explore throughout part 3 of this book.

Cryptocurrency Wallets and Exchanges

Your ownership of crypto is defined by your key pairs: no keys, no crypto. Your keys enable you to initiate a transfer of crypto or to receive it from others. Your approach to storing keys is a major decision. This is particularly critical for your private key(s), which must remain, well, private. The importance of this decision has inspired entire product lines of hardware and software solutions, known as wallets. Exchanges, meanwhile, are the venues that bring buyers and sellers together. Many exchanges will also manage your private keys on your behalf—a service referred to as a *custodial wallet*. Most cryptocurrency investors will need to find the right wallet and the right exchange for their needs.

Wallets

The main functions of a cryptocurrency wallet are to facilitate access and management of private keys and to check crypto balances. Wallets have a wide range of forms. They may be simple software programs that you install and run on your computer. Alternatively, they may take the form of detachable, transportable hardware. They may also be embedded within a network node that you operate.

When it comes to her cryptocurrency, Tori is committed to extending her trust only when and where it is absolutely warranted. She holds a significant quantity of Bitcoin as an investment. Rather than extend her "circle of trust" to include a third-party app, Tori opts to run Bitcoin Core software, which requires hundreds of gigabytes of hard drive space. This *full node wallet* contains a complete and constantly updating copy of the Bitcoin blockchain, and it also has a built-in wallet that allows her to send and receive Bitcoin.

The use of wallets is essential to cryptocurrency's core value proposition. Your claim of ownership on your cryptos begins and ends with possession of your private keys. No bank or other institution is standing by on your behalf, prepared to verify that your money is where you say it is. If you send a payment to someone by mistake, *no one*—and by that I mean no one—will be able to reverse that payment. With crypto, you alone are responsible for your money. This concept has been referred to as "monetary sovereignty."

While monetary sovereignty is a cool concept, there are some obvious drawbacks. The irreversible errant payment is one. Another is related to general security: unlike your typical bank, the individual crypto owner is not a security expert, but securing your private keys is still of utmost importance. In fact, the securing of one's private keys is one of the cryptocurrency system's biggest vulnerabilities. It makes your choice of wallet especially crucial. So, what are your options?

» **Online Wallets:** An online wallet is procured after setting up an account with a third-party vendor who generates and stores the keys on the user's behalf. This is also called a custodial wallet. Access to an online wallet may be provided to you by certain cryptocurrency exchanges after you open an account. Online wallets are also known as *hot wallets*, because they are connected to the internet. Wallets that store keys offline are called *cold wallets*. You can review the differences between hot and cold wallets in figure 62.

fig. 62

HOT WALLETS VS. COLD WALLETS		
	HOT WALLETS Types: Mobile, Web, Desktop	**COLD WALLETS** Types: Hardware, Paper
Security	Generally thought to be less secure, can be hacked	Generally thought to be more secure and less vulnerable to hacks; just don't let it get lost, damaged, or thieved
Cost	Often free	Hardware must be purchased, $50 - $250
Transactions	Coins and tokens are delivered and signed for entirely online	Transactions begin online but the final private key signing is done by the cold wallet offline; private key data therefore never needs to be broadcast
Who can benefit?	Crypto users who wish to complete fast payments and transfers	Crypto owners who want to maximize security
Lost wallet recovery options	Generally good, most can be backed up and accessed via multiple devices	Not great, recovery options are available for lost passwords, but if you lose your wallet, you're out of luck
Connecting to exchanges	Definitely, hot wallets are simple to integrate with most of your go-to crypto exchanges	A little more clunky, you have to take an extra step or two to connect your cold wallet to an exchange

NOTE

Online wallets may also be referred to as light wallets. "Light wallet" is a term used to categorically identify relatively simple and lightweight software programs that connect to the internet and interface with the nodes of your crypto's blockchain. In addition to your private keys, these wallets contain your public keys, referred to as the wallet address, which can be shared with other parties from whom you are requesting payments.

» **Software Wallets:** Like online wallets, software wallets are typically a type of *light wallet*. They are basic software programs/apps that run on your computer or smartphone and don't necessarily require internet access when they are not transmitting or receiving transaction information. There are some free software wallets, several of which provide a feature called "cold storage," whereby your private key information is kept offline.

» **Full Node Wallets:** This is the antithesis of the light wallet. It is the wallet preferred by Tori Forrest. A full node wallet is technically a software wallet; it's just a whole lot heavier—it's the difference between about a hundred MB and several hundred GB—because in addition to storing your keys, the full node wallet is maintaining and updating the complete blockchain ledger.

CAUTION

While using a software program to obtain and make transactions with cryptocurrency can be extremely convenient, it's essential to have a backup option in the event that your computer hard drive fails or your phone is lost. Some software wallets provide users with a recovery phrase, also known as a seed phrase, which is a list of 12–24 words that can be used to reenable access to your wallet. The recovery phrase is generally copied into a file on your computer, in the cloud, or on your external hard drive. It may also be handwritten on paper and kept in a secure place.

NOTE

A best practice is to split your recovery phrase into two parts and store each part in separate locations known only to you and those whom you trust (figure 63). You may be tempted by the convenience of storing your keys in an online wallet, as they tend to be a degree more convenient than using a cold wallet. However, know that in doing so you are making a trade of reduced security for convenience.

fig. 63

ALONE	SUBMIT	GRIEF	SHIELD
GLARE	CORAL	CHASE	TRIGGER
PURITY	CONSIDER	BEST	MAID
INNER	INNOCENT	SCREEN	STATE
LIAR	MISERY	TANK	ENEMY
WIRE	BLOOM	SHUFFLE	COOL

» **Hardware Wallets:** A hardware wallet is a physical device used to store your keys. Many hardware wallet vendors make devices that are similar to thumb drives with added features including key pair generation, encryption, and passcodes. Hardware wallets are an example of a cold wallet.

» **Paper Wallets:** You can write down your private key on a piece of paper. Technically speaking, this is another approach to a cold wallet. But this method obviously isn't very secure. You'll still need to enter your key into a computer if you want to make a transaction, so you're not going completely off the grid if you choose this method. If you do write your private key down physically, do so on acid-free paper, using high-quality indelible ink, and store it someplace fireproof.

Though it's not as long as a public key (2048 bits), the private key itself is very long at 256 bits. That's 256 characters when formatted in binary (1s and 0s only) and it's 64 characters long when formatted in hexadecimal (using all ten decimal numerals plus the six alphabetical characters A through F). It's a lot to record manually, so be sure to do so carefully!

Here are a few other cybersecurity tips for maintaining a secure crypto wallet:

» **Use a VPN (virtual private network),** especially if you are regularly accessing public WiFi. A VPN masks your computer's IP address and may prevent you from being a target of hacking attacks. VPNs are relatively common and affordable in the cybersecurity marketplace. They are easy to download and install.

» **Routinely run and update your antivirus and anti-malware software.** A reputable solution here may prevent you from falling victim to malware, such as CryptoShuffler, which can steal your cryptocurrency assets. Other malware can hijack your computer's processing power and turn your machine into an unwitting miner or "zombie." Your machine will be encumbered, and you'll foot the higher power bills.

» **Use an email account with anti-phishing protection.** Even the savviest among us may fall prey to the latest phishing attack—this is where a hacker elicits your submission of sensitive login names and passwords, usually by posing as a trusted third party. Anti-phishing protection won't stop all attempts, but a high volume will be caught and will never make it to your inbox.

» **Use multi-factor authentication.** Make life more difficult for the bad guys by enabling multi-factor authentication on all your wallets and all your exchange accounts. Account access will then require a standard password and at least one other authentication method such as an OTP (one-time password) that will be sent to a separate device and/or account.

» **Choose a hardware wallet.** The hardware wallet will minimize exposure of your assets to the internet and thus to hacking risk. Just don't lose it!

For more, see the Crypto Research and Analysis links included with your digital assets at go.quickstartguides.com/crypto.

Regardless of how you store your private keys, consider sharing access with at least one person you trust. This can include listing your key pairs in (or alongside) your will. After all, if you become seriously incapacitated or pass away, and no one else can access your private keys, then nobody else can access your crypto, ever. That would be a shame if your portfolio was worth something.

Exchanges

A *cryptocurrency exchange* is a business that enables users to buy and sell cryptocurrencies through the exchange of cryptos for fiat currencies or through the exchange of one crypto for another. According to CoinMarketCap, at the time of writing, there are over 400 crypto exchanges in existence.[2]

Getting set up on a cryptocurrency exchange is relatively straightforward. You create an account online, then fund it with a fiat currency via credit card or bank transfer. Once your account is funded, you can use the money you have on deposit to buy crypto.

Here are some suggested questions to ask when determining which exchange is right for you:

» **How secure is the exchange?** Historically speaking, even the established and popular exchanges have been hacked, creating devastating losses. The well-known Mt. Gox exchange, for example, was hacked not once but twice and about a half billion dollars' worth of crypto was stolen, and FTX, once the third-largest crypto exchange, faced collapse in November 2022 when it was unable to meet demand for customer withdrawals.

You can begin to discern an exchange's commitment to security by paying attention to some of the finer details. For example, does the exchange:

- Store its account holders' cryptos in a hot wallet, or does it use the less vulnerable cold storage option?

- Insist that user passwords are sufficiently complex?

- Offer multi-factor authentication—that is, the request for at least two proofs of identity prior to account access—to prevent unauthorized logins?

Assess the security track record as well: how long has the exchange been in operation and is there any record of notable breaches?

DIGITAL ASSETS

Included with your Crypto Research and Analysis links at www.clydebankmedia.com/crypto-assets is a comprehensive listing of cryptocurrency exchange hacks.

» **What cryptocurrencies are supported?** There are thousands of cryptocurrencies, and some exchanges will only support a small number of them. If you are interested in trading or investing in a particular crypto, then verify that the exchange you're considering maintains a market for it.

» **What are the fees?** The fee structures, types, and amounts vary greatly from exchange to exchange. If you're planning on doing a lot of trading, then you'll want to use an exchange that accommodates affordable high-frequency trading. If you're planning only to buy and sell a few times a year, then transaction-based fees won't be as relevant. Here are some common types of fees to watch for and assess when selecting an exchange:

- *Transaction fee*: a specific percentage fee based on the value of your trade. The Gemini exchange, for example, charges customers 1.49% of the value of their ether or bitcoin trades. The transaction fee varies for other cryptos.

- *Spread fee*: the difference between what you pay to own a cryptocurrency and what the exchange pays to procure it. The Coinbase exchange, for example, charges customers .5% more for the crypto than what Coinbase pays for it. When you sell your crypto, the spread works against you in the opposite direction.

- *"Whatever" fees*: if there wasn't money to be made through owning and operating an exchange, then there wouldn't be nearly 400 of them out there. "Whatever" fees, such as Coinbase's "Coinbase fee" or Gemini's "convenience fee," are fees charged "just because" and may be based on the value of the trade or the type of crypto being purchased. These fees are often stacked on top of the transaction and/or spread fees.

» **Is the exchange available in the country where I live?** Given the legally hazy area that crypto inhabits (see my discussion about this in chapter 13)—with some countries banning all cryptocurrency outright (e.g., China, Colombia, etc.) and others making it their nation's legal tender (e.g., El Salvador)—it's not uncommon to discover that a particular crypto exchange is unavailable in your home country. Most famously, the popular Binance exchange—which continues to lock horns with the United States' Securities and Exchange Commission (SEC)[3]—was for a time unavailable in the United States.

The Forrest Family: A Cryptocurrency Purchase Walk-through

Corporate lawyer Peter Forrest has decided to take the cryptocurrency plunge. Though he remains unsure of the exact amount he wants to invest, he's agreed to have his daughter Tori walk him through the process of purchasing Bitcoin "the right way," which entails moving crypto assets to your own self-administered wallet as soon as possible.

"Tori, before we get into the thick of this," Peter says, "I want you to tell me honestly: how complicated is it going to be?"

Tori shrugs. "Most cryptocurrency exchanges require that you verify your identity. You'll have to scan in a copy of your government-issued photo ID and a separate proof of address. After that it's as easy as linking a payment method, and clicking on the crypto and quantity you wish to purchase. Once the crypto is purchased through the exchange, you can move your private keys wherever you like, including to your own cold wallet."

Buying Cryptocurrency on an Exchange

Tori proceeds to walk her father through purchasing $100 worth of BTC on the Coinbase exchange and then moving his private keys into a software wallet (Electrum).

Hot wallets such as Electrum, while generally secure, are not as secure as cold storage wallets, such as Trezor, which store your private keys offline.

Electrum, at the time of this writing, supports only BTC. There are many other wallets, however, that function similarly to Electrum and support a variety of other cryptos.

Tori shows her dad how to connect his bank account to Coinbase. From there they use the Buy/Sell button (see top right of figure 64) to purchase crypto with fiat currency.

fig. 64

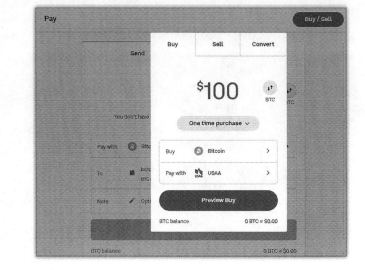

Let's buy $100 worth of Bitcoin.

fig. 65

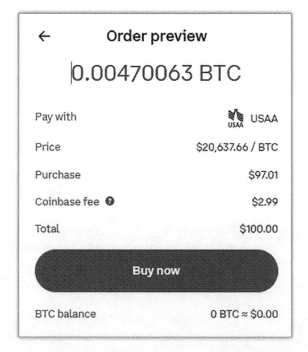

Take note of how much crypto Peter is buying (4.7 mBTC) and what he's paying in fees ($2.99 Coinbase fee).

After submitting his order, Peter waits for confirmation that the order has been filled (figure 66). Tori explains that this is one of several ways that using a cryptocurrency exchange is similar to buying stocks, or government-based currencies such as Japanese yen or the euro. Peter travels abroad frequently and is very comfortable with basic exchanges of currency—perhaps this crypto thing will end up working out after all.

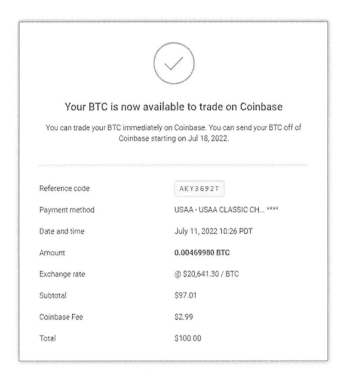

Your BTC is now available to trade on Coinbase

You can trade your BTC immediately on Coinbase. You can send your BTC off of Coinbase starting on Jul 18, 2022.

Reference code	AKY3692T
Payment method	USAA - USAA CLASSIC CH... ****
Date and time	July 11, 2022 10:26 PDT
Amount	**0.00469980 BTC**
Exchange rate	@ $20,641.30 / BTC
Subtotal	$97.01
Coinbase Fee	$2.99
Total	$100.00

fig. 66

NOTE

In the time it took for Peter to preview his order (figure 65) and to actually transact, the price of BTC appreciated slightly, causing Peter to get slightly less Bitcoin for his $100.

Peter has procured 4.7 mBTC. He can keep his private keys in a wallet managed by the Coinbase exchange or, per his daughter's insistence, he can transfer them to a wallet that he controls directly. He can also use the "Convert" tab on Coinbase to exchange his BTC for another crypto (figure 67).

Peter's intention, however, is not to convert his Bitcoin to another coin—not yet. What he wants to do is to transfer the private keys associated with his recent Bitcoin purchase into his Electrum wallet.

fig. 67

There's a bit of a waiting game, as Coinbase requires a few days to confirm the transfer of his fiat currency into his Coinbase account. Tori explains that this holding period is referred to as a "withdrawal lock" and is also a feature of another major exchange that she frequents, the Binance Exchange, which requires that customers wait 10 days before withdrawing fiat currency or crypto that was funded by new deposits on the exchange.[4]

MY TAKE

I prefer to keep my exchange accounts funded with verified funds before I purchase crypto. It means I'm always free to move my private keys at my own discretion as soon as I conclude any transaction on the exchange. From an investor's perspective, however, such flexibility may not be necessary. If you were interested in a crypto's price and funded your account on the day of your purchase (as Peter Forrest is doing), you could still lock in your price and buy the crypto immediately, well before the withdrawal lock expires. You just wouldn't be able to transfer your private keys off the exchange for another several days.

NOTE

It may be possible to short-circuit the withdrawal lock, for a price. The Coinbase exchange offers customers "instant withdrawals" via Visa and Mastercard using capabilities known as "Visa Direct" and "Mastercard Send." Coinbase attaches a 1.5% fee to this service for US customers.[5]

Moving Your Cryptocurrency to Your Own Wallet

As soon as his withdrawal lock expires and the funds used to purchase the crypto are verified, the crypto is in Peter's full control, and he's now ready to move his private keys to his Electrum wallet.

He will first need to obtain a public key "address" for his wallet. He'll do this by downloading, installing, and setting up the Electrum wallet software.

Once the software is installed, Peter will access the Receive tab and generate an address he can use to receive Bitcoin (figure 68).

IMAGE

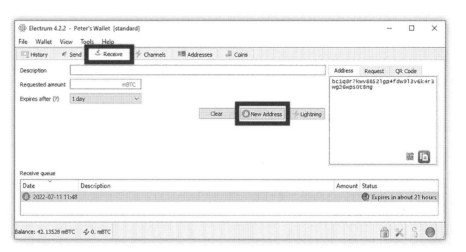

fig. 68

Notice how the address generated in the right-hand window (figure 68) is not formatted in hexadecimal. What you're looking at is another layer of encoding (the address) that's been hashed from Peter's public key. Peter's public key, as expressed in hexadecimal format, is as follows: 035ce673c73ea039bd9a1c185da5a0105929038e3ed0d28eaf402e67f18f9d4b2e.

DETOUR

The wallet software will automatically create private-public key pairs for Peter to use on the Bitcoin network. Why key pairs, plural? Electrum is a *hierarchical deterministic wallet* or "HD" wallet. In the interest of security and manageability, these wallets don't use only one public-private key pair but rather a series of them, all generated in a predetermined sequence from a "master root seed," which is recoverable via the wallet's *recovery phrase*/seed phrase. This feature sets the HD wallets apart from the older cryptocurrency wallets. Though some old wallets would, as a security feature, continually generate new key pairs, they'd do so at random, with no thread of connection from one key pair to the next.

The next step is to access the Send/Receive panel on the Coinbase website and copy the address into the To field (figure 69). Note that Peter is sending only $50 worth of BTC to his software wallet. The remaining $50 (*approximately*) of his crypto has a different destiny, which I discuss later in this chapter. For now, it will remain in his Coinbase account.

IMAGE

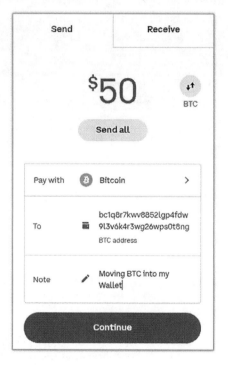

fig. 69

Peter and Tori will wait around 10 minutes for confirmation that their transfer has gone through. The Electrum wallet, however, will indicate within a matter of moments that an "unconfirmed" transaction has been initiated and will report the amount as well. The unconfirmed transaction will be listed in the History tab until the confirmation process is complete. Upon confirmation, the transaction is complete, and the keys are now stored in Peter's Electrum wallet (figure 70).

NOTE

In my example, Peter purchases his crypto using Coinbase, a *centralized exchange (CEX)*, where customers' cryptos are (at least initially) stored in wallets controlled by the exchange itself. In my example, Peter transferred half of the crypto (appx. $50 worth) to a wallet that he directly controlled. There are other exchanges, known as *decentralized exchanges (DEXs)*, where cryptos purchased are immediately placed under the direct control of the customer. I talk more about DEXs in chapter 12.

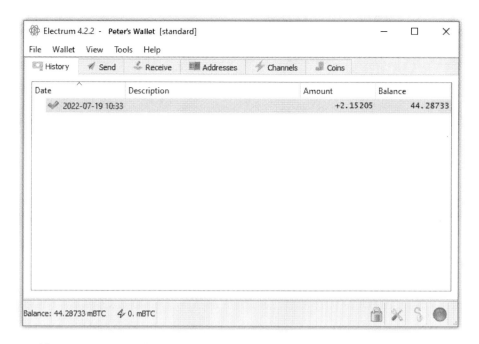

fig. 70

The keys themselves of course are not visible here. Otherwise, they wouldn't be private.

Other Ways to Buy Crypto

Given the popularity of cryptocurrency, many players in fintech are finding ways to add crypto to their services. For example, several stock brokerage firms now allow customers to trade in some cryptos, and services like PayPal and Venmo (a PayPal subsidiary) are including a limited selection of cryptos in the currencies they support.

DETOUR

Forrest Family: Buying Crypto through Your Bank

Despite Tori's and Alan's best efforts (including Tori's step-by-step tutorial of how to move Peter's private keys off the exchange and into his own wallet), Peter Forrest has decided that going forward he's against the purist approach to monetary autonomy. Rather than maintain his own crypto wallet, he's going to work with his financial advisor and tennis buddy, Mariana, who's had dollar signs in her eyes ever since Peter first brought up the idea of moving a portion of his assets into crypto. The world of traditional finance has finally come around to crypto, offering all manner of cryptocurrency products to investors. Their customers, by and large, tend to be high-net-worth individuals like Peter who are more comfortable putting big bucks into crypto when a big-name financial brand brokers the deal. To Mariana's delight (and Tori's and Alan's annoyance), their father's decision to use traditional finance ("TradFi") will come with excessive fees and a forfeiture of direct control over the assets.

Peter, no dummy when it comes to money and business, understands his children's objections. He tries to explain to them that according to his research, a new era of crypto is arriving, one where banks, acting as custodians of their customers' crypto assets, can offer a degree of real security as well as some limited guarantees. He compares it to an investment he knows better: stocks. Though market losses in crypto can't be insured, long-standing securities regulations, when applied to crypto holdings, may help remedy any losses that are the result of bank error or fraud.[6] As Peter sees it, the convenience of working with his preferred institutions, along with the simplicity and security they can offer, more than justifies the substantial percentage that Mariana and her partners will collect from his investments.

It seems likely that some other investors will feel the same way. Back in July of 2020, the regulators at the Office of the Comptroller of the Currency under the US Department of the Treasury gave banks permission to hold private keys on behalf of their customers. In 2021, financial services firms such as Deutsche Bank, Wells Fargo, Citigroup, Capital One, Barclays, Credit Suisse, Bank of America, and others hired three times as many cryptocurrency professionals as they did in 2015.[7] While the early offerings from banks are geared toward high-net-worth and institutional investors, the longer-term strategy appears to favor more broad offerings of cryptocurrency services. I expect such democratization will be inevitable if the popularity of cryptocurrency continues. As with any investment decision, there are pros and cons to consider with this approach.

Pros of Buying Crypto through Your Bank

» **Regulations**: There' s a baseline level of liability assumed by the banks in most cases.

» **Security**: Legacy banks tend to have longer track records with general account security, boasting the latest and greatest in multi-factor account authentication, cyber-defense, fraud prevention, and so forth.

Cons of Buying Crypto through Your Bank

» **Cost:** This is the most obvious downside to working with a bank to manage your cryptocurrency investments. What you'll want to do is compare the bank's fees to those of the cryptocurrency exchanges, which range from around .1% to 1.5% per transaction. Given that the bank is offering presumably a more robust custodial service and abiding by tougher regulation, you may be hard-pressed to find bank fees lower than the typical fees you'd pay to use an exchange.

» **Selection:** Similar to Venmo and other mobile payment platforms that offer crypto, the bank's selection of coins is still not nearly as robust as that offered by your typical cryptocurrency exchange.

In chapters 9 and 10, I discuss cryptocurrency derivatives (options and futures), IRAs (individual retirement accounts), ETFs (exchange-traded funds), and other crypto investment vehicles offered by both traditional and nontraditional institutions.

Buying and Selling Non-Fungible Tokens (NFTs)

In chapter 7, I introduced you to the fascinating, original, and sometimes zany world of NFTs. As I write this book, non-fungible tokens have experienced a rather dramatic decline in popularity and value relative to where they were in 2021, when they were one of the hottest areas in crypto. Rather than prematurely suggesting NFTs have no future role or value, I'd say this downturn is likely more indicative of how the NFT market is quickly evolving. In any case, Tori Forrest insists on showing her dad how to buy an NFT before he completely abandons the DIY approach to all things crypto and hands over the keys to Mariana. Peter has no interest in NFTs as a serious investment, but he can't deny that he's curious about them. *People paid thousands and millions of dollars for what, exactly?*

Tori attempts to simplify the topic, telling him that NFTs are sold on marketplaces or by auction, and they are purchased with cryptocurrency. Peter agrees to see it in action and go NFT shopping.

"Just like cryptos," Tori explains, "the price of NFTs can be volatile. If you want to make agile moves in the NFT marketplace, buying and selling on your own terms, then you need the ability to transact quickly. Let's make sure you have access to the cryptos you'll need to buy the NFTs that you're interested in. Let's get started."

STEP 1

Get the Crypto You'll Need to Participate in the NFT Marketplace: In Peter's case, he has access to Bitcoin but nothing else. Using the Buy/Sell button on the Coinbase exchange, Peter is going to convert his remaining $50 worth of Bitcoin holdings into ether (figure 71), ether being the most prominent cryptocurrency used in the NFT trade.

fig. 71

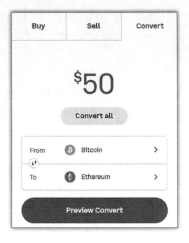

fig. 72

The "Order preview" screen shows the rate of exchange and any associated fees.

STEP 2

Move Your NFT-Friendly Crypto (Ether) into a Compatible Wallet: To buy an NFT, Peter will need to move his ether off of the Coinbase exchange and into an ether wallet (Electrum can only hold Bitcoin). At this point, Peter hands the controls over to Tori. He figures this is likely to be his first and only NFT purchase, so he's fine with standing on the sidelines as Tori takes care of it.

Tori opts to install the Coinbase wallet app as a Chrome extension on her browser. She also installs this wallet as an app on her smartphone. This will facilitate an easy transfer of the ether now held in Peter's Coinbase account to his new Coinbase wallet.

NOTE

Up until this point, Peter only had an account on the Coinbase exchange. Coinbase held his keys via a custodial wallet. After moving $50 worth of BTC to an Electrum wallet and now moving the remainder to his own Coinbase wallet, Peter has complete control over all his crypto, because he controls the private keys for each wallet.

Tori writes down the new seed phrase for the Coinbase wallet and tells her dad to store it in a secure place. Now .0321 ETH is easily moved from Peter's Coinbase account to his Coinbase wallet. Those funds are now ready to be used in the NFT marketplace (figure 73):

fig. 73

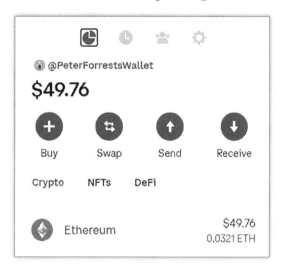

Notice in figure 73 that the main user interface on Peter's Coinbase wallet has a designated section for NFTs. That's because the keys associated with his purchase or sale of an NFT are actually stored in his wallet. They are the same private keys that authenticate his claim on the crypto he used to make the NFT purchase.

STEP 3

Go Shopping! Tori and her dad search through several NFT marketplaces. Peter recognizes big names such as Sotheby's and Christie's, known for their auctions of expensive art, property, and other hard assets. These organizations have now moved into NFTs. After half an hour of perusing, the Forrests decide to purchase an NFT listed for sale on a marketplace called OpenSea.io. It's a low-cost variation on the famous "Bored Apes" series (figure 74). The cost is .01 ETH (currently around $16). The transaction also includes gas fees (see chapter 5) to compensate the Ethereum network participants whose computational work makes it possible for Peter Forrest to acquire a digitally signed version of this artwork:

IMAGE

fig. 74

Peter Forrest's possession of a digitally signed version of this artwork has now been recorded and confirmed on the Ethereum blockchain. From here forward he may do with it as he pleases. He can give it away to another party or bring it back to the marketplace to sell.

"You think Sotheby's would be interested in auctioning off this little guy for me?" Peter asks his daughter. He's half-kidding, but not entirely.

"Maybe someday, Dad," Tori says. "Anything's possible."

For more guidance on NFTs, refer to the "Creating, Publishing, and Selling Your Own NFT" section of chapter 7.

What Is Crypto Worth?

In all this discussion of buying and selling cryptos and NFTs, I haven't addressed one central question: what is a given cryptocurrency or NFT worth? I provided the short answer at the beginning of chapter 1. Specifically, its value is whatever you're willing to pay for it, and its worth is whatever someone else is willing to give you for it!

Similar to stocks, an exchange will quote a price for a cryptocurrency that reflects the approximate average price of recent transactions plus whatever spread fees the exchange cares to add in order to pad its bottom line. In short, the market wants what it wants at whatever price it thinks it can get.

NFTs are even more speculative in nature. These digital artworks, similar to traditional artworks, are assigned a "buy now" price or are auctioned off to the highest bidder. In many (though not all) cases, the purchaser of the NFT claims ownership only over a digital copy with a digital signature attached—the digital equivalent of a signed print of a painting, where the buyer retains no rights to the original painting itself. It's also possible to create an NFT where the buyer would also purchase full ownership rights to the digital "original" itself. This all means that the dynamics of the pricing are as whimsical and unpredictable as they are in the traditional art sphere, where the final price paid could be influenced by any number of factors.

I discuss the art and science of trading cryptos in chapter 9 and investing in them in chapter 10. As a summary, here are factors that can be considered when assessing any cryptocurrency's true value:

» **Supply and demand**. From an economist's standpoint, the value of a cryptocurrency can be understood in terms of supply and demand, with the value (price) increasing when its demand goes higher than the supply. The supply side of the crypto trade tends to be very transparent. According to The Motley Fool, it is "always known," because "each crypto publishes its token minting and burning plans."[8] Bitcoin famously limits total supply to 21 million, and Binance coins (BNB) have quarterly burnings (chapter 6). Demand, of course, is more subjective in nature, but several of the other key factors noted on this list can influence it.

» **The strength of the teams behind the cryptocurrency**. In my discussion on altcoins in chapter 6 I noted that two of the major altcoin founders (Charles Hoskinson of Cardano and Gavin Wood of Polkadot) were veterans of the Ethereum development team. Their demonstrated skills, relevant experience, and past crypto efforts suggest that their new endeavors are worth considering.

While they are no guarantee of success, crypto founders like these add credibility over new, unknown players in the crypto market.

NOTE

When assessing crypto personnel, don't limit your focus to only the technical teams. It's also important to take a hard look at the investors behind any new cryptocurrency or blockchain project.

» **Noteworthy applications.** Where function goes, value follows. Here are a few questions to ponder when assessing the functionality of a given cryptocurrency:

- What's the cryptocurrency going to be used for?

- Are smart contracts going to be in play?

- Does the crypto solve a unique problem?

- Is there innovation in the crypto that sets it apart from others?

- Might the functionality attract unnecessary attention from regulators?

- Does the functionality solve a temporary need or does it have long-term value?

EXAMPLE

The Stacks cryptocurrency (STX), used to power the CityCoins application (discussed in chapter 6), may be more worthy of investment than a coin that's built solely on hype with no discernible purpose.

» **Market longevity.** If a cryptocurrency has been around for a while, then there's a much better chance that the coin will be viable. Not to discount the massive return potential of buying the right altcoin fresh out of the gate, but generally speaking, longevity tends to boost value and the lack thereof tends to reduce it. "Here today and gone tomorrow" is the calling card for many cryptocurrency scams.

» **Competition.** In certain ways, the world of crypto can be brutally Darwinian, as a large number of cryptos compete for limited resources. One such resource, for example, is the pool of developers. A cryptocurrency that can attract top development talent is generally going to fare better than one that nobody wants to work on. You may also find cryptos in the marketplace with fundamental similarities to one another, but one has become better-known. This will in turn make it more widely used, and, presumably, more valuable. The point is that cryptocurrencies compete with one another for market share.

» **Strength of community**. For reasons that are sometimes mystifying, some communities of users and developers may flock to cryptocurrency A while ignoring a similar cryptocurrency B. This is the *network effect*—the organic value-add bestowed upon a product or service due to widespread usage. The network effect is a big deal in the world of crypto. It can crown the leaders in the space and make it harder for upstarts to break in.

» **Media attention**. Whether it's social media attention or mainstream media coverage, cryptocurrencies that are widely discussed often accumulate more value. For this reason, you can try to understand the media outreach strategy behind a cryptocurrency, especially a lesser known one, before you invest. For example:

  • Search for mentions of the coin on social media and probe the quality and influence of the social media accounts devoted to promoting the coin. Does this look like a solid PR operation?

  • Study the content (articles, blog posts, studies, project summaries) that are circulating on behalf of the coin.
    - Who is penning this content? Are they influential?
    - What is the quality level of the content itself? Is it compellingly presented?
    - Is the content being shared widely?

» **Exchange presence**. Take note of where your prospective cryptocurrency is available (and where it's not available) to trade.

Chapter Recap

» Cryptocurrency transactions mostly take place on exchanges and through wallets. Wallets store the private keys needed for a cryptocurrency transaction.

» When choosing a cryptocurrency exchange that's right for you, consider factors like security, fees, accessibility, and the range of available cryptos.

» The private keys for your cryptocurrency can be moved off the exchange to your personal wallet.

» The buying and selling of NFTs takes place on special marketplaces, for sale or by auction, most often using ether.

» Cryptocurrency prices are largely driven by supply and demand. Demand, in turn, is driven by a number of factors, which can also be used when attempting to determine a crypto's value and viability. These factors include competition, media attention, proven longevity, and the network effect.

| 9 |

Trading Cryptocurrency

While Peter Forrest is pursuing a "set it and forget it" *investing* approach to his crypto portfolio (an approach affectionately known as "hodling" and something I discuss in more depth in chapter 10), many crypto enthusiasts are primarily interested in *trading* these assets in the dynamic cryptocurrency marketplace. With rapid price swings in cryptocurrency, it's no wonder that this space attracts seekers of fast fortune. Take young Alan Forrest, for instance, who recently turned eighteen. In an effort to emulate and impress his older sister Tori, he has decided to hone his skills as a cryptocurrency trader.

In this chapter, I walk you through Alan's foray into cryptocurrency trading. I also provide you with an overview of the basic terminologies, methods, and risks that inhabit the cryptocurrency trade. Much of the information here may be redundant for anyone with a basic understanding of trading, for example, stocks, futures, options, and forex. For readers who are new to this topic, I provide a lay-of-the-land "QuickStart" overview of this fast-paced and exceedingly risky approach to the buying and selling of volatile digital assets. For readers who are simply uninterested in trading, consider proceeding to the next chapter.

Trading vs. Investing

What's the difference between trading and investing? In brief, trading is short-term. It seeks to capitalize on the near-term "price action" (the change in an asset's price), typically by buying low and selling high.

Investing, on the other hand, is long-term in nature and relies more heavily on the fundamental analysis of an asset's worth, which I discuss in chapter 10. In the case of cryptocurrencies, this means taking into account those factors discussed at the tail end of chapter 8, such as supply and demand, noteworthy applications, and market longevity. Investors stake their money on assets they believe will deliver value back to them over the long term. They access a wide variety of investment vehicles such as bonds, mutual funds, and ETFs in an effort to maximize their returns. Unlike traders, they are less concerned with day-by-day trends in price changes. They are uninterested in attempting to guess at the emotional states of other buyers or sellers, which is what can lead to those big day-to-day changes.

Given the effects such behavioral factors can have on daily price fluctuations, traders are constantly wondering and wagering on when other market participants will take action en masse. For example, what price point, when reached, will trigger a massive sell-off, or what low price will trigger an onslaught of new buyers?

Why Trade Crypto?

Newbie and veteran traders alike are drawn to the cryptocurrency market for many of the same reasons traders are drawn to any market: it's volatile and accessible. Cryptocurrency traders are looking to make relatively short-term profits from changes in coin and token prices, and the high volatility of the space ensures that such price changes are frequent and often dramatic.

I buy $1,000 worth of Litecoin (LTC) on December 3 and hold it for eight days (this is known as a "swing trade," which I discuss shortly). When I sell it on December 11 the price of LTC has gone from $100 to $400, and I receive $4,000, with $3,000 in profit. This is a true story with regard to the LTC price change from December 3, 2017, to December 11, 2017, and I wish it were a true story with regard to my having actually placed a trade.

Why is the cryptocurrency market so volatile?

The fact that the cryptocurrency market is relatively new contributes to its volatility. Concrete norms of valuation just haven't been broadly established, with new cryptos coming and going on a routine basis. There's also a near-constant flow of news stories about different uses for crypto or potential government regulatory actions under consideration even if they don't come to fruition. These stories ripple through the market, drawing in new buyers and causing existing crypto owners to ramp up their holdings, or to tamp them down, or to sell off everything.

Still, despite a general volatility, in recent years crypto has had a tendency to follow the broader market. For instance, as inflation and gas prices went up in 2021 and 2022, the stock market declined and crypto followed suit. When the broader market began showing signs of recovery, crypto did the same.

Accessibility is another big draw for would-be cryptocurrency traders. Foreign exchange has always been popular among traders because the market is open every day and night, except for Sunday in London, compared to the US markets, which are open from 9:30 a.m. until 4:00 p.m. eastern standard time. Cryptocurrency markets are open around the clock, with no pauses for weekends or holidays. No matter when you like to trade, you will find price action in the crypto markets.

Trading Terminology

Before delving into the particulars of trading cryptocurrencies, I want to make sure you're familiar with some basic trading terminology. Aside from the note on the unique arbitrage opportunities within the cryptocurrency market, these terms are quite generic and speak to the basic elements of trading in general.

Arbitrage

Arbitrage refers to the simultaneous buying and selling of assets in different forms, in order to take advantage of price differences. In a classic arbitrage trade, you buy an asset from one market where it is cheaper and resell it almost instantly in another where it is more expensive. Arbitrage is difficult in most assets because there are so many professional investors with sophisticated automated trading. Opportunities to profit are fleeting, as they are quickly spotted and capitalized on.

NOTE

The crypto market is less developed than the other popular trading markets such as futures, commodities, and options, etc., that have been around for decades. There are hundreds of cryptocurrency exchanges, and you can more easily identify a price discrepancy in crypto than you can in more established markets.

To capitalize on arbitrage in crypto, you will need to have accounts on the different exchanges in play, and you will need to consider the fees charged by either exchange (see chapter 8), as they will bite into your profits.

If arbitrage trading is something you're interested in pursuing, then consider the following tips:

» **Check out the various software offerings that facilitate and automate arbitrage.** Given the thousands of cryptocurrencies in existence and the hundreds of exchanges, trying to root out arbitrage opportunities by way of manual browsing may prove difficult. Why not let a software program do some of the work for you?

» **Overestimate your transaction costs.** Remember, in order for this to work, you'll need to find spreads big enough to overcome the costs you incur during your transactions. Give yourself some room for error by overestimating your transaction costs on your prospective arbitrage trades.

» **Favor cryptos with faster transaction times and higher liquidity; use limit orders as needed.** One of the major risks of arbitrage trading is that you transact at prices that are not the prices you thought you were going to get. Minimize this *slippage* by favoring cryptos that transact fast in markets that are highly liquid. You can also add a layer of safety by using *limit orders*, orders that will only transact when your specified price point is available.

» **Favor less popular cryptos.** This tip will need to be balanced with the "higher liquidity" tip I just mentioned; less well-known cryptos are less likely to have highly liquid markets. And yet, these less popular cryptos are the ones most apt to reveal rapid price differentials market by market.

Day Trading

Day trading involves making a high volume of relatively small transactions, then closing them out at the end of the day. This can help limit your risk because you do not hold any positions overnight when you are not trading, so you won't get blindsided by news events or big price changes occurring outside your watch.

Swing Trading

Traders who hold positions overnight, or for a few days, are said to be *swing trading*. Swing traders, unlike day traders, don't revert to an all-cash balance at the end of each day but give their positions some time to play out.

Position Trading

Position trading entails holdings your positions for a month or more, often while waiting for a news event to play out. This entails more risk, but it also gives you more time to see the return you want.

Scalping

If you're interested in really rapid, high-volume trading, consider *scalping*. This trading style involves making a series of small profits by buying and selling within the span of short-term price movements. The risk is relatively low, as are the profits, but scalpers can sometimes be flattened by prices that move too fast and in opposition to their trade. Scalping is sometimes euphemistically referred to as "picking up nickels in front of a steamroller."[1]

Trading in the Cryptocurrency Market

I mentioned how arbitrage opportunities may be a little easier to come by in the cryptocurrency markets relative to those of more traditional trading assets. The relative immaturity of the cryptocurrency marketplace has several other ramifications as well. For example, Jacob Canfield, host of the *Crypto Trader Podcast*, believes that many basic chart-analyzing and trend-spotting techniques have become played out in the traditional world of trading due to overuse, but that these techniques remain viable in crypto trading because of the market's relative youth.[2]

The cryptocurrency market is thought to retain more *inefficiencies* than the more established markets. For those of you unfamiliar with what is meant by market efficiency, allow me to introduce you to a concept known as the *efficient market hypothesis*. This idea states that markets are always rational and will ultimately create accurate, fair transaction prices for goods and services.

Consider the stock market, with its market makers, brokers, retail traders and investors, institutional traders and investors, and analysts hoping to detect, examine, and capitalize on even the most minimal of price inefficiencies. If a JPMorgan algorithm finds that the Coca-Cola Company (KO) is undervalued by 30 cents, it will motivate buyers to take action, which will in turn serve to bid the price up to the level that the algorithm thinks is appropriate based on its meticulous analysis of both the company's fundamentals and the current state of the market. In other words, this hypothesis suggests that the mechanisms, tools, and information infrastructure that drive the price of stocks are mature and efficient.

There is some debate over whether this hypothesis overvalues the so-called "invisible hand" of free-market capitalism and its ability to assign fair and just values to goods and services. But even if there's some disagreement over how efficient traditional markets actually are, a less mature market like cryptocurrency still offers theoretically greater opportunities to capitalize on market inefficiencies. Examples of these inefficiencies could include significant arbitrage from one exchange to another, or an excessive price swing in a crypto that a trader might judge to be a temporary product of emotion, rather than sound market analysis.

A celebrity tweets that they are abandoning their sizable position in ether (ETH) to invest in a new cryptocurrency called Reichental Coin (RCC). ETH drops by 3% soon after the story breaks and RCC shoots up by 40%. The smart cryptocurrency trader may recognize a degree of over-emotionalized price movement and may seek to capitalize. This is how a less mature crypto marketplace can be influenced more heavily than more established trading venues.

Long-term success in cryptocurrency trading requires a strong fundamental grip on the market. You will need to study the rise and fall of individual coins in larger market cycles within the space. You can do this by examining the price action of cryptocurrencies and learn to identify common patterns. Put on your market analyst's hat and try to describe some basic, testable rules for how cryptocurrencies typically react to various types of events. Test your hypotheses using historical price data—a process known as *backtesting*, which I discuss later in this chapter. You will also want to become proficient at assessing the valuation factors I explored at the end of chapter 8. Pair your crypto-specific market knowledge with a thorough understanding of basic trading methodologies and you'll improve your odds of success.

Many of these fundamental skills can be developed with the aid of the ClydeBank Media QuickStart Guide Series. *Day Trading QuickStart Guide* and *Forex Trading QuickStart Guide* offer in-depth information about essential trading methodologies and are both available at www.quickstartguides.com.

The Forrest Family: The Adventure of "Alan the Great"

Alan Forrest has just turned eighteen. A month ago, he was walking across the stage to receive his high school diploma, having graduated at the top of his class from Caruthers Preparatory School. He's headed to Stanford University in August as a business major.

He also feels that he could become a millionaire imminently. To his parents' chagrin, Alan is already fantasizing about dropping out of college and starting his own tech start-up. He's interested in creating an on-demand in-home cleaning service.

"It's like Uber," he explains. "Except they're not giving you a ride or bringing you food. They show up at your house and wash your dishes for you, or they vacuum or, you know, all that stuff you're always making me do."

"Why don't you try going to college first *before* dropping out?" admonishes his father, Peter. "You never know, you might learn something."

"I'm just going to play it by ear, Dad. If I can get the capital together for the CleanItUp App, then I may need to focus on that full time. School will always be there."

"Interesting idea, little bro," Tori says. "But how are you planning on raising capital? The bank of Mom and Dad?"

Alan looks at his mother expectantly. It's a look he's honed and practiced since he was a little boy, one that's often led to his mother giving him exactly what he wants.

"No," Peter replies quickly. "No, I don't think Alan's going to do that. Pretty sure he's aware that we already gave away all of our money to Stanford."

"Relax," Alan says. "I've already got it all figured out."

"Have you?" His father is intrigued.

"I'm going to start trading cryptocurrency," Alan says confidently. "All I need is a few weeks here to work my magic, and I'm sure I can get enough money to launch my app. I've already made about five grand just from *hodling* Bitcoin and ether. Once I start tapping into the right altcoins and making the right moves, I'll be generating funds faster than I can spend them!"

This leads to an animated discussion between Peter, Lynn, and their two children. Lynn has long disapproved of Alan risking his money in the crypto markets when he should, in her mind, be saving it for college expenses. Peter implores Alan to take a look at the hard realities of trading, stressing that less than 5% of all traders make money over a long period of time.[3] And Tori, for her part, is quick to point out that the cryptocurrency market is unique in that traders have more opportunities to exploit inefficiencies, though she stops short of offering Alan a full vote of confidence on his proposed crypto-trading and capital-raising initiative. Instead, she suggests that Alan begin his crypto-trading endeavor by using a trading simulator where no real money is involved.

"Let's see how well you do with play money first," Tori says to her kid brother. "Tell ya what: if you can double the value of your account in a month, I'll even pitch in a few thousand cowries to help you kickstart your app. Let's see what you can do."

"You're on," Alan says.

Later that evening Alan selects from among several crypto trading simulators, landing on one called CryptoParrot. He is delighted to find that the username "AlanTheGreat" is available.

Types of Orders

The method of "practice trading" that Alan is pursuing with CryptoParrot is often referred to as ***paper trading***. I'd encourage beginner crypto traders to paper trade first before putting anything at risk. And when you do move into real money, I must reiterate the common mantra, ever-present in the crypto universe: *only risk what you are prepared to lose*.

Through paper trading, Alan is able to get a feel for how to enter his trading orders correctly and how to take advantage of tactical tools for trade management, such as the stop order and the limit order, as well as margin.

Long and Short

Beginning with the basics of opening a position, you are said to be *long* an asset when you own it, and *short* when you sell it. Trading currencies is somewhat unusual in that there is always a clear long and short position taken on any given trade. If you buy BTC with US dollars (USD), you are long BTC and short USD.

Alan begins his paper trading endeavor by taking long positions in Litecoin (LTC), Cardano (ADA), and Ripple (XRP). A listing of his executed trades and the prices paid for each crypto can be seen in figure 75.

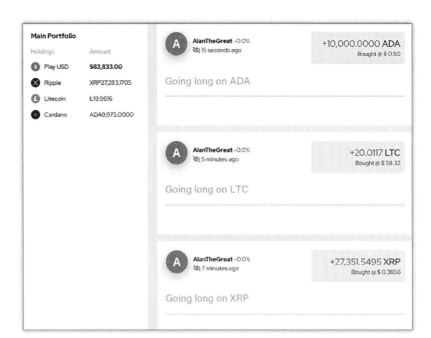

fig. 75

Alan decides to pursue a swing trading strategy, where he'll hold his cryptos overnight (for a few nights) before closing out his trades and taking his profits (or losses).

He liquidates his ADA first (figure 76). He has a total of 9,975 ADA to sell, after having paid a fee of 25 ADA on his initial long trade. The price of ADA has fallen to $0.47 from his purchase price of $0.50. Alan will take a loss on this trade. Moreover, there will be a fee of $11.80 on the short transaction.

fig. 76

When Alan went long on ADA (figure 75) he spent $5,000 to buy 10,000 ADA and then paid 25 ADA as a fee for that transaction, leaving him with 9,975 ADA, which he later sold for a total price of $4,688.25. Subtract a fee of $11.80 and Alan recovered a total of $4,676.45. He took a $323.55 loss on that trade ($5,000 - $4,676.45).

Alan sells out of his positions in XRP and LTC as well (see the order screens in figure 77).

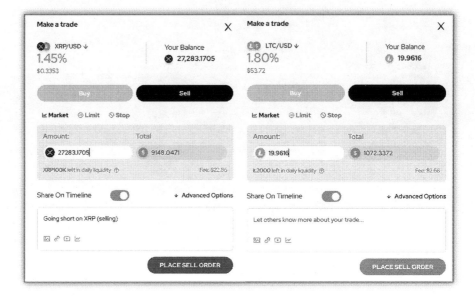

fig. 77

Unfortunately, Alan will take losses on LTC and XRP. He entered the trade on LTC at 20.0117 and will exit at 19.9616. He'll take a loss of about $100 there, but the biggest loss is in XRP, where he initiated a big $10,000 long position when the currency was trading at $0.3656. He's going to exit his XRP trade at $0.34 and will take a loss of over $800.

He's quietly grateful to his sister for insisting that he paper trade before putting real money at risk!

In the same six-day period in which Alan executed his swing trades, the price of BTC plummeted alongside those of the cryptos Alan was trading. This correlation between BTC's value and that of other coins is a well-known phenomenon with several plausible causes. For example, if a regulatory crackdown causes several BTC mining operations to close up shop, the impact will often be felt throughout the greater crypto ecosystem and altcoins will decline in value alongside BTC.

So, what's Alan doing wrong? Taking losses is an inevitable part of trading. The key is winning more than you lose. This takes practice, discipline, and commitment, and even then success is found only by the few (less than 5% of traders make money at it).

Trading and investing are two very distinct disciplines. Traders attempt to capitalize on short-term price changes in assets, whereas investors take long-term positions based on their assessment of an asset's fundamental viability and growth potential.

There are countless theories and techniques used by day traders and swing traders involving the analysis of charts and trends. Traders are apt to stay on top of the news cycle and assess the impacts that various headlines inject into the marketplace. They may also attempt to identify various chart patterns that purport to show common forms of price movement, to lend them a leg up on predicting what the immediate future may hold.

Backtesting

Many traders evaluate the behavior of the buyers and sellers in the marketplace to gain a sense of how price action may be predicted. A specific form of this evaluation is called *backtesting* and it involves proposing a trading technique based on, for example, patterns and news cycles. From there, you study the historical price action of the asset you wish to trade, and test whether your proposed technique would have produced winning results. When you begin trading in real time, keep a record of your trades and their results, so you can continue to refine your strategy. If the backtest is successful, the trader may implement the technique with a greater level of confidence in its success.

Stops and Limits

Trading cryptos, or any asset, isn't for the faint of heart, but Alan isn't ready to throw in the towel just yet. Anxious to chip away some at his swing trading losses, Alan is going to attempt a bit of scalping, using some additional tools at his disposal. He notices that Polkadot (DOT) is up 7.12% for the day. He looks at a daily chart and sees more running room. The price is currently at $7.06 and Alan is convinced that if the price climbs as high as $7.08 it will be sufficient *price action confirmation* (an indication that the price really is moving up) to warrant a trade. He places a *buy stop order* with a stop price of $7.08 (figure 78). When the price hits $7.08 his buy stop order will convert into a standard market order and he'll be long DOT to the tune of 3,540 DOT, or about $500.

fig. 78

AlanTheGreat -1.3%
👁 17 seconds ago

+3,540.0000 DOT
⏱
Buy @ $ 7.08

Long on DOT once price hits 7.08

Notice the clock icon in the upper right, indicating that the order has not executed yet but is waiting on a condition to be met—the stop price being reached, in this case.

The order executes and after fees (≈ 9 DOT is paid in fees), Alan now controls 3,531.15 DOT. The price, as Alan predicted, continues to run upward after his buy order executes, touching $7.19 before going back down to $7.16. Alan decides to put in a *limit order* which will attempt to sell all of his DOT at a price of $7.19, as soon as that price becomes available again—which it will, hopefully, before the day is out.

fig. 79

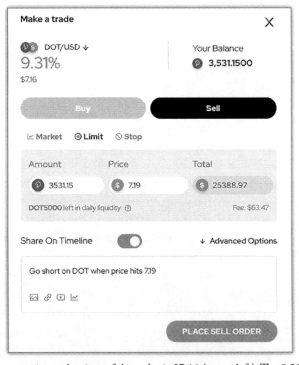

Notice the current price at the time of the order is $7.16 (upper left). The 9.31% depicts the extent of a crypto's appreciation or depreciation throughout the day. The down arrow indicates that the price has gone down, depreciated.

As you may have gathered, stops and limits are used to control the price of your purchase or sale. They are critical to risk management, given how fast crypto markets move.

Here is a summary of the different order types:

» A *market order* is the most basic order type. It indicates that you want your asset bought or sold on the market at the prevailing market price at the time of the order's execution. These orders are executed quickly, but you still may not get the exact price you want. Rapid price swings, particularly in volatile assets like crypto, may lead to a situation where your buying price is more expensive (or your selling price is cheaper) than you anticipated. Use a market order when your main objective is to ensure that your transaction executes. If you are very concerned about transacting at a precise price point, then you'll want to use a limit order.

» A *limit order* allows you to declare the price at which you want to buy or sell an asset—sort of like an eBay bid. In the preceding example, Alan wanted to exit his trade precisely at $7.19, so he used a limit order. Limit orders generally stand for the duration of a trading day, or you can set them up as GTC (good till cancelled), which will allow them to stand for 30–90 days while you wait on a buyer or seller to agree to your limit price.

» A *stop order*, which Alan used when entering his DOT trade, requires the specification of a predetermined price (the stop price), which, when hit, will trigger a market order for the asset. Stop orders are used when you need assurance that you will be able to enter or exit a position when a certain price point is reached. These order types are most frequently used to limit losses during a trade, as I illustrate shortly.

» A *stop limit order*, like a stop order, gets triggered when the specified stop price is reached, but rather than triggering a market order, it triggers a limit order. A stop limit order may be used when you want to transact once your stop price is reached, but you want to do so at a very specific price point. If you're unable to transact at that price point immediately after the order is triggered, then you're willing to hold your position and wait for another opportunity to get the exact price you want. This type of order is used less frequently in trading and more so in investing.

Returning to Alan's Polkadot (DOT) trade: as with all trades, it is important that Alan limit his potential losses. Alan does this by placing a sell stop order that will sell out of his position should the price drop to $7.06, two cents below where he entered the trade at $7.08. If this order triggers, then Alan will take a loss, but it will be a limited loss. Good traders typically define their targets and their stop losses prior to entering a trade.

REMEMBER

A stop order (sometimes known as a *stop loss order*) should be placed with every trade to limit losses. Failure to do so can expose you to catastrophic losses, especially in a market as volatile as cryptocurrency.

Alan's limit order price of $7.19 finds a buyer (figure 80) ten minutes or so after he enters the trade at $7.08. This one is a winner and Alan nets just over $300 in profit (figure 81).

fig. 80

| A | AlanTheGreat -1.0% | | -3,531.1500 DOT |
| | 23 hours ago | | Sold @ $ 7.19 |

Go short on DOT when price hits 7.19

fig. 81

#	ORDER	PAIR	PRICE	VOLUME	COST	LEVERAGE	FEE	OPENED
● 219589	Sell	DOT/USD	7.19	3,531.1500 DOT	25,389.0	n/a	$ 63.4724	27 Jul, 2022
● 219581	Buy	DOT/USD	7.08	3,540.0000 DOT	25,063.2	n/a	DOT 8.8500	27 Jul, 2022

Notice how the "cost" of the sale at the $7.19 price point was a little over $300 more than the cost of the purchase at the $7.08 price point—a textbook case of buy low, sell high, and bank the difference minus fees.

The exhilaration of a big win has left Alan hungry for more. He's curious about using margin on his trades, because he's heard that doing so can lead to sizable paydays. Somewhere in the back of his mind he also recollects hearing that it's incredibly risky, but at the moment he's riding high and has no trouble throwing caution to the wind. He's more eager than ever to prove his family wrong.

Margin

Margin, also known as *leverage*, refers to the use of borrowed money to trade. Traders use margin when they wish to control a larger trading position by putting up some of their own capital and borrowing the rest from their broker or another entity.

For his first margin trade, Alan decides to put up $10,000 leveraged three times (3×) to initiate a long position on BTC. BTC is currently trading at $23,800, so $10,000 would allow him to buy 0.4202 BTC. However, his 3× leverage means that he's borrowing $20,000 from his broker and initiating a long position worth $30,000, or 1.2605 BTC. Both his winning and losing potentials are now magnified.

But Alan is paying for this privilege to magnify his potential gain or loss. On the CryptoParrot trading platform, Alan is charged a 0.25% fee per leverage multiple. At 3× he's paying 0.75% of his initial capital outlay in fees, or $75, *on top of* the standard trading fees he'll pay when opening and closing the position.

NOTE

The fees paid when using margin are often referred to as "interest" owed on the borrowed money.

The extra cost doesn't bother Alan. He's still riding high from his big win with Polkadot and thinks his BTC long play is a sure thing. He diligently defines his stop and his target by placing a sell stop order (with a stop price of $23,730) and a buy limit order at $23,875.

He places all of his orders at once: the leveraged buy order and the standing stop and limit orders. As noted, he gets in at $23,800 and is looking to find a buyer at $23,875. If the price drops to $23,730 before he does so, a market order will trigger, and he will exit the position with a loss.

Alan watches the price hover and vacillate between his stop loss and target markers. He gets up from his computer to grab a snack and refill his coffee.

When he returns, he is greeted with bad news (figure 82).

Alan's long position closed out at $23,689, a whopping $41 below the stop price he had set. You'll recall that the stop price merely triggers a market order. If the price is moving too fast you may get a far worse price than what you anticipated, a frustrating phenomenon known as "slippage."

fig. 82

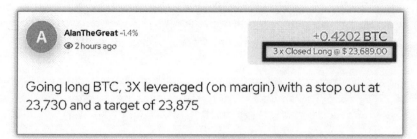

AlanTheGreat -1.4%
👁 2 hours ago

+0.4202 BTC
3 x Closed Long @ $ 23,689.00

Going long BTC, 3X leveraged (on margin) with a stop out at 23,730 and a target of 23,875

Taking losses on margin are never fun, especially knowing that you've actually paid extra for the privilege of losing more than you would have had you not levered up your position. Here's a breakdown of the damage:

Alan put up $10,000 to go long on BTC, at 3× leverage; that's $30,000 being risked to control 1.2605 BTC (@$23,800).

Alan's 3× long position was closed and his 1.2605 BTC was sold (@$23,689) for a total of $29,859.98.

$30,000 - $29,859.98 = a loss of $140.02 on the trade. Not so bad, right, especially considering he just made over $300 with his successful scalp of Polkadot? Not so fast. I haven't taken into account the fees yet.

The 0.75% leverage fee plus the standard trading fee comes to a total of $223.94. This amount must be added to $140.02 in order to calculate his true loss on the trade, which comes to $363.96.

So much for those winnings on Polkadot. Faced with the likely prospect that he's not the innate trading super genius he thought he was, Alan decides that he's going to put in some serious time to study trading techniques and strategies before he proceeds any further. He may just end up sticking it out for a while at Stanford before dropping out to become a millionaire. Only time will tell.

When to Buy, When to Sell

You have some of the essential vocabulary now and a sense for the mechanics of trading, but you still don't have two key pieces of information that together make up the holy grail of trading: knowing when to buy and knowing when to sell. In other words, how do you win at trading?

Unfortunately, this knowledge doesn't come easily. You can read more about the trading process beyond its applications to crypto (again, my publisher offers *Day Trading QuickStart Guide* and *Forex Trading QuickStart Guide* titles for a broader view). But reading about it, whether here or in another book, is just the starting point—you've got to put in the work, defining and executing your trade plan and determining which trades you think will win more than they lose and why. You will also need to acquaint yourself with the many tools of the trade.

For instance, take a look at this bar chart from Yahoo! Finance (figure 83) tracking three months' worth of price action on Binance Coin (BNB). Each of the vertical bars at the top represents the range over which BNB traded during the course of one day. The vertical bars on the bottom represent the trading volume for BNB: how many units were traded that day from one party to another.

fig. 83

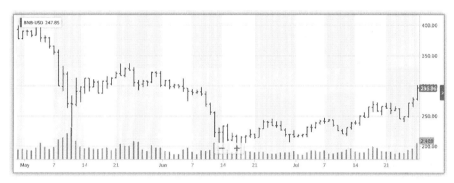

Source: Yahoo! Finance

By looking at the changes in the bars over time, you can get a sense of the amount of demand for a given currency. It can help you identify trends in the market and changes in its sentiment. Perhaps (and I do mean *perhaps*) if Alan had used a chart like this to study some of the common price fluctuations of Bitcoin during a typical day, it would have helped him define more favorable parameters for his leveraged trade of Bitcoin.

Veteran traders have learned how to identify different patterns in charts to help them find good trading opportunities. You can start working with charts as you make your practice trades to see how your trades play out.

Note in figure 83 how each of the little marks jutting out of a given price bar offers an additional piece of information. The mark on the left tells you where the price opened for the day, and the mark on the right tells you where it closed for the day. The very top and very bottom of the vertical bar reveal the highest and lowest price point reached during the course of that day.

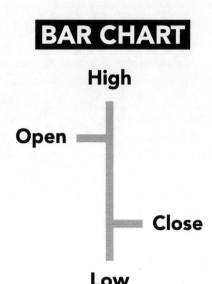

BAR CHART

High

Open

Close

Low

fig. 84

The bar chart is just one of hundreds of chart types and indicators used by traders to cultivate a "trading edge" that allows them to win more than they lose. Even the very best traders still lose on a regular basis—they just win more! But many traders, unfortunately, end up losing more than they win; they are lured by the prospect of fast money but are unwilling to put in the real work required to master the process. They are essentially gambling—and there's nothing wrong with that so long as they are fully aware of the risk they are taking. Unfortunately, some people may try to make a living without realizing that they are entering a casino and expecting to support themselves.

As indicated by Peter's warning to Alan, the evidence suggests that around 90–95% of day traders lose more money than they gain. Separate studies tracking futures traders in Brazil and day traders in Taiwan found a success rate between 3% and 5% over periods ranging from 300 days (Brazil) to several years (Taiwan).[4]

Automated Trading

Over time, some chart trends have become so popular that traders have created tools such as a trading bot to automate their trading. A *trading bot* is a utility that identifies specific market conditions and places trades accordingly. Some exchanges offer bots to customers for free, while others charge a fee. Many traders, specifically those who are proficient in computer programming, opt to create their own.

If you decide to create your own trading bot, it might be best to test it in your practice account before using real money.

Many serious traders use a separate trading platform for the purpose of research, chart analysis, and so on, but they rely on their exchanges for their actual trading. Some of these platforms, such as Altrady and Coinigy, will connect to your exchange account to make trading simpler. Consider working with one of these integrations if you are seriously committed to crypto trading.

In chapter 10, you will learn about other ways to generate income with your crypto, such as yield farming and staking. Before you go out and fully commit yourself to the arduous course of becoming a cryptocurrency trader, consider the pros and cons of all routes available to you.

Cryptocurrency Derivatives

So far, I've discussed trading via the straightforward buying and selling of the cryptocurrencies themselves. Another way to trade crypto is through derivatives. *Derivatives* are contracts whose value is *derived* from the value of the underlying currency. They are agreements to buy or sell (or offering the option to buy or sell) a given asset. These agreements have parameters specifying that the purchase be made at a particular price and point in time (or within a given time period).

Right now, there are derivatives available to trade on Bitcoin and ether. As other currencies increase in scale, they will likely spawn their own derivatives.

Here are some common derivatives that are in play now and will likely expand more broadly into the cryptocurrency space:

The appeal of derivatives in trading has always been their price volatility. A derivative of a stock, for instance, will experience more dynamic fluctuations in price than the stock itself, attracting traders who hope to capitalize on quick price changes. Since cryptos are already highly volatile, crypto derivatives will further compound that volatility. Proceed with caution.

Call Options

A *call option* gives you the right, but not the obligation, to buy an asset at a specified price on or before a specified date in the future. Buying calls is a way to bet on a future price increase.

Suppose the price of Bitcoin is $23,000, and I buy a call option contract (for a price of $1,000) that entitles me to purchase 1 bitcoin at $23,500 *within thirty days*. The price of Bitcoin climbs to $25,000 *within twenty days*. My call option contract is now much more valuable than the $1,000 I paid for it. I can resell the contract at a profit (this is what typically happens). Or I can "exercise" the option and purchase 1 bitcoin for $23,500, $1,500 less than what it's actually worth.

Put Options

A *put option* gives you the right, but not the obligation, to sell an asset at a specified price on or before a specified date in the future. Buying *puts* is a way to protect yourself against a future price decrease.

I buy 1 ETH at $1,700. I may, in lieu of placing a sell stop order, purchase a put option contract (for a price of $300) that entitles me to sell 1 ETH for $1,650 within a thirty-day period. If the price of ETH plummets, say to $1,000, then the put option insures my loss to an extent, allowing me to take a $350 loss rather than a $700 loss. Alternatively, say I never purchased any ETH but only the put option itself. When the price of ETH plummets to $1,000, my put option (at $1,650) will be worth a lot more than the $300 I paid for it. It will be worth, at the very least, $650, because I could buy 1 ether at $1,000 and then exercise my put option to immediately sell it for $1,650.

Futures Contracts

Futures contracts give you the obligation to buy or sell an asset in the future at a specified price on a specified date.

Bitcoin is currently selling for $23,000. I decide to "go long" on $20,000 worth of Bitcoin futures contracts (each "contract" typically corresponds to $1, so I'm technically agreeing to 20,000 contracts), which oblige me in summary to pay another party $20,000 for 1 bitcoin exactly one month from the current date. This other party is "going short." If the price of Bitcoin goes up, I make money and the opposite party takes a loss. If Bitcoin goes down, I take the loss and the opposing party makes money.

Perpetual Swaps

Unlike options or futures, *perpetual swaps* are contracts with no expiration or settlement date. They allow traders to manage risks and hedge positions (like the example from the *put options* section) without having to continually open new positions every time an option expires or a futures contract comes due. Like the other derivatives I've discussed here, perpetual swaps can be used for trading as well.

Pay Attention to the Risks

Trading cryptos is easy. Making money while trading cryptos is not. I want to highlight two risks that are common to all forms of trading: volatility and emotion. Traders also need to watch out for dangerous "pump and dump" schemes, which are rampant in the crypto world.

Volatility

Volatility creates opportunities for traders to make fast money, but it's important to understand that this same dynamic also creates opportunities for traders to lose money fast. The volatility that makes crypto so attractive to so many is exactly what makes trading it especially perilous. Always mitigate your risk by using stops to protect yourself when prices start to move against you.

Doubt, Fear, and Greed

Traders are undone by psychology more than anything else. Doubt and fear can make traders cash in prematurely when they should hold; greed can make them hold, or buy more, when they should be selling. That's why paper trading is so helpful. While practicing, keep a trading diary to document both your trading techniques *and* your emotional state. Practicing your trading builds confidence, and confidence can offset the emotional bugbears.

Pump and Dump Schemes

In a *pump and dump scheme*, some influencers or promoters buy into a cryptocurrency, promote the heck out of it, and sell their coins while other people are bidding them up. The promoters are out before the new buyers realize that their holdings are worthless. These schemes often involve very small cryptocurrencies that don't have an interesting use other than for trading. If you see a celebrity posting on Instagram about a sure-fire cryptocurrency, apply a healthy dose of skepticism.

Chapter Recap

» Cryptocurrencies tend to be volatile, which creates opportunities for traders to make short-term profits. The risks, however, are significant, and losses are more common than gains.

» Traders (of cryptocurrency and other assets) use a variety of order types to limit and define their desired entry and exit.

» Cryptocurrency derivatives offer an added degree of volatile price action to an already volatile trading arena.

» Before trading with real money, take the time to practice. Learn how to place an order, study charts, backtest your strategies, and keep records of your trades.

» Watch out for emotions that can undermine your trading, use stops to prevent losses, and stay on guard against hype directed at a particular crypto—there's a good chance it's a pump and dump scheme.

| 10 |

Investing in Cryptocurrency

Chapter Overview

- » Cryptocurrency as an asset
- » How to invest
- » Cryptocurrency portfolio management
- » Fundamental analysis
- » Generating income

Back in 2013, a contributor on a forum for cryptocurrency enthusiasts called BitcoinTalk.org posted a message titled "I AM HODLING." He meant to type "I AM HOLDING" (he also admitted to drinking while posting). Over time, however, this typo has taken on a life of its own. For some, *hodl* has come to mean "hold on for dear life," and it is used to describe buying and holding crypto for the long term. This is exactly what asset investors do. They identify assets with long-term price appreciation potential and then hold them, sometimes for decades. "Hodlers" believe in the long-term potential for crypto. Rather than worry about the haphazard, difficult-to-predict short-term movements of the asset, hodlers buy their crypto and wait.

In addition to *hodling*, there are several other ways to invest in crypto. Some investors buy assets that run adjacent to the crypto economy, such as crypto exchange-traded funds (ETFs) and shares of stock in companies such as Coinbase (COIN) and Riot Blockchain (RIOT). There are other methods, such as staking and yield farming, that enable crypto owners to derive income from their crypto portfolio, similar to how stockholders derive income from dividends. In this chapter I discuss these methods and more.

Recent Market Performance of Cryptocurrencies

In the early days of Bitcoin, it wasn't uncommon for the crypto-curious to build their own home-based mining apparatus. Back then it was easier to mine coins from the comfort of your own home (see how to build your own mining rig in chapter 11) without a warehouse full of computing tech. Any of these Bitcoin pioneers who held their bitcoins for a few years would have seen extraordinary returns, as the price rocketed up from pennies to tens of thousands of dollars over the course of a decade.

This shocking appreciation in value made plenty of people rich at breakneck speeds. Countless others, fearing a bubble, pulled the trigger prematurely and cashed out, only to see BTC soar to ever greater heights. In truth, despite the many compelling arguments for a decentralized, all-digital currency, the extraordinary appreciation of Bitcoin was a black swan event, meaning it was unanticipated and carried profound implications.

Not all cryptocurrencies have shared Bitcoin's meteoric rise. The practice of hodling spans the gamut of coins in the crypto universe, and in the midst of the remarkable gains there are many who pursued a *hodl* strategy with one cryptocurrency or another and have seen the value tank.

In chapter 7, I discussed initial coin offerings or ICOs, and noted that, according to one study, a large number of ICOs were scams. Many investors who took bold positions during the height of the ICO craze—from 2017 to 2018—ended up seeing the value of their assets shrink away to nothing. Richard Malone, a writer for a website called www.dailyhodl.com, compares the larger crypto market to that of the many ".com" businesses that were publicly traded in the late 1990s and early 2000s: "86% of companies with a ".com" at the end of their name from 1996–2006 went to zero," Malone wrote in 2018. "It is my opinion that the current crypto market is even frothier, and therefore, I believe over 90% of cryptocurrencies out today will be worthless in five years."[1] Yikes!

The tendency of cryptos to come and go at breakneck speeds can make the assessment of Malone's 2018 prediction a little tricky. At first, the raw numbers may look far more positive: in March of that year, the total number of cryptocurrencies in circulation worldwide was a paltry 1,658,[2] whereas there are approximately 19,000 in circulation at the time of this writing. But that doesn't mean those cryptos from 2018 were all or even mostly successful. According to www.coinopsy.com, a website that tracks cryptocurrency failures, the total number of all-time crypto failures is around 2,415 at the time of this writing— and about 1,266 cryptos failed between the years 2018 and the summer of 2022.[3] This data would suggest that around 76.3% of the cryptos that were up and running in 2018 have since failed. That's a lower rate than Malone predicted—but then again, it wouldn't be impossible for that number to climb closer to 90% before his five-year period is up.

I mention these numbers up front because they provide good context for a discussion of crypto investing, particularly when it comes to the question of what coins should and should not be *hodled*. Malone, with his grimmer outlook on altcoins, argues that hodling should be reserved for the "blue chip" cryptos such as Bitcoin or ether, as these are thought to have a much lower risk of complete failure.

When it comes to altcoins, however, our friend Lynn Forrest has a different idea, one I explore later in the chapter. First, though, comes a discussion of how to categorize crypto as a financial asset, and how it compares to other, more established assets.

Cryptocurrency as an Asset

Let's say you badly miscalculated throughout the year on your taxes, and in April you discover that you owe the IRS $25,000 after penalties. But, lucky you, you've amassed a small fortune in Bitcoin due to a series of hodling investments you've made over the last five years. You proceed to sell off a portion of your Bitcoin holdings and pay your tax bill.

Your ability to liquidate your cryptocurrency in order to service a debt is a key feature of an *asset*—which can be defined as a property having some kind of value, owned by an individual or company, and able to fulfill debts or legal commitments. Cryptocurrency is categorized as a "digital asset."

The world is still trying to figure out how cryptocurrency compares to more traditional assets in terms of its characteristics. Is it similar to gold or to a high-flying tech stock? If you're serious about investing intelligently in cryptocurrency, then you need to at least have a sense of how this asset fares among its more established peers.

Crypto as a Growth Asset

A "growth asset" is thought to have a large potential for appreciation. The downside is that they also tend to be risky and can end up losing value or even becoming totally worthless.

Examples of growth assets include the following:

» **Tech stocks,** especially of the "small cap" variety (smaller companies) that have very high price-to-earnings ratios (the price of the stock relative to the annual income of the company).

» **Real estate** such as land or buildings, is a long-term investment that can provide capital growth. It can also provide investors with income when the property is rented.

NOTE

For a deep dive into general investing and real estate, check out the bestselling *Investing QuickStart Guide* and *Real Estate Investing QuickStart Guide* from ClydeBank Media.

Cryptocurrency has shown signs of being a growth asset; it certainly has the high risk and high reward dynamic in play. There are two distinct areas of risk that should be considered when assessing cryptocurrency as a growth asset:

1. Is the cryptocurrency space as a whole going to continue to grow and flourish, or will it retract and possibly disappear?

2. What are the specific concerns and opportunities presented by the cryptocurrencies you're looking to invest in?

Crypto as a Store of Value

An investor knows that holding all your extra wealth in your savings account is generally unwise. Left alone, cash will steadily depreciate in value due to inflation at an average rate of 3–4% a year. For this reason, investors find it useful to devote portions (often 10% or so) of their portfolios to strong "store-of-value" assets, which are expected to offset the degrading effect of inflation.

Examples of store-of-value assets include the following:

» **Precious metals,** such as gold, silver, or platinum
» **Treasury bonds,** with reliable yields that blunt inflation

NOTE

Ironically, even though investors consider store-of-value assets a buffer against inflation, stronger fiat currencies such as US dollars and British pounds can be viewed by some as "store-of-value" assets, despite the inflation factor. Consider an investor whose home country is undergoing hyperinflation (in excess of 50%); in such a context the US dollar's annual rate of 3-5% seems a quite reasonable store of value.

Though many cryptocurrency enthusiasts have made the case for its qualities as a store-of-value asset—Bitcoin, especially with its finite supply, has been likened to digital gold—cryptos have yet to demonstrate inflation-hedging properties. Chapter 4 includes a review of some of the specific numbers that speak to this conclusion.

Crypto as an Income Investment

An income investment is an investment that can be relied upon to generate income at regular intervals.

Examples of income investments include the following:

» **Rental property**: When tenants pay rent on a property it's an example of an investment creating income.

» **Dividend stocks**: These are stocks that pay out dividend income, usually on a quarterly basis. The amount of the expected payout is usually listed publicly and expressed as a percentage of an investor's total holdings in the stock.

Income investment may be the most reliable categorization available for cryptocurrencies, an asset that too often defies categorization. There are several opportunities available to cryptocurrency investors who want to use their portfolio holdings to generate income, usually in the form of more cryptocurrency. I discuss the specifics of certain "crypto income strategies" later on in this chapter.

Inherent Risks of Crypto Assets

Cryptocurrency as an asset presents a multitude of risks. Some of these risks are distinctly double-edged swords; the immutability of transactions (see more on this in chapter 2), for example, allows crypto to function properly while also adding risk to market participants. Here are a few of the broader risk factors to consider when assessing any crypto asset.

» **Getting out can be tough**. The nascent marketplace and the strong correlations between cryptocurrencies (i.e., when Bitcoin crashes, the rest will likely follow) can create harrowing conditions for investors looking for an exit. If you find yourself looking to sell in a wave of panic-selling, you may wind up selling for much less than you wanted.

» **Bankruptcies in the industry have unclear implications**. As expected, many exchanges have not survived the ups and downs of this turbulent industry. Many declared bankruptcy during the "crypto winter" of 2022.[4] The rights of customers to retrieve their assets managed by defunct crypto exchanges are as yet undefined.

Your crypto assets are not insured by the government the way assets in a bank account are.

» **Access to private or other insurance is unclear.** Most crypto assets and businesses either cannot be insured at all or, best case, are underinsured. Though some insurance companies are interested in further engagement with the crypto space, the intangibility and illiquidity of this asset makes insuring it very difficult.[5]

» **Transactions are immutable.** Once consensus is reached, there's no way to reverse erroneous transactions.

» **Crypto is uniquely susceptible to misinformation and social engineering.** There are literally open forums of crypto-conspirators who are hard at work planning their next pump and dump scheme. The growth of crypto as an asset class has drawn all manner of predatory opportunists. The US Securities and Exchange Commission has even created a fake initial coin offering website (www.howeycoins.com) to draw attention to the problem of these "shiny object threats"[6] that entice both opportunists and their victims.

» **There are no standardized security standards for custodial services:** Banks have rigorous protocols to follow when it comes to the handling of cash and electronic records. No such requirements yet exist for custodial entities such as exchanges in the crypto world.

» **Legal redress is limited.** Legal recourse for victims of fraud or theft is often somewhat limited, and in the past has been nearly nonexistent—though more recently, additional regulatory frameworks have been advanced in the US and abroad aiming to protect consumers from fraud (see chapter 13).

» **Human error plays an outsized factor.** Spill a cup of coffee on your cold storage wallet, and you could be facing a catastrophic financial loss. Send money to the wrong address? Tough luck.

Ways to Invest in Crypto

Now that you have a somewhat better sense of cryptocurrency as an asset, it's time to look at the common ways that this asset gains admittance to a typical investment portfolio. From buying coins directly to making strategic investments in the larger cryptocurrency ecosystem and its supporting players, there are several options available to investors seeking exposure to this space.

Here are the essential entry points for making direct and indirect investments in cryptocurrency.

I'm not a financial advisor and the data and anecdotes I present in this book should not be construed as investment advice. My role in your journey through the crypto-verse is that of a guide and educator.

Buying Crypto Directly

Buying crypto on an exchange and then keeping your keys secured in your wallet is the most common and direct approach to cryptocurrency investing. By now, if you've read this book straight through, you understand the role played by exchanges and wallets and how to make intelligent selections on this front.

Investing in Cryptocurrency Companies

A timeless problem in all kinds of investing is how to best gain exposure to an industry that is of interest to you. Many are looking for some level of exposure, but maybe not *direct* exposure—like Peter Forrest.

Instead of investing directly in cryptocurrencies, these investors look to invest in businesses that have cultivated roles in the cryptocurrency ecosystem. Several crypto exchanges are publicly traded—Coinbase, for instance (NYSE: COIN)—and companies like PayPal (NASDAQ: PYPL), Block (NYSE: SQ), and Mastercard (NYSE: MA) are embracing cryptocurrency payments as part of their long-term growth strategies.

One place to look for these companies is the NASDAQ Blockchain Economy Index (NASDAQ: RSBLCN). This was introduced in 2017 and currently has 62 constituent companies from around the world that are committing material resources to develop and utilize blockchain technologies.

Exchange-Traded Funds

Going back to the investor's problem of how best to gain exposure to a target industry or asset, there has been a fair amount of chatter in recent years on the topic of a cryptocurrency-based *exchange-traded fund*, or ETF. An ETF tracks the price of an asset or an index (a group of investments) but is traded on stock exchanges throughout the day just like stocks.

For years, would-be sponsors have tried and failed to gain regulatory approval for a cryptocurrency ETF, one that would operate similarly to commodities ETFs such as State Street Global Advisors' Gold Shares ETF or iShares' Silver Trust. The US Securities and Exchange Commission, however, wasn't willing to approve an ETF that invested in unregistered assets that were subject to dramatic swings in valuation and liquidity.

In 2021, a loophole was found by way of the commodity futures market, and for the first time ever in the US an ETF became available that would closely follow the performance of Bitcoin. This ETF is known as the ProShares Bitcoin Strategy ETF (NYSE Arca: BITO). It doesn't invest directly in Bitcoin but in Bitcoin futures contracts (see chapter 9). These are traded on the Chicago Mercantile Exchange and registered with the Commodity Futures Trading Commission. Crypto ETFs lack certain benefits that come from owning your crypto directly, such as anonymity and the opportunity to earn yields on crypto under your control through staking and yield farming.

IMAGE

fig. 85

Source: Yahoo! Finance

The expense ratio for this ETF indicates that nearly 1% of all the money you put into this ETF will go toward management or other fees not related to the purchase of investable assets. That's about double the average expense of any given ETF in the marketplace.

NOTE

Many of the crypto ETFs introduced after BITO are also tied to the Chicago Mercantile Exchange's futures contracts.

While a crypto ETF is a quick and easy way to introduce cryptocurrency into your investment portfolio (you can purchase them through your standard brokerage platform such as TD Ameritrade, Schwab, or Robinhood), there will be an associated expense to this asset, costs that you pay that don't go directly to the purchase of assets held in the ETF. These costs are quantified in all ETFs in the reported "expense ratio" (figure 85). Compare that cost with the fees incurred when buying and selling your cryptos directly.

If you want a crypto option in your 401(k) or other employer-sponsored retirement savings account, ask your human resources department about adding a crypto ETF to the array of offerings.

Funds that Invest in Crypto

For cryptocurrency investors willing to accept and pay for an extra layer of professional management, there are cryptocurrency-based mutual funds and trusts.

Mutual Funds

Like ETFs, cryptocurrency-based mutual funds don't have regulatory approval to hold actual cryptocurrencies, but hold cryptocurrency futures whose market performance roughly reflects that of the base asset.

Mutual funds, unlike ETFs, are not traded throughout the day like stocks. The assets in a mutual fund are valued at the end of each trading day. This valuation, known as the Net Asset Value or NAV, determines the price of the fund's shares. All investors get the same price quote on any given day. That price will reflect either the previous day's NAV or, if the markets have already closed, the current day's NAV.

You may be able to buy into a mutual fund without paying a commission on your trade, but the expense ratios generally veer higher. Similar to ETFs, mutual funds have an expense ratio, which will tell you what percentage of your money is going to costs other than those of the asset itself.

Trust Funds

Another type of fund that may invest in crypto is a *trust fund*. A trust fund pools money from investors and uses the money to buy assets. The investors are then given shares in the trust.

The majority of the trusts that hold cryptocurrencies are **statutory trusts**. The shares of these trusts can initially only be sold to institutional investors (companies representing investors) and to accredited investors. Following a seasoning period of 12 months, the shares may be sold in secondary markets to the general public.

Under SEC regulations, an **accredited investor** meets the following criteria:

» You have earned income that exceeded $200,000 (or $300,000 together with a spouse or spousal equivalent) in each of the prior two years, and reasonably expect the same for the current year, or

» You have net worth over $1 million, either alone or together with a spouse or spousal equivalent (excluding the value of your primary residence), or

» You have a Series 7, 65, or 82 license. These are licenses obtained by financial professionals that govern the sale of securities.

As always, pay attention to the expenses when considering buying into a cryptocurrency trust.

The Grayscale Bitcoin Trust charges annual fees of around 2% to 2.5% of your investment. You are paying for professional management of the assets in the trust and for the convenience of being able to sidestep the crypto exchanges and just trade shares in your trust via a standard brokerage account.

Cryptocurrency and Your Portfolio

Here I discuss investment portfolio management from two different perspectives: fitting cryptocurrencies into a more conventional investment portfolio, and how to build and maintain the cryptocurrency investments within that crypto slice of your portfolio.

The Crypto-Inclusive Traditional Investment Portfolio

Conventional wisdom advises that investment portfolios should be diversified—that is, they should include a mix of assets. Diversifying your assets spreads out your risk and reduces your vulnerability to catastrophic losses. An investor may, for example, seek a general portfolio asset allocation of 45% domestic stocks, 35% international stocks, and 20% bonds with multiple different positions (investments) within each category. Another investor may wish to carve out 10% or 15% of their asset allocation for precious metals, such as gold or silver. Others may want at least 15% of their investment portfolio to include real estate or artwork. You get the idea. Different assets provide different benefits. "Growth stocks," for instance, offer the opportunity for robust price appreciation. Bonds offer regular interest payments. Precious metals may offer a low-volatility hedge against inflation.

> **How does cryptocurrency fit into a typical investment portfolio?**

It has become commonplace for institutional investment advisers to recommend a cryptocurrency asset allocation of up to 5% (figure 86).

POSSIBLE ASSET ALLOCATION IN A LONG-TERM INVESTMENT PORTFOLIO

fig. 86

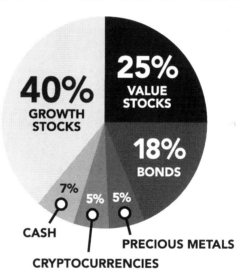

It's interesting that the 5% figure has come to represent the conventional wisdom for cryptocurrency allocation within a larger portfolio. This was the figure that Peter Forrest's advisor Mariana suggested when he came to her with crypto on his mind. In truth, there's no single concrete reason so many advisors have arrived at the 5% figure as a benchmark for crypto allocation. It primarily seems to be based on the fact that advisors have only recently begun including cryptocurrency investments in their product lines and aren't necessarily crypto enthusiasts. They focus on how it's a volatile and risky asset class that could depreciate or disappear rapidly.

But that's also what makes 5% about as good a guideline as any. After all, in any form of investing, you shouldn't risk any more than you are prepared to lose; 5% should suit the interests of most investors, who may be excited by cryptocurrency's application potential but not so bullish that they want to risk a major drawdown in their larger portfolio. Really, that 5% figure could be used to justify all kinds of asset allocations that stimulate the curiosity of investors: 5% in art, 5% in rare vinyl records, or even 5% in NFTs. It's not a magic number, but it is a useful rule of thumb.

The Crypto-Specific Portfolio

What might the asset allocation within a crypto-specific portfolio look like? (See figure 87 for a visualization of this question.)

THE CRYPTO-EXCLUSIVE PORTFOLIO

fig. 87

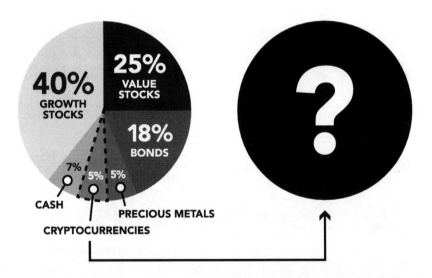

If cryptocurrencies make up 5% of a portfolio, what specifically should that 5% consist of?

In order to define a strategic asset allocation for a crypto-specific portfolio, the investor should begin by answering a few introspective questions.

» **What do I hope to gain from my investment in cryptocurrency?** Am I looking for dramatic growth, a store of value, or something else? For example, if store of value is your thing, then you'll want to pay more attention to the currencies that have a finite supply, like Bitcoin, and maybe those that reliably burn off units, like Binance Coin.

» **How long will I hold my crypto assets?** If my assets skyrocket in price, will I sell some or all of them off or will I continue to buy more? Maybe you're all about riding that one breakout coin "to the moon." Make note of which coins you intend to *hodl* and which ones you intend to prune and why.

» **Am I more comfortable owning the cryptos themselves, or would I prefer to own a basket of stocks related to cryptocurrency?** If you have mixed feelings on the topic, you're free to invest on both fronts.

» **Am I interested in generating passive income from my crypto holdings, such as interest and staking fees?** If so, would I prefer using my cryptos to generate a reliable but small amount of income or would I rather take more risk if it gives me the chance to generate higher levels of income? You'll want to take some time to study this approach before deciding how much of your resources should be deployed here. I discuss "Crypto Income Strategies" later in this chapter.

» **Are there any blockchain applications or projects that are of particular interest to me?** If so, should I overweight my crypto portfolio with the coins or tokens used in these projects? If a particular altcoin project has won your enthusiasm, then perhaps it makes sense to consider devoting 10% or even 15% of your crypto portfolio to that coin.

Your answer to these questions may lead you to any number of crypto investment strategies. For example, your self-analysis may reveal that all you really care about is not missing out on another round of skyrocketing gains in the general cryptocurrency space. You may thus pursue a strategy of broad exposure to the most popular cryptos with significant overweighting on the blue chips: Bitcoin and ether.

The cryptos included in the figure 88 asset allocation are the eight coins with the highest market cap at the time of this writing (not including stablecoins). The idea here is to reduce downside risk by only investing in coins that have an established reputation while giving extra weight to the two biggest players in the space, BTC and ETH.

SAMPLE CRYPTO PORTFOLIO

fig. 88

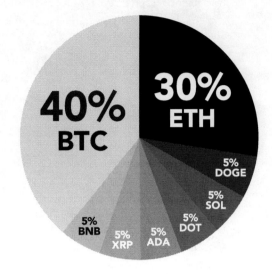

(Re)Balancing Your Portfolio

As with all other forms of investing, the idea of keeping your portfolio balanced comes into play within the crypto-specific portfolio. Balancing and rebalancing your portfolio is a straightforward concept. Don't put all your eggs in one basket, right? Diversify your risk lest your entire enterprise go up in smoke due to the cratering of one particular position.

Rebalancing refers to the practice of routinely—perhaps quarterly—reestablishing your original asset allocation. Take, for instance, the portfolio in figure 88. Say Ripple (XRP) goes on a wild tear and appreciates drastically over the course of a quarter and suddenly you've got 20% of your crypto portfolio value in XRP. The investor who believes in rebalancing would sell off a portion of her XRP to bring the allocation back down to the original 5%. She would then buy the coins that had fallen below their original allocation percentage in the portfolio. If the portfolio's Bitcoin component, initially configured for 40%, was down to 30% in the same quarter that XRP skyrocketed, the "rebalancer" would proceed to buy more BTC in order to reset the allocation back to the BTC target—40%.

Now that I've covered rebalancing, perhaps it's a good time to tell you that some amazingly successful investors positively despise the notion of rigid rebalancing, particularly when it comes to diminishing a position that has been serving them well. Returning to the wisdom of Peter Forrest's favorite investor, Peter Lynch; "Selling your winners and holding your losers is like cutting the flowers and watering the weeds."

Different approaches to rebalancing or not rebalancing are appropriate at different times and depend on an investor's circumstances, risk tolerance, and objectives. It may be unwise to abandon the idea of maintaining a balanced portfolio, but there's nothing wrong with adjusting your asset allocation in favor of those coins or tokens that appear, by your analysis, to be in line for big runs.

Using a Crypto Portfolio Tracker

It's not uncommon for crypto investors to have assets scattered about in multiple different locations: hardware wallets, software wallets, exchanges, brokerage accounts, etc. This decentralized custody of crypto assets is probably smart, as it spreads out hacking and fraud risk over a multitude of custodians. But when you're attempting to build a general portfolio with specific, strategic asset allocations such as in figure 88, you need a centralized view of your holdings and their present values (see the interface depicted in figure 89).

The software you select should reflect your interests as an investor. Here are some factors to consider when selecting your software:

» Is the software configured for tax reporting? Will it keep track of your taxable losses and tax-deductible gains? Will it generate a 1099-DIV or other pertinent tax documentation for you?

» Does the software integrate easily with one or more major cryptocurrency exchanges, providing you with a one-stop shop for your crypto trading/investing and management needs? Will it allow you to visualize your holdings across other exchanges as well?

» Does the platform provide access to trading bots to help you automate your trading, or will you need to personally execute each transaction?

Recall that trading bots are automated programs that can place trades on your behalf. You may program them yourself or run those that have been programmed by others whom you trust. Traders and investors alike may elect to use trading bots in order to remove the often counter-productive emotional human dimension from their decision making.

SAMPLE PORTFOLIO TRACKER INTERFACE

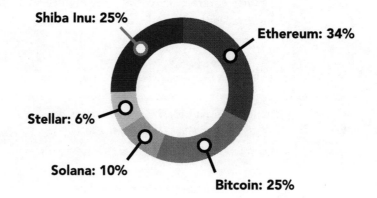

Shiba Inu: 25%

Ethereum: 34%

Stellar: 6%

Solana: 10%

Bitcoin: 25%

GRAPHIC

fig. 89

$6,856	-$650	$1,856
Total Balance	24h Portfolio Change (-10.5%)	Total Profit/Loss (+37.1%)

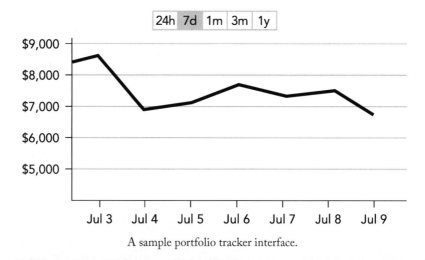

A sample portfolio tracker interface.

DIGITAL ASSETS

As with any software applications, free, premium, and DIY crypto portfolio management solutions exist. Fortunately, you don't have to look further than the free digital assets that come with this book. Request free lifetime access to our Crypto Portfolio Manager that tracks sales, purchases, and portfolio performance with one easy-to-use dashboard from go.quickstartguides.com/crypto

For those of you who believe—emotions notwithstanding—that you have the keen insight necessary to pick the next big breakout crypto, you'll need to know how to analyze and assess coins and tokens based on their individual merits. I discuss this later in this chapter. But before I get to that, I want to quickly check in with Lynn Forrest, who has come to believe that building an oversized position in the altcoin MANA is surely the path to unbridled financial success. What could possibly go wrong?

Lynn Forest's Altcoin Affinity

With her son away at college and her daughter Tori busy with her budding career in DeFi, Lynn Forest now feels the full void of the empty nest. Her practice in clinical psychology fills her days, but in the evenings and on weekends, she's begun to dabble in new hobbies. One of her patients recommended that she explore a project known as "Decentraland," a sprawling 3D virtual world, accessible via a Web browser, that was launched in 2020 by the nonprofit Decentraland Foundation.[8] Lynn, like the rest of the Forrest family, has an entrepreneurial bent and has become captivated by the idea of setting up a virtual counseling station for the frequenters of the Decentraland metaverse.

In order to buy the virtual land[9] and materials she will need to construct her offices, Lynn must acquire sufficient quantities of Decentraland's native cryptocurrency, MANA.

fig. 90

The emblem of Decentraland's MANA token.

Lynn soon discovers that MANA is listed in the top fifty of all cryptocurrencies by market cap.[10] She purchases some MANA to spend on her creation. With the limitless metaverse at her fingertips, she decides against building a dull conventional office building for her practice. Instead, she creates a tower that extends up into the clouds with a private open-air parapet on top, complete with an analyst's couch. It's a relaxing, private environment perfect for her virtual counseling sessions. She'll charge a modest fee in MANA for her services.

Sensing the potential in this innovative virtual space, Lynn begins to wonder if making a major investment in MANA may be a good idea. Her husband, Peter, is quick to point out the extreme riskiness of such a proposition. "As cool as it is, we're talking about a lesser-known altcoin that could very well be wiped out of existence by Mark Zuckerberg's Meta in a few years."

Lynn isn't ready to let the idea go. She believes there's something special and empowering about a metaverse governed by a distributed autonomous organization (DAO, see chapter 5), and one whose commerce runs on a decentralized currency built on the Ethereum blockchain.

After much back-and-forth, Peter agrees to take Lynn's idea to his advisor, Mariana, who recommends that the Forrests keep the majority of their crypto exposure limited to the blue chips, BTC and ETH, but suggests they accommodate Lynn's hunch by overweighting MANA in their collection of smaller altcoin positions.

Analyzing and Evaluating a Cryptocurrency Purchase

It's clear that some crypto investments pose greater risk than others.

If you have $1,000 that you could afford to lose, putting it into ether (ETH) or Bitcoin (BTC) likely carries less risk than investing the money in ZombieVerse (ZBV), a token that can be earned while playing a post-apocalyptic zombie game.

As an investor, you are not betting on the short-term price action of an asset and whether it will be more or less valuable tomorrow. Rather, you are staking your capital on the belief that the asset is *fundamentally* strong and on a long-term positive growth trajectory. Any asset, cryptos especially, can vacillate in price over the short term, but as an investor, you're not concerned about these short-term fluctuations. You're interested in making a long-term commitment based on research, analysis, and insight that shows a particular crypto as being imminently viable. If you see yourself as the kind of person willing to dig deeper and make such assessments, then you need to understand *fundamental analysis*.

The beginning of this understanding is seeded in the section at the tail end of chapter 1 that answers the question, "why does cryptocurrency have value?" To summarize, in the early phase of their analysis, investors may want to view and assess cryptocurrencies as they would any other currency, the key evaluation points being *fungibility*, *divisibility*, *limited supply*, *portability*, and *durability*. Even though the fundamental analysis of a crypto is broader in scope than this, assessing a crypto's strengths as a currency is still a good place to begin. If the asset is to be fundamentally viable for the long term, it must provide a viable means of exchange.

So, what else goes into a good fundamental analysis of a crypto or other digital asset? Consider the fundamental analysis of a stock, whereby an investor must assess the strengths and weaknesses of the underlying business that has issued the stock. A fundamental analysis will include a review of the business's earnings. You might ask, are they reliable and sufficient to cover expenses while generating strong profits? Is the company able to service its debts while also investing in its growth? Do the profits or growth potential justify the market's asking price for the stock? In short, to pass muster on a rigorous fundamental analysis, the business must show strong, reliable profits and/or have highly compelling growth prospects.

As you might imagine, the fundamental analysis of a cryptocurrency has some major differences from that of a stock—but at the same time, it's not entirely dissimilar. While digital assets like cryptos are not the same as equity shares in a business, and as such don't provide the investor with a claim on business profits, some do generate income or yield for their owners. Furthermore, cryptos and other digital assets are almost always fueled by a growth story of some sort, even if it's not a good one. Their proponents are aiming to win or engineer favorable coverage in the media and to articulate reasons why cryptocurrency X, Y, or Z is destined to be the next breakout sensation in the crypto-verse. In this latter, more abstract dimension, the fundamental analysis of a crypto mirrors that of a traditional growth stock.

The savvy crypto investor knows, however, that not all growth stories are created equal. Consider the following examples.

EXAMPLE 1: A cryptocurrency investor decides to make a long-term investment in a new cryptocurrency because it is being aggressively promoted on social media by a celebrity chef.

EXAMPLE 2: A cryptocurrency investor decides to make a long-term investment in a cryptocurrency that has been in circulation for two and a half years and has demonstrated the essential components of a functioning currency: fungibility, divisibility, portability, etc. In the last year, this crypto has attracted the attention and support of a number of qualified developers who are pursuing several different projects that integrate the crypto into various dapps and DeFi applications. The investor has looked closely at some of these applications and feels they will attract customers and capital investment, be competitive, and ultimately add value to the marketplace.

Clearly, the second example represents the stronger fundamental analysis, with an emphasis on the qualitative factors that are somewhat akin to those used in the fundamental analysis of a stock.

NOTE

I've outlined these key qualitative factors at the end of chapter 8 under the header "What Is Crypto Worth?"

While the qualitative side of the analysis sets the stage, there are some key quantitative factors that provide insight into the unfolding drama of a good crypto story. These metrics should also be considered when pursuing a fundamental analysis of a cryptocurrency. Pay specific attention to the following:

» **Market Capitalization**: If all positions in a given crypto were liquidated at today's price, what would the final price tag look like? *Market capitalization* refers to the total amount of money currently invested in a given crypto. As a prospective investor, you should know how many total dollars are in play. Be careful, though; in this highly volatile space, bigger isn't always better.

» **Transaction Values**: Get a sense for how the cryptocurrency circulates by looking up its average transaction value. (If you search for "average transaction value" and the crypto you're looking for, various charts should come up. Be sure to look at multiple sources and make sure the information looks consistent.) Are people using this currency primarily to buy and sell out of big investment positions, or, alternatively, is there evidence of an active ecosystem where smaller (micro) transactions are commonplace?

» **Active Addresses**: Continue to define the character of your crypto by looking up the number of active addresses—participants in transactions with that crypto. (As with transaction values, searching for a particular crypto and the term "active addresses" should give you some idea. The site ycharts.com often has information like this available.) Remember, you're investing as much in the community as you are in the crypto itself. How big is it currently? Is there reason to think it might be on track to grow bigger?

» **Hash Rates**: How quickly are transactions being processed? (Coindesk.com may have this information; otherwise, search the crypto name and "hash rate.") It's possible that a crypto may be precluded from certain functions—retail point-of-sale transactions, for instance—if the transactions take too long.

» **Supply Mechanisms**: How many units of the crypto are currently in circulation? (Ycharts.com is a possible source for this information.) Keep in mind that some currencies are deflationary (with a finite number of units). Others are inflationary (able to expand their unit quantity indefinitely). Some are systematically "burned off" at regular intervals (see chapter 6). Also remember that a crypto subject to indefinite inflation may not possess the *limited supply* attribute that defines a viable currency.

» **Liquidity and Volume**: How many units of currency can be readily bought or sold? If a crypto is widely traded across several highly liquid markets, then it's a sign that the crypto is well-known—held by many and sought by many. You can also expect a correlation between a given crypto's liquidity and volume and the prevalence of media coverage surrounding the crypto. (Livecoinwatch.com is a site that keeps track of a crypto's liquidity, among other figures.)

Before you invest, you should use these quantitative factors to augment your qualitative factors. They may confirm or invalidate critical aspects of the growth story that underpins your fundamental analysis.

Check out appendix III for a list of some of my favorite resources for crypto research.

For the most up-to-date crypto research links, access the Crypto Research and Analysis Link Library found with your digital assets at go.quickstartguides.com/crypto.

Fundamental Analysis vs. Technical Analysis: You will often find these terms coming up together. They are representative of two distinct methods of asset analysis. Fundamental analysis is what I have just described. Technical analysis refers to the study of price charts and the search for patterns that may predict the behavior of an asset's pricing in the marketplace. Technical analysis is more relevant to traders, while fundamental analysis is more relevant to investors.

Where to Start? Get the White Paper!

A great place to start your fundamental analysis into a particular crypto is with its white paper. Following Satoshi Nakamoto's lead, crypto developers have been writing white papers when they launch their currencies. These explain the structure, the capabilities, and the consensus mechanism used. With this information, you can begin to identify the crypto's value proposition. Find the white paper using your search engine. You will likely land on the crypto's official website, another good source of information about the asset and its developers' take on its long-term potential.

After hearing it from the home team, diversify your research sources. Identify the experts and publications that are the most helpful and trustworthy. In this vibrant and active space, you will have no shortage of options when it comes to information brokers.

Weathering Volatility

If you're going to invest in cryptocurrency, you must be prepared to ride out the highs and lows. Volatility is a persistent feature of this marketplace. It's not uncommon for a *hodler* to see their investment drop by 25% or more over the course of a day or two. By the same token (pardon the pun), a good week might see a portfolio increase by that same level, or more.

For some investors, unaccustomed to seeing these dramatic price swings in their investment portfolios, crypto's volatility can be off-putting. For those who are more risk averse, yet still crypto-curious, it may help to offer some perspective on why high levels of volatility exist in this space.

Consider the price dynamics of Bitcoin, which often correlates with and seemingly influences the price dynamics of other coins.[7] Bitcoin has a limited supply. New coins are issued on a regular basis as a reward for miners. In this way, the supply is regimented and fixed along a steady trajectory. Unlike with fiat currencies, there is no option available to dramatically increase supply in response to a spike in demand. To put it more plainly, demand rather than supply has an outsized influence on the price of the asset. And whereas supply is clear-cut, demand is an abstract and finicky thing subject to the whims of consumers, analysts, and the media buzz of the moment.

DETOUR

The demand-driven dynamics of the crypto marketplace also drive this market's unique impressionability—that is, its vulnerability to manipulation. Criminals like to exploit vulnerability using a tactic known as *spoofing*. They create fake buy or sell orders in the marketplace without the intent of ever having them filled. Instead, the aim is to influence market trends in one direction or another. In some cases, the criminals actually execute the trades, but with themselves or with one another. The objective is to lure investors into bad trades on inflated or deflated assets that the spoofers can then capitalize on. Spoofing is easy to detect after the fact, but difficult to detect when it's actually happening.

Using Stablecoins to Counter Volatility

Stablecoins, discussed in chapter 6, are the coins designed to stay on par with a given fiat currency. Whereas your typical crypto is not pegged to any underlying asset and is highly volatile, stablecoins—in most cases—have a reserve asset available, such as a fiat currency or gold, that is equal to their value. These reserve holdings allow the crypto to continually reflect the value of the reserve asset. This makes their value predictable and removes fluctuations, while letting owners enjoy the crypto benefits such as peer-to-peer payments. Investors, meanwhile, can use stablecoins to quickly trade in and out of other cryptos without incurring the costs and overhead of cashing out to fiat currencies.

For investors put off by volatility in the cryptocurrency market, stablecoins provide a mechanism to lock in profits and reduce the overall volatility of their portfolio.

EXAMPLE

A cryptocurrency investor's portfolio includes ten coins. Each coin has a target price point. Once the target price is reached, the investor could convert all or part of the position into stablecoins until such time as a new coin or a new target for the same coin is pursued. Similarly, the investor may convert to stablecoins as part of a stop-loss mechanism, following a predetermined maximum allowable loss in any given position.

NOTE

The same tools discussed in chapter 9 on trading can also be applied to investing. Though investment objectives are more long-term, limit, stop, and stop limit orders can be used by investors as a method of locking in profits and managing risks.

Crypto Income Strategies

There are several techniques crypto investors can use to generate income from holdings (and hodlings). These involve different degrees of risk and return, but they can help you get more value from your crypto positions.

Yield Farming

Yield farming, sometimes known as liquidity farming, is a cryptocurrency investment strategy that involves lending cryptocurrency out to others who are attempting to maintain a liquidity pool. These liquidity pools are maintained by blockchain-based companies that often prefer to crowdsource their capital, rather than to rely on traditional investors or bank loans. For them, crowdsourcing their liquidity is easier and quicker, and if you're willing to loan out some of your crypto to help them achieve their liquidity targets, they'll gladly compensate you.

The precursor to yield farming is the traditional savings account. In a savings account, you put your money in, and then the bank loans it out to someone else. The borrower pays interest, and the bank gives you some of it. The bank is essentially compensating you for helping it maintain liquidity. Yield farming is more layered than a typical deposit into a traditional savings account. It is a combination of putting money on deposit to earn interest *while also* holding a volatile asset in anticipation of an increase in price.

As an investment tactic, yield farming is highly compatible with the *hodler's* mindset. Hodlers want to accumulate and hold as much crypto as they can—volatility be damned—while they await greater and greater heights of growth. Well, why not put this crypto to use generating passive income in the meantime rather than letting it sit idle?

Interest rates paid via yield farming are higher than those paid via savings accounts, but so is the level of risk. Your funds on deposit are not federally insured and, if you want to make big returns, then you'll need to hold large amounts of whatever crypto you're lending. That crypto will be locked up and unsellable while it's in the pool, and its value may change rapidly. If it goes up, that's great, but if it goes down, then you have to watch and wait until your loan is repaid.

In addition, some liquidity pools may be fraudulent or unwittingly open to hackers, leading to deposit losses. It's also wise to be aware of the added costs in play here. Even though the pool needs the liquidity you're supplying, the pool operator will likely charge you a fee to participate. On balance, I consider yield farming to be a high-risk proposition, but high risk can often result in high returns.

Another distinction between yield farming and savings accounts is that yield farming occurs entirely on the blockchain. It is but one example of decentralized finance, or *DeFi*, in action, whereby standard financial services operate on the blockchain in place of intermediaries such as banks or insurance companies. The world of DeFi is discussed further in chapter 12.

For a "QuickStart" on yield farming, you can consider buying some ether. Then connect your wallet to a liquidity pool that allows people to borrow ether for speculation or other purposes. When they repay the loan, you will receive interest back on top of your principal, usually in the form of more ether.

Staking

In chapter 3, I covered proof-of-work, which is the consensus mechanism used to verify Bitcoin transactions. Because it involves considerable computing power and electricity, participating miners make big up-front investments in equipment that keep most crypto users out of the game.

Newer cryptos have other consensus mechanisms designed to work faster and with lower electricity requirements, making them open to broader and more eco-friendly participation. One of these mechanisms is proof-of-stake, currently used by several notable blockchains, such as Ethereum, Cardano, Solana, and Polkadot. To put it simply, staking earns income through a crypto owner (known as a validator in this context) offering up substantial crypto as collateral for a chance to validate blocks. These validators are selected at random (the more you stake, the greater your chances of being selected) and they receive a crypto reward.

For a "QuickStart" on generating income through staking, start by buying a crypto that uses proof-of-stake. Next, connect your wallet to the crypto's staking pool. You'll need to specify how much of your currency you are willing to commit. Once staked, your currency will be locked up for a while. The exact amount of time depends on the terms of the stake. When a transaction appears for verification, the blockchain protocol will select one of the validators to validate the block and receive a fee.

The primary risk of staking is similar to that of yield farming. Your currency is out of your control for a fixed period, and prices may move against you while you've put up a stake.

NOTE

In chapter 14 I further expand on the topic of crypto income when I introduce you to crypto savings accounts and the *crypto-accumulative model*.

Chapter Recap

» Crypto's wild price action and peculiar properties make it difficult to categorize as any particular type of asset.

» In addition to direct investment, several other investment vehicles can provide exposure to crypto, including mutual funds, ETFs, and trusts.

» The proper fundamental analysis of a cryptocurrency investment encompasses many qualitative and quantitative factors.

» Investors in crypto should anticipate volatility and can use available resources, such as stablecoins, to limit volatility as appropriate.

» Yield farming and staking are examples of income generation available through cryptocurrency investment.

| 11 |

Mining Crypto for Profit

Chapter Overview
» The rewards of mining
» Mining vs. minting
» Mining methods
» Getting started with crypto mining

Cryptocurrency mining has two main purposes: it's a way of validating transactions in a decentralized network and it's also a way that new cryptocurrency is generated and distributed. In chapters 2 and 3, I discussed the role that mining plays in the proof-of-work consensus algorithm. In this chapter I go deeper into the crypto-mining process and discuss how and why you might want to consider it as a pursuit—and the obstacles you might face if you do.

I also discuss minting, the preferred term for the creation of new cryptos through the proof-of-stake consensus mechanism utilized by Ethereum, Cardano, Solana, BNB, and others.

Earning Bitcoin Rewards

In chapter 3, I discussed that once a block is mined and a block hash created, the solved block is attached to the blockchain. The mining node that solved the block receives both the transaction fees and a fixed amount of the cryptocurrency as a reward.

Transaction fees. The transaction fees associated with a given block have been collected from spenders (those sending Bitcoin to new public key addresses). Spenders are required to pay fees as a method to abate network congestion, and in some cases they can elect to pay fees of varying percentage amounts in the interest of having their transactions prioritized over others waiting in the mempool (see chapter 2). Selected transactions are assigned to a block-in-progress or **candidate block**, which is a block that has not yet been verified and appended to the blockchain. Transactions entering the mempool with a higher fee in tow will be assigned to a candidate block faster than ones that enter with a lower fee.

The fixed payout amount is paid to each winning miner. This payout is halved about every four years. From approximately 2009 to 2013, it was 50 bitcoins per block, a figure that was subsequently halved to 25 and then 12.5. As of 2023, the reward is 6.25 bitcoins, as shown in figure 91:

fig. 91

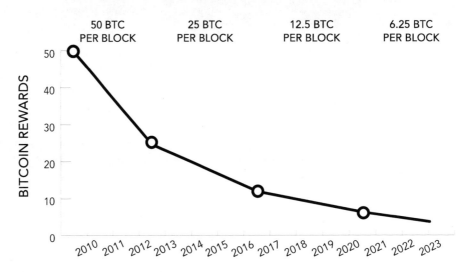

THE HALVING OVER TIME OF BITCOIN REWARDS (PER BLOCK)

While the amount of Bitcoin being awarded has gone down, the value of that Bitcoin has generally increased. In November 2021, when Bitcoin's price hit a high of $68,000, the **block reward** for a single solved block was the equivalent of $425,000. Now it's easier to understand why individuals and businesses are interested in becoming crypto miners—and are willing to invest the money needed to succeed.

Meanwhile, not only has a validated block been added to the blockchain, but 6.25 bitcoins have been "mined" and rewarded to the miner. This is how the proof-of-work consensus mechanism creates new Bitcoin.

While the mined Bitcoin is sent to the miner, it can't be spent until 99 more blocks are added to the chain. This is in order to assure that the new block is legitimized by the "longest chain" rule (see chapter 2).

Cryptos that use consensus mechanisms other than proof-of-work of course provide rewards in different ways. Let's delve a little deeper into *minting*, which, aside from mining, is the most prominent way to earn crypto rewards.

Mining vs. Minting

In chapter 5 I discussed a second validation method, proof-of-stake (PoS), that is becoming a popular alternative to proof-of-work. PoS is a process where a selected group of nodes serve to verify transactions and add blocks to the blockchain, with holders staking crypto for this privilege.

Staking requires depositing a substantial sum of cryptocurrency. Ethereum requires a minimum stake of 32 ether, for example, which is currently worth around $40,000. The proof-of-stake system chooses the validating node, favoring those nodes that have staked the highest amount of crypto. If the validating node is found to act maliciously, its stake will be forfeited. You keep your stake only if you act honestly.

I've added a useful website, stakingrewards.com, to the Crypto Research and Analysis Link Library included with your digital assets at go.quickstartguides.com/crypto. There you'll find a sorted list of PoS cryptos alongside their reward amounts.

fig. 92

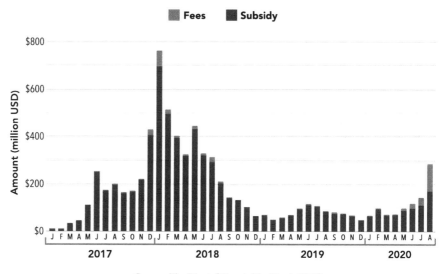

ETHEREUM'S MINER REVENUE BY MONTH

Source: The Block (Khatri, The Block 2020)

Just as with proof-of-work, proof-of-stake performs two essential functions: 1) building and adding new blocks to the blockchain, and 2) adding more cryptocurrency to the network in the form of rewards paid to successful validating nodes. Figure 92 shows the amounts (converted to millions of US dollars) that Ethereum stakers earned between January 2017 and September 2020.

Similar to how proof-of-work calls the reward component of this two-part process *mining*, proof-of-stake's process is called *minting*. Mining refers to the "work" part of proof-of-work, and proof-of-work nodes are known as miners. Minting is a term more commonly used to describe the creation of additional currency, and its proof-of-stake nodes are called *validators*. Proof-of-stake solves the energy-consumption problem associated with proof-of-work by eliminating the energy-intensive problem-solving work. There are several other consensus mechanisms available, and a list and description of each can be found in appendix II.

Other Ways to Earn Money from Mining

Anyone with a computer and internet access can become a crypto miner. However, as proof-of-work-based cryptocurrencies become more valuable, more miners are attracted. As this happens, requirements for computer processing go up. The average computer, such as a business laptop, currently has little chance to win mining races against heavier-duty, more powerful hardware.

In Bitcoin, a new block is solved approximately every ten minutes to prevent too many blocks being formed at once, which could create a blockchain traffic jam. To maintain this timing, the hashing problem's complexity, also known as the *cryptocurrency difficulty*, is increased. This keeps pace with the more powerful computers becoming miners. Miners are incentivized by their potential earnings, which in turn stimulate the race for more computing power.

This is all to say that for mining to make economic sense, there has to be the possibility of earning more than you spend on equipment, maintenance, and electricity. In the case of Bitcoin, it's been a long time since that's been possible for the home user with a laptop. But if you're interested in mining and don't have the resources for a mining rig (which I discuss in greater detail shortly), there are options.

Mining Pools

It's still possible even for those with home computers to mine many altcoins. If you're open to combining your computer power with a group of miners to form a mining pool, you can even tackle Bitcoin and other big-ticket cryptos. In pools, miners combine their computational resources with those of the other pool members, enhancing their joint processing power and helping achieve the desired output more quickly.

The first step is to identify the mining pool you want to join.

I've included some links to mining pools for you. Find them included with your Crypto Research and Analysis Link Library at www.clydebankmedia.com/crypto-assets.

Once you've joined a pool, you are rewarded in proportion to the share you have established. Your "share" is defined by the amount of work your computer contributes to the mining pool. The rewards for solving a block hash are distributed among all the pool's members, generally in proportion to each member's share.

Cloud Mining

Instead of buying or building an expensive computer to mine coins yourself, you can rent computing power from a dedicated crypto mining company. These companies have powerful computers, accessible via the cloud, whose speed at guessing a nonce could give you a fighting chance to earn some of the associated rewards.

fig. 93

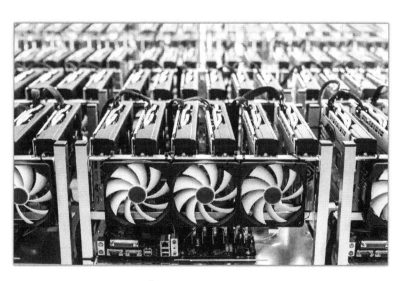

Source: www.exame.com
A professional mining rig.

I've included some links to cloud mining services in the book's Digital Asset Library. As with mining pools, the costs associated with cloud mining will reduce any profits you may see from the process.

Mining Rigs

If you're serious about competing with high-performance computing power, you will need what's called a mining rig, a computing system with high processing power (figure 93). Computers can increase their performance by adding more GPUs (graphical processing units). These are optimized for performing large parallel calculations quickly. A good mining rig can start off with at least six GPUs. A special housing unit is needed to keep a rig with this much processing power from overheating, and you will probably need additional external cooling as well. Count on the rig being noisy, and on its consuming 1,200 watts of electric power at a minimum, as opposed to the 500 watts a regular computer uses.

These rigs can be tethered together to produce even more powerful systems. Cryptocurrency mining has now become a big business, with systems taking up entire warehouse floors and large data centers.

Application-specific integrated circuit (ASIC) miners are a type of specialized high-performance computer. These systems have only one purpose: to mine crypto. They contain special computer chips optimized for proof-of-work.

How to Become a Crypto Miner

Are you still intrigued by the idea of becoming a crypto miner? Here's a brief step-by-step overview of the process:

1. **Choose which crypto to mine**. Focus on those that deliver on your crypto income goals. Of course, Bitcoin is the most lucrative today but also the most competitive. You'll find a good list at coinmarketcap.com.

2. **Identify the right hardware.** You'll find more details on this in the next section.

3. **Build the hardware.** For more detail on this, see "Building Your Own Mining Rig."

4. **Download and configure the crypto software**. This software will be unique to the crypto you wish to mine.

5. **Choose a wallet**. Choose a crypto wallet capable of receiving any fees or rewards you earn while crypto mining. See chapter 8 for more on wallets.

6. **Create keys**. See chapter 2 for more on keys. Your key pair enables you to participate in a blockchain network and to send and receive crypto.

7. **Run and monitor the system**. Monitor your system from time to time to ensure that it is actively mining.

Building Your Own Mining Rig

Guru99 and PC Guide are two mining rig websites where you can go comparison shopping and buy the necessary equipment to build a mining rig. The initial investment will of course depend on the price of the various components you use.

Here's one example for illustrative purposes:

- » Motherboard (main circuit board): $450
- » CPU (central processing unit): $125
- » RAM (active memory): $65
- » Storage (extra space for data retention and management): $95
- » PSU (power supply unit): $100
- » PCI-e-Riser (external frame): $60
- » NVIDIA graphics card (for additional processing power): $550
- » AMD graphics card (for additional processing power): $1,100

The total here is $2,545. But depending on the price of the individual components and your preferences, the cost could be anywhere from $500 to $10,000, which in turn would affect how long you might need to use it break even and then turn a profit on your mining. You can also buy and install a pre-built mining rig. The costs for these vary considerably.

A mining rig also takes up a bit more space than a typical desktop computer. See figure 94 for an example of what a completed DIY mining rig may look like.

Graphical Processing Units (GPUs)

Fans

fig. 94

Motherboard

Source: https://tekhouse.co.uk/product/6-gpu-mining-rig

Other Ways of Earning Crypto: Faucets and Airdrops

Mining and minting are by far the most potentially lucrative ways of earning crypto—but not the only ways. Smaller rewards are sometimes offered through initiatives often used to market new cryptocurrencies. The two most prominent are crypto *faucets* and *airdrops*.

Faucets

Bitcoin faucets are websites that were introduced in 2010 as a way of spreading awareness of the new cryptocurrency. Bitcoin was given to community members who did such simple tasks as filling out forms as an incentive for people to adopt Bitcoin and get involved.

Crypto faucet sites are still easy to find, although the amount of crypto to be earned is limited. They are called "faucets" because rewards come out in drips rather than gushes. The rewards are generally paid out of income from advertisements on the sites. One example of a crypto faucet is Bitcoinker, which offers up to 100,000 satoshis (0.001 bitcoins; currently about $20) for solving simple CAPTCHAs. Another faucet is Cointiply, which gives rewards of an average of 200 satoshis per activity—things such as clicking ads, completing surveys, and looking at videos.

Airdrops

Blockchain developers, especially of new crypto initiatives, will often send out newly minted, free coins or tokens to different crypto wallet addresses for promotional purposes. These airdrops, as they are known, are meant to inspire recipients to become part of the project. Airdrops involve greater amounts of crypto than faucets, although at an early stage of development, currencies generally have limited value. The hope is that their value will increase in time.

Interested in being part of an airdrop? Lists of current and upcoming offers can be easily found on the Web. One good resource is airdrops.io Once you choose an airdrop, you'll be asked to register and connect your crypto wallet to receive funds.

The Energy Implications of Proof-of-Work

Miners and validators are the guardians of many crypto networks, ensuring consensus and generating new crypto. Most are economically motivated. But as you've seen, mining rigs can be expensive and may not be an option for many would-be miners. But with rigs, cloud mining, and mining pools as viable options, crypto mining isn't going away—and neither, for the moment, are debates about its environmental impact. These debates are colored by negative attitudes, even cynicism, toward crypto, a system many believe to require unsustainable levels of energy growth over the long term.

It's true that proof-of-work requires a substantial use of energy, much of which is still derived from fossil fuels. The fact that proof-of-work cryptos rely heavily on old-fashioned energy consumption has led to some controversy and debate. The Tezos Agora wiki states, "Reasonable estimates from the University of Cambridge place Bitcoin's current annual energy consumption at 130TWh, a continuous draw of 15 gigawatts of electricity. If Bitcoin were a country, its annual energy consumption would place it between the mid-sized countries of Ukraine and Argentina."[1]

Others maintain the problem is not as dire as it sounds. Defenders of proof-of-work mining point out that many other enterprises, such as Netflix, Google, Amazon, and Facebook, expend just as much energy. They also maintain that Bitcoin mining uses less than 0.1% of global energy, which, annually speaking, would put it roughly on par with Christmas tree lights.[2]

No doubt, the debate about proof-of-work energy use is important, and it will continue. This will be a space to watch in the months and years ahead. In the short term Ethereum will be one to monitor for energy results, as it moved from proof-of-work to proof-of-stake in September 2022, in large part because of power considerations.

The debate over proof-of-work can still affect the overall credibility of cryptocurrency; Bitcoin is so well-known that it is easy for casual observers to equate that particular crypto's shortcomings with the entire crypto ecosystem.

Chapter Recap

» Mining is used in proof-of-work calculations to both add new blocks to a blockchain and create new crypto.

» New crypto is a reward for the winners of proof-of-work competitions. The amount of Bitcoin awarded in this way is halved approximately every four years.

» Proof-of-stake, a second validation method, is becoming a popular alternative to proof-of-work. It requires "staking" a sum of crypto, and the process is referred to as "minting" rather than "mining."

» Mining with your own hardware can be a rewarding activity, but the computing power it requires can be prohibitively costly. Some alternative methods include mining pools (combining your computing power with that of others) and cloud mining (renting computing power from others).

» There is a debate over whether the energy required to mine crypto is excessive or not that different from any number of other activities.

| 12 |

DeFi (Decentralized Finance)

Chapter Overview
- » Fintech and DeFi explained
- » How DeFi works
- » Exploring DeFi services
- » Understanding DeFi opportunities and risks

DeFi is a portmanteau constructed from the first syllables of "decentralized" and "finance." The meaning of finance is relatively well understood, and decentralization is a fundamental feature of both blockchain and cryptocurrency. But what does their combination signify? Decentralization replaces the typical centralized model of finance with a peer-to-peer architecture in which the system functions without the direction of a central authority. This is a paradigm shift for the traditional financial industry, whose entire business model is based on intermediaries and centralized control.

In this chapter, I discuss the specifics of DeFi: how it differs from centralized finance, how it works, and how it is already beginning to make an impact in areas as diverse as banking, real estate, and insurance. While there are any number of risks currently associated with DeFi, it remains arguably one of the most promising and interesting applications of blockchain and crypto technology. That's why Tori Forrest is determined to leave her current programming job behind and become an entrepreneur in the DeFi space. Expanding on the possibilities, she has lit a fire under her brother Alan and is even wearing down the resistance of her skeptical parents.

Starting with Fintech

DeFi is a type of fintech, another portmanteau made up of the first syllables of "finance" and "technology." The use of technology in finance is nothing new. It goes back to the first handwritten ledgers and has continued on to the abacus, mechanical and then electronic calculators, mainframe computers, ATMs, and the current era of laptops, tablets, and smartphones.

Today, fintech encompasses companies that deliver financial services through software and other technologies, especially (though not limited to) smartphones, AI, cloud computing, and big data. Historically, the bigger the conventional financial institution, the more dominant and powerful it generally is. But in fintech, small and agile can also win the race. It can become a question of who can respond fastest to quickly changing consumer needs. Even better, reduced size also often means reduced costs, which can be passed on to the consumer as lower fees.

While fintech has often been used to describe financial institutions' back-end systems, this newfound digital agility now applies to any number of consumer-focused applications, enabling people to manage their finances easily and conveniently. For instance, apps like Venmo now make it simple to split the check among several people at the end of a restaurant meal. Other apps, such as Robinhood, have made it a breeze to trade stocks.

DeFi has the potential to take this financial industry transformation further. With the addition of crypto and blockchain technologies, the focus of control shifts closer to the user, rather than the institution.

What Is DeFi?

> *DeFi is an open and global financial system built for the internet age—an alternative to a system that's opaque, tightly controlled, and held together by decades-old infrastructure and processes.*
>
> – ETHEREUM WEBSITE

All DeFi is fintech, but not all fintech is DeFi. DeFi refers specifically to *fintech that operates with and on blockchains.* Cryptocurrency may or may not be involved, but often is.

DeFi transactions, including payments and other records, are stored on a blockchain constructed according to smart-contract-based rules. Centralized systems, by contrast, grant users less control over their finances and often require human gatekeepers, who can slow transaction times.

Blockchains running DeFi applications are increasingly enabling ever more sophisticated financial transactions, some of which have only been made possible by this leading-edge technology. For example, decentralized exchanges (DEXs) are an innovative, entirely peer-to-peer method of investing in crypto. I explore DeFi applications in greater depth below.

Today, the primary blockchain on which DeFi applications are built is Ethereum, which was specifically built to extend blockchain use cases beyond buying, selling, and holding cryptocurrency, using its smart contracts. Other blockchains, such as Tezos, also have smart-contract capability, and even Bitcoin has add-on software for this purpose.

DeFi applications benefit from blockchain's security features. For example, blockchains make it remarkably difficult to alter records of transactions once they are recorded. This fraud-reducing feature is particularly important when dealing with financial matters.

Just as DeFi is an important subset of fintech, DeFi applications can also be decentralized autonomous organizations, or DAOs, which I discuss in chapter 5. In a DAO, trust is encoded in the blockchain software and does not need to be extended to human participants in the system.

The advantages of DeFi DAOs include the following:

» A democratic design that means everyone in such an organization has an equal opportunity to participate

» No centralized management system: you report to the system, not individual administrators or executives

» Transparency in transactions, which may well contribute to renewed trust in the banking system, which may well contribute to renewed trust in a banking system with a lowered consumer reputation

» The potential for opening new markets among currently underserved populations

DeFi is growing quickly because of a variety of advantages beyond increased security. For example, DeFi transactions eliminate many of the common delays experienced in traditional financial transactions. These solutions are also permissionless, meaning that third parties cannot exert authority over them. Also, anyone with an internet connection and a crypto wallet can access DeFi blockchains, making the solutions more inclusive.

DeFi vs. CeFi

Indeed, DeFi is defined largely in contrast with traditional finance—which DeFi advocates call centralized finance or CeFi. One of DeFi's principal advantages over traditional financial services is cutting out the middleman. This places each individual participant—in other words, you—in direct charge of their finances.

Figure 95, which contrasts the two approaches, will probably look familiar:

CeFi
CENTRALIZED FINANCE

DeFi
DECENTRALIZED FINANCE

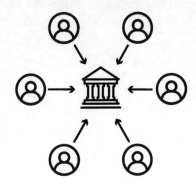

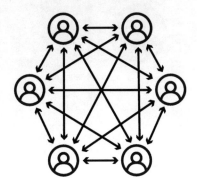

fig. 95

Accordingly, the differences between CeFi and DeFi closely parallel those between fiat currency and cryptocurrency, as the following table shows:

fig. 96

CeFi	DeFi
Fund transfers often take days.	Fund transfers usually take minutes.
Transactions are prone to human error.	Transactions are largely free from human error.
Banks and markets close at night and on weekends.	DeFi blockchains are open 24/7.
User identity is revealed in most transactions.	Transactions are pseudonymous, increasing security.
Institutions manage (or mismanage) user money.	Users retain control over funds.
Users must apply for access to services.	Access is available to anyone with an internet connection.
Institutions can turn down applicants for any reason.	There is no central authority to deny services or block usage.

On a macro level, it is estimated that there are a billion people on the planet who don't have access to banks. DeFi advocates argue that more of these people will now be able to access banking and related financial services, because traditional financial institution requirements—such as a permanent address—may be unnecessary.

How Does DeFi Work?

The shortest answer to the question of what enables DeFi to work is smart contracts. That's why Ethereum, which was originally created to add smart-contract capability to blockchain technology, is the most prominent DeFi network.

A smart contract is self-executing code that follows a set of instructions, which are then verified and carried out on the blockchain. These contracts are trustless, autonomous, decentralized, and transparent. Once they're executed, they are irreversible.

One way of looking at smart contracts is as a replacement for the procedures of traditional financial institutions in DeFi transactions. Smart contracts manage transactions based on the unalterable conditions programmed into them. In every case, a smart contract will run as it has been programmed to run.

Beyond the ability to use smart contracts, DeFi usually requires a software stack with four layers:

1. **Settlement layer**: the blockchain in use and its accompanying cryptocurrency, which is used in DeFi transactions.

2. **Protocol layer**: a layer of rules, written in code, defining what a DeFi protocol can do.

3. **Application layer**: where the DeFi applications live, and where users interact with them.

4. **Aggregation layer**: where outside applications, like noncustodial wallets or fund deposits, connect to the DeFi software.

Though Ethereum is the most popular blockchain for DeFi, this does not mean that ether is DeFi's default currency. Ethereum supports token creation that can be used for a multitude of purposes, including DeFi. There are some issues with Ethereum's speed and scalability, though the recent Ethereum 2.0 upgrade, moving from proof-of-work to proof-of-stake, is meant to address and improve upon those limitations. And there are alternatives to Ethereum: the Compound lending platform uses its native COMP tokens, while Solana, the self-proclaimed "world's fastest blockchain," has consciously set itself up as an alternative to Ethereum in the DeFi space.

Not to be left out of the DeFi action, Bitcoin loyalists can participate in Ethereum-based smart contracts through *wrapped* Bitcoin (WBTC), a token specifically created for this purpose. Also, so-called Bitcoin *sidechains* have been created to support smart contract capability.

A sidechain is another blockchain, connected to a main blockchain through a two-way bridge, enabling assets native to a particular chain to be transferred between multiple blockchains. RSK is a prominent Bitcoin sidechain specifically built to give Bitcoin Ethereum-compatible smart-contract capacity.

To summarize, any DeFi initiative has five essential components:

1. A blockchain
2. Smart contracts (also known as protocols)
3. Assets in the form of cryptocurrency
4. Tokens
5. One or more financial services

So far, I've discussed the first three components. Next, I examine the fourth and fifth; beginning with the role of DeFi tokens and then moving to the types of DeFi services being implemented today.

DeFi Tokens

Much of DeFi runs on tokens. DeFi tokens are blockchain-native assets that operate using smart contracts, enabling, among other things, users to access DeFi services and applications. They are used in DeFi applications built on top of an existing blockchain.

Though their current market cap is relatively small compared to the overall cryptocurrency market, DeFi tokens are also growing fast, in part because of their many uses: savings, loans, insurance, gaming, and network staking in some proof-of-stake validations, as discussed in chapter 11. In other words, they facilitate access to decentralized versions of many of the same services presented by traditional financial service providers.

There are several types of DeFi tokens:

» **Fee tokens** enable the collection of fees generated in a DeFi application.

» **Governance tokens** represent voting power within DeFi protocols and enable holders to influence a DeFi application's operations and development. They thereby enable their holders to participate actively in the development of the DeFi sector as a whole.

» **Collateral tokens** function the way the collateral functions in conventional loans: they are tokens with an assigned value that in turn mitigates risk for lenders.

» **Asset tokens** can represent physical assets such as real estate, vehicles, etc., in DeFi-based transactions.

DeFi Services

DeFi services fall into a number of subcategories that are gaining traction in the marketplace—illustrated in figure 97 and explained in greater detail in this section.

fig. 97

Banking: Lending, Borrowing, and More

DeFi is making some of its greatest inroads into services formerly rendered by traditional, centralized banks, most prominently lending and borrowing.

DeFi companies have made borrowing money simpler than with conventional banks and credit unions. Often, consumers only need to go online to apply, and processes are automated; software, not bank officers, determines a borrower's creditworthiness, primarily using on-chain data. This data is based on the borrower's ability to provide collateral, most commonly their existing crypto, and their crypto use history. With data on the blockchain indicating whether the borrower has the necessary collateral or not, intermediaries like centralized credit bureaus are no longer needed. (If the borrower is using ether as collateral, they're not even required to reveal their identity or credit score) The system is not perfect; someone with little or no on-chain data might still need to fall back on more traditional information to be approved for credit, which would undermine the potential for anonymity—as could the data itself, even if it's on-chain. This is a space to watch for emerging innovation, as alternatives to traditional creditworthiness processes would be a game-changer for so many potential borrowers.

One DeFi lending platform that connects crypto lenders and borrowers is Compound, one of the first providers in this space, which determines interest rates algorithmically. The greater the demand for a certain cryptocurrency, the higher the interest. Another DeFi lending platform is Liquity, which provides interest-free loans using ether. Revenue is generated through a one-time 0.5% fee.

Insurtech

Like banking, insurance is one of the oldest, most highly regulated, and most conservative industries. It's also quite inefficient, as almost anyone who has filed a claim will attest. There is ample opportunity for both streamlining and cost-cutting. This is what DeFi insurance solutions, collectively known as *decentralized insurance*, are setting out to do. Just as DeFi is the form of fintech that operates on blockchains, decentralized insurance is a blockchain-based subset of what's known as *insurtech*.

As with banking, there's no question that further automating processes can boost efficiency. Blockchain can help automate outdated processes, giving the potential to save enormous quantities of paperwork and reduce human error in the process.

Insurtech is opening up new possibilities. Instead of getting insurance from a single company, it's now possible to purchase coverage from a decentralized pool of insurance providers. This increases the options for insurers as well as the insured: any company or individual can, in effect, become an insurance provider by providing capital for that decentralized pool, and customers no longer have to rely on traditional insurance companies to agree to the right policy. Insurance policies can be written as smart contracts where the insured agrees to pay the insurer in return for the insurer's contractual promise, for example, to help cover the insured's future medical costs.

Smart-contract logic can process claims far more efficiently and perhaps even more fairly, given that subjective judgment calls are removed from the process. The immutable data about the insured stored in the blockchain makes it possible to evaluate any number of types of claims immediately, in real time, rather than based on the availability and schedule of a human insurance adjuster.

With this ability to streamline claims processing while boosting cybersecurity protocols, blockchain could potentially optimize the efficiency, safety, and transparency of the insurance industry. This in turn could make it easier for insurers to serve currently underserved populations.

Mark Wales, CEO of Galileo Platforms, a blockchain-based insurance company, notes that the microinsurance products offered by his firm in Thailand and elsewhere can be used to "cover someone who rides on the back of a different motorbike to get to and from work each day." He goes on to say, "It can offer you insurance before boarding a plane at the airport. The possibilities are limitless."[1]

DeFi Insurance

Throughout this book, I emphasize both the opportunities and risks associated with crypto. It's not surprising, then, that a specific policy type, known as *DeFi insurance*, has emerged to help mitigate some of the risks of crypto and DeFi. DeFi insurance, provided by organizations such as InsurAce and Blockdaemon, is a means of insuring against losses caused by DeFi industry events. Perhaps you have invested capital in a

DeFi platform, while remaining aware that this capital might be lost if the platform is hacked. You could insure yourself against this risk. Other examples include policies insuring against exchange hacks, attacks on DeFi protocols, smart contract failures, or stablecoin price crashes. In all of these cases, the consumers are insuring themselves against specific risks that might occur in a DeFi network, such as losses due to hacking or a smart contract failure. This form of insurance is becoming increasingly prominent as institutional capital continues to pour into the DeFi space.

Decentralized Exchanges (DEXs)

DeFi is also impacting cryptocurrencies themselves through decentralized exchanges. In chapter 8, I discussed centralized crypto exchanges, also known as CEXs. A CEX handles transactions by means of an "order book" that establishes a crypto's price based on current buy and sell orders, much as traditional stock exchanges do.

By contrast, a decentralized exchange, or DEX, connects crypto buyers, sellers, and traders directly, in a peer-to-peer model. As there is no central authority, like there is in a CEX, smart contracts govern the ensuing transactions. While transactions on a centralized exchange are recorded on that exchange's internal database, DEX transactions are settled directly on the blockchain. You can think of a DEX as a DeFi network that allows for the buying, selling, and trading of cryptocurrency.

After starting small in 2019, DEXs exploded in popularity, accounting for over 80% of crypto trading in June 2021. A balancing correction occurred the following year, with DEXs accounting for 55% and CEXs for 45% of trading volume.[2]

DeFi Portfolio and Asset Management

While it's still early in its maturity, DeFi is beginning to make inroads into brokerage functions such as the buying, selling, and management of crypto-based and other digital assets. DeFi's portfolio management advantages are familiar:

» **Speed**: completing transactions takes seconds or minutes, rather than hours or days.

» **Transparency**: the real-time status of digital transactions on public blockchains can be examined in depth and detail.

» **Control**: brokerages are disintermediated, putting investors directly in charge of their assets while also bypassing transaction and related fees.

Some DeFi tools parallel those in traditional finance. For example, traditional exchange-traded funds (ETFs) track the prices of several assets together. DeFi indexes do the same, except that the assets invested in such funds are a variety of crypto tokens. The index provider does the research and analysis needed to select the tokens the fund manages, meaning the individual investor is freed from doing the legwork. Again, the fees for such AI- and smart-contract-based services can be reduced or eliminated altogether.

There's a bigger story emerging here, and at its core is the disruption to the current system of *active management* in portfolios and funds. An actively managed fund is a type of investment that is essentially the opposite of an indexed fund. Whereas index funds are a preset, static group of investment positions (for example, all the stocks listed in the S&P 500), actively managed funds are managed by analysts—generally of the human variety. The conventional wisdom, backed by a multitude of studies, has long held that active portfolio management doesn't help and may actually hinder your investment returns. The idea is that because so few professional money managers beat the market, it's unlikely that the gains from your holdings in an actively managed fund will surpass those of simple index funds, especially after you deduct the overhead costs incurred by those managers. In the same vein, common investing wisdom urges investors to refrain from constant over-active management of their own portfolios. Instead, they are urged to rebalance their portfolios (chapter 10) two to four times a year and let the market do the rest of the work. The assets will then, in theory, appreciate, accumulating interest and dividends with little overhead by way of trading fees and advisor fees.

This passive approach to portfolio management is particularly prevalent among middle-class investors whose overall financial needs aren't overly complex. Active management, by contrast, is considered more the area of hotshot fund managers and the wealthy individuals who provide them with capital—those with a little more money to gamble on the market. Meanwhile, *robo-advisors*—centrally controlled algorithms capable of analyzing and "advising you" on the contents of your portfolio—offer a less costly alternative to human advisors, but, as noted, these centralized protocols operate behind a corporate black box, giving advisees very limited control or insight into the process.

So, what does this have to do with DeFi? With DeFi, you can now access countless active management protocols on-chain and apply them to your own crypto assets. DeFi protocols are less expensive than robo-advisors, and wholly transparent. Think of it as having access to the granular investing wisdom of famous fund managers like Peter Lynch or Michael Burry, but all open source and on the blockchain. Users can institute or modify their favorite DeFi protocols—basically mimicking whatever crypto investing experts they care to emulate—with fast and automated implementation. Compare this to the cumbersome and frustrating process of trying to copy the stock trading of your favorite hedge fund manager; by the time you get the information about their savvy trade, the opportunity has often already passed.

The ability to efficiently copy the experts is but one of the exciting developments that DeFi brings to portfolio and asset management. Another relates to the data used to develop active management strategies. Alexander Fleiss, CEO of Rebellion Research, argues that data quality is essential to sound investment strategy and that blockchain opens the door to better data quality.

Decent input can be turned into a good product with an inferior algorithm, but bad data cannot be made into a worthwhile product, no matter how powerful or awesome the machine learning or math behind your algorithm… [Open blockchains in lieu of centralized databases mean that] funds will be able to see in more real-time fashion the movements of a number of industries. Funds pay to have forward knowledge and blockchain is ideal for showing inflection points in consumer or society behavior as soon as possible.[3]

– CHAINALYSIS TEAM

Derivatives Markets

A derivative, in traditional finance, *derives* its value from an underlying asset (see chapter 9 for a more detailed explanation). Crypto and DeFi derivatives are contracts whose value is *derived* from the value of the underlying currency. They are agreements with specific parameters, obliging the sale or purchase of a given asset, at a given price, at a given point in time. Owners of derivatives may profit from the price movement of a given asset without owning the asset. In this way, certain risks are limited and various opportunities become available.

For instance, if you purchased a smart contract for a Bitcoin call option (a type of derivative), then you might find your position more agile than had you purchased actual Bitcoin. The transaction times for Bitcoin at the time of writing are around ten minutes. So if you were looking to capitalize on what you see as a burst of fast-moving upward price action within an otherwise volatile fifteen-minute pattern, then you may prefer to operate at a faster pace, and without using an exchange that could subject you to fees. By using a derivative, you could go long on BTC by simply executing a smart contract on the Ethereum network, guaranteeing you the right to purchase BTC at a price that will be much lower than where you think the price is headed. There is no cumbersome transfer of crypto in this scenario unless you decide to execute the option and purchase the BTC per your right under the contract. This rarely happens; most options and futures contracts aren't executed but are *offset* by symmetrical contracts. In other words, if the price of BTC moved in your favor, then you'd end up selling the option itself (via a separate, offsetting contract), for a price in excess of what you paid to own the contract.

Given their importance in centralized finance, it isn't surprising that DeFi derivative markets have begun to spring up. Crypto derivatives, not subject to the same regulations as those in CeFi markets, can easily be created. Moreover, the liquidity of DeFi derivative markets can be automated (via smart contract) to create perpetual supplies of product (derivatives) to allow traders and investors ready access to long and short derivative-based positions. By removing the human element from the market-making process, some DeFi derivative firms claim they can provide customers with more precise control over their trades (entry and exit prices) than the CeFi markets ever could.[4]

On the downside, the lack of regulation in this space carries plenty of risk; even traditional derivatives are already controversial for their potential to destabilize markets with waves of big losses and defaults. This is why investment guru Warren Buffett has called them "financial weapons of mass destruction."[5] Tori Forrest's father, Peter might tend to agree with the wizard of Des Moines. After all, the collapse of subprime mortgage derivatives was perhaps the principal cause of the Great Recession of 2008–2009.

Nevertheless, derivatives are an important part of our financial system, and decentralized derivatives will therefore almost certainly play a role in establishing the cryptocurrency industry as a recognized mainstream asset class.

The Future of DeFi

At this time, DeFi is arguably one of the most promising and dynamic areas of the blockchain and crypto ecosystem, with the potential to upset and reshape banking and other financial services. It's a bit of a David-and-Goliath situation, with DeFi's David wielding the weapons of cryptocurrency and blockchain against the gigantic financial industry.

These weapons seem perfectly suited to attack several of the financial industry's weaknesses. Fraud, for example, is a major challenge facing financial services, especially in the digital age. Blockchain's unalterable, easily verifiable records, which enable crypto-based systems to bypass the need to trust third parties, go a long way toward solving this problem, because it's so difficult to manipulate or tamper with them. Contributors can store and share digital information in a security-rich environment.

With blockchain, information can be shared in real time, and the ledger can only be updated when all parties agree. In addition, blockchain can reduce the processing time and costs of transactions, and decrease the opportunities to commit fraud. That said, in some instances DeFi can increase transaction costs, so keep a close eye on the details of any service you might use.

Since so much of the blockchain ecosystem is open source, many DeFi functions are *composable*, which means that they can be reused as the building blocks for new apps and potentially innovative, previously unavailable financial instruments and services. As with everything crypto, there is ample creativity in the DeFi community, which will likely lead to further innovations in the future.

Despite the risks involved, DeFi has the potential for remarkable innovation and to provide answers to real, global problems involving banking and investing access, such as the expansion and democratization of access to financial services. Regulation will likely be required to bring order to the space, including a process for taxation and protections for consumers.

Given the flexibility of blockchain and crypto, expect the DeFi ecosystem of financial services to expand, with new innovations yet to be seen. Some major players, like Goldman Sachs, have already joined in. This may indicate that in the next few years, DeFi could be poised to become an increasingly significant factor in the global economy.

Chapter Recap

» Fintech refers to firms that use technology to provide financial services more easily and conveniently than conventional methods do.

» DeFi is a type of fintech whose transactions are recorded on a blockchain and managed using smart contracts.

» In contrast to centralized finance, DeFi eliminates intermediaries and enables users to directly control their assets.

» Applications of DeFi include banking, insurance, real estate, decentralized exchanges (DEXs), asset management, and derivatives.

» While DeFi demonstrates promise in a wide range of financial services, caution is warranted as the space matures.

| 13 |

Different Countries, Different Approaches

Chapter Overview

- » Crypto regulation and its possible impact
- » Understanding US crypto regulations
- » Exploring regulatory approaches in other countries
- » The future of crypto regulation and the Fourth Industrial Revolution

The World Wide Web, as its name implies, is borderless, and so is crypto. The internet and cryptocurrency's common ethos is wide-open communication and exchange, unimpeded by national boundaries. On the ground, however, as crypto has become a more significant player in the financial system, nations have begun to consider issues of sovereignty and regulation. While many countries have so far remained open to crypto, others have restricted its use or outright banned it. The same reason that some have advocated for crypto and blockchain technology—that it would serve to revolutionize the international financial system—has alarmed plenty of world leaders.

For example, Hillary Clinton, calling attention to the risks of crypto and the need for regulation, said at a Bloomberg conference in Singapore in 2021, "One more area that I hope nation states start paying greater attention to is the rise of cryptocurrency because [it] has the potential for undermining currencies, for undermining the role of the dollar as the reserve currency, for destabilizing nations, perhaps starting with small ones but going much larger."[1] Strong words, and governments have begun to take claims like these seriously. Despite crypto's decentralization, regulation appears inevitable and could profoundly alter its development and adoption worldwide. In this chapter, I examine where regulations stand at the moment, in the US and around the world, and where these regulations might be heading next.

The Regulatory Environment

In general, financial regulations supervise the world of finance, setting up restrictions, requirements, and guidelines for its institutions, with the goal of keeping financial systems stable and establishing and maintaining their integrity. For traditional financial institutions across the world, these rules have been evolving for decades. The cryptocurrency market, as a comparably new area of finance, does not have this larger history, and given its rapid growth and maturity, now faces the prospect of regulation.

As the crypto market has grown, governments and international organizations, such as the International Monetary Fund (IMF), have taken notice of its potential to *disrupt* the established economic systems—in both the forward-looking, tech-world sense of the word and the more troublesome sense of creating problems, such as those associated with the collapse of the crypto exchange FTX in November 2022. In other words, the cryptocurrency industry is now extensive enough that financial analysts worry that it may have adverse macroeconomic consequences if not properly regulated, even if it also has potentially positive effects. The increased risk has led to a call for more regulation. The World Economic Forum, for instance, has said regarding cryptocurrency regulation that—as with other financial regulations—the aim is to "support financial stability, transparency, protection for consumers and investors, and a level playing field for different market participants."[2]

So far, most regulatory activity in this space, which I discuss later in this chapter, has been on a national level. But cryptocurrency use is not restricted, or meant to be restricted, to national borders, making international regulatory cooperation something of an ideal—and one whose realization still seems far off. But regulatory agencies have reason to pursue it: as of this writing, one in five Americans claims to have already been involved in cryptocurrency trading on some level. In Singapore, those numbers are even higher. And as the market grows, everyone will be eager to avoid a repeat of the 2008 financial meltdown. In general, the larger the market, the more likely it is to be regulated; this is based on the assumption that as the market grows, it is more likely to affect the common good.

On the other hand, crypto advocates point to the possibility that crypto itself is attempting to avoid a 2008-style meltdown by its very nature. It constitutes an alternate financial structure not dominated by major financial institutions that more urgently need to be checked by regulations. There is a definite tension between crypto's underlying independent ethos and the nature of regulation. Will this be a creative tension or a destructive one? It may be too early even to speculate, but, whatever the case, governments have begun to assert their authority.

Regulating Cryptocurrency in the US

The history of cryptocurrency regulation in the United States reflects that of most Western nations. Early on, the US government's perspective was that Bitcoin and other cryptos were a fascinating innovation but required little attention from federal agencies. This frictionless system may have exhilarated early adopters, but the more skeptical felt crypto was doomed to failure.

However, to many people's surprise, crypto not only didn't go away but continued to grow in both value and popularity. Still, US regulatory agencies such as the SEC (Securities and Exchange Commission), whose function is to supervise markets and protect investors, held on to a wait-and-see attitude for some time. Eventually the crypto market became too prominent to ignore: problems with initial coin offerings (ICOs) prompted their regulation in 2017. Additional regulation seems inevitable, for instance, in the wake of the collapse of Sam Bankman-Fried's FTX in November 2022. The question, then, becomes which regulations will be put in place and what areas they'll address.

TIMELINE OF US CRYPTO REGULATIONS

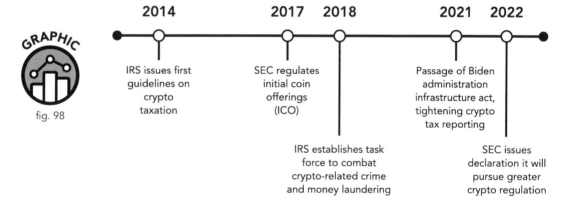

fig. 98

2014 — IRS issues first guidelines on crypto taxation

2017 — SEC regulates initial coin offerings (ICO)

2018 — IRS establishes task force to combat crypto-related crime and money laundering

2021 — Passage of Biden administration infrastructure act, tightening crypto tax reporting

2022 — SEC issues declaration it will pursue greater crypto regulation

Figure 98 has a timeline of some major US crypto-specific regulation milestones so far, including in taxation, which I cover in the next section.

Government concern actually first centered on fraud and the use of cryptocurrencies for illegal activities on the dark web. But existing laws cover such cases; until Congress passes additional laws directly related to crypto, the SEC's approach will continue to be what's called "regulation by enforcement" of existing statutes. Current regulations include provisions against money laundering and financing terrorism; these could apply to crypto-related cases but are not regulations written with crypto in mind.

In March 2022, President Biden signed an executive order to "ensure responsible development of digital assets."[3] Broadly speaking, this order encourages close government study of digital currencies, including initiatives to do the following:

- "Identify and mitigate" broad economic risks associated with digital assets

- Report on how technological breakthroughs in financial services can be used to address inequity among underserved communities

- Examine technological advances in digital assets, emphasizing "privacy, security, combating illicit exploitation, and reducing negative climate impact"

- Research the possibility of a US Central Bank Digital Currency

In September 2022, SEC chair Gary Gensler, who has taught a course on blockchain and crypto at MIT, made a speech stating that regulations covering securities should be applied to crypto, with crypto exchanges to be treated as brokerages. The crypto community responded that, while crypto is often used as an investment vehicle, its nature and potential differ widely from the traditional investment vehicles, such as stocks and bonds, generally treated as securities. In their view, these comparisons to familiar investment vehicles only serve to limit the potential applications of crypto. Given the polarization of these attitudes, prospects for reconciliation may be remote—although history does have a way of surprising us.

Crypto Taxation in the US

The designation of crypto as a currency, a security, or both has clear tax implications. Many approach crypto not as a currency but as an investment. As is true for most tax-related issues, the relevant agency is not the SEC but the IRS—the Internal Revenue Service, which in general taxes crypto as it would a security or asset.

Currently, the IRS defines cryptocurrency as a form of "virtual currency." How it is taxed ultimately depends on how it is used. If someone pays you for a good or service in crypto, those amounts are taxed as income, based on their value in US dollars on the day received. If you hang on to your crypto and treat it more like a longer-term investment, it will be taxed differently.

A piece posted on Forbes Advisor puts it this way: "If [long-term crypto investors] hold onto their coins for at least a year, they can benefit from lower long-term capital gains taxes, which range from 0% to 20%, depending on your income level. Short-term crypto gains on purchases held for less than a year are subject to the same tax rates you pay on all other income: 10% to 37% in 2022, depending on your federal income tax bracket."[4]

Also, if you use crypto to make purchases, you're required to pay state and local sales taxes. There is a confusing disparity among the ways the various states define crypto for tax purposes. For instance, proposed legislation in Arizona treats Bitcoin as legal tender. Alabama, by contrast, exempts cryptocurrency from "ad valorem" taxation; that is, based on its assessed value.

The bottom line is that the SEC and IRS apply current regulations to crypto covering both securities and income. Requirements around reporting crypto buying, selling, and trading became stricter with implementation of the Biden administration's Infrastructure Investment and Jobs Act, passed in November 2021.

Moreover, given crypto's growing prominence, it is likely that Congress will consider and pass further regulations focusing on its unique properties and characteristics. There have been, for instance, several bills introduced aiming to repeal the Infrastructure Act's strict reporting requirements, which sponsors believe may obstruct innovation in this space. Obviously, these regulations will apply only to US citizens, even though US crypto participants will probably buy, sell, and trade crypto internationally, bringing up issues traditionally associated with offshore investments.

Differing National Approaches

Just as in the US, it's legal to own and trade crypto in other prominent Western democracies. Many other national governments, however, are taking a more conservative approach, viewing the potential for monetary and economic destabilization with greater alarm. They view issues such as poor consumer protections, no oversight of the interface between traditional finance and crypto, taxation avoidance, criminal activities, and unregulated financial instruments as major national risks.

Additionally, governments of nations with less stable economies take the possibility of crypto undermining their role in the global financial system most seriously and are acting to forestall this lack of control. The ripple effects of a crypto failure in such countries have the potential to be quite harmful in a country's greater economy—and, in great enough numbers, perhaps the global economy as well. Combined with how crypto's decentralized nature thwarts existing regulations and provides potential utility for criminals, the emergence of crypto poses challenges to governmental authority.

Some countries, such as Kuwait and Vietnam, have placed restrictions on crypto, while stopping short of an outright ban. Others, including Algeria and Bolivia, have restricted banks' abilities to deal with crypto, or barred crypto exchanges, in ways that amount to an indirect ban—call it a strong discouragement.[5] Such bans generally cite illegal crypto activities such as money laundering and tax avoidance. Those charged with and convicted of trading and holding crypto face possible fines and time in jail.

The following countries have notable approaches to crypto:

China

China outlawed cryptocurrency in September 2021, the culmination of a year when it had already banned banks and other financial institutions from crypto transactions in May and banned crypto mining in June.

China had already had a prior history of regulation. In 2017, it closed its cryptocurrency exchanges at a time when they made up 90% of the world Bitcoin trade. Two years later, the country banned crypto trading, although transactions continued through foreign online exchanges, a loophole closed in 2021.

The official argument provided by the People's Bank of China is that the ban was enacted to curtail financial crime and forestall economic instability. However, it is also part of a policy trend, known as the "common prosperity" campaign, toward greater state intervention in the economy. Specifically, the ban is a reaction to fears that crypto, bypassing normal restrictions, enables capital to flee from national markets.

China currently shows no sign of lifting these bans. The difficulty it is facing lies in enforcement, which is also the case in its ban on crypto mining. Surreptitious mining operations have been creeping back, making Chinese miners once again a force in the industry, albeit illegally.

El Salvador

The Central American country of El Salvador lies at the other end of the spectrum from China in many ways. It adopted Bitcoin as legal tender on November 10, 2021, at the instigation of its president, Nayib Bukele.

Bitcoin adoption enabled El Salvador and Bukele to achieve political as well as economic goals. According to cointelegraph.com, the main reason for recognizing Bitcoin was to offer banking services for unbanked Salvadorans—and 70% of that population was reached and onboarded within six months, giving them access to payment services without an official bank.[6] Bitcoin adoption also facilitated cross-border payments, helping rebuild the country's tourism industry.

Unfortunately, the country bought into Bitcoin in November 2021, just as the currency hit its peak. Shortly thereafter, it fell considerably in value and subsequently went on a downward roller-coaster ride. Even with losses in the many millions, President Bukele announced that the country was going to stay the course with Bitcoin. Meanwhile, less than a quarter of the country's population used the currency in the year following adoption.

Central African Republic

In June 2022, the Central African Republic (CAR) became the second country to accept Bitcoin as legal tender. The move may have been intended to facilitate investment in the mineral and mining industries of the country, which is rated as one of the poorest in the world and might have trouble attracting investment through fiat currency.

The Middle East and North Africa (MENA)

Middle Eastern and North African (MENA) countries are sending far more mixed, indeed often contradictory, crypto regulation signals. The region showed the highest growth in crypto adoption between 2021 and 2022. This is despite the fact that Egypt's highest Islamic authority declared crypto "haram," or forbidden, in 2018. In Turkey, crypto adoption rose especially sharply when the country's fiat currency, the lira, plummeted in value. The government then issued a series of regulations banning the use of crypto as payment for goods and services. Despite these bans, crypto adoption in MENA's Islamic countries rose almost

50% in the twelve months ending in June 2022, often as a hedge against inflation and the devaluation of fiat currency. Morocco even rescinded a 2017 crypto ban.

The United Arab Emirates (UAE), and particularly its capital, Dubai, has become a leader in crypto exchanges. This continues the UAE's recent pattern of embracing new ideas and technologies as a defining quality of a nation on the rise. In addition, as CoinDesk.com puts it, "The UAE has become an attractive gateway for expansion for crypto firms in recent months, particularly in Dubai thanks to its helpful regulatory regime."[7] That regime has argued that crypto is another way to continue to diversify its wealth beyond oil, and that the UAE is geographically well positioned to serve as a hub between the Middle East, Northern Africa, India, and the West. Dubai's influence is in fact spreading further afield to East Asia, possibly in response to the opportunities offered by the Chinese ban.

All of this is by design. Emirati authorities have created a regulatory environment conducive to crypto, at the same time that many other nations increased their oversight of the digital asset industry. The UAE's openness to crypto contrasts significantly with the restrictive attitudes of other governments, such as India and China.

In 2018, the Emirates also formulated a blockchain strategy that outlined a plan to transform half of all government transactions using blockchain technology. In February 2022, the Dubai Virtual Assets Regulatory Authority was created, with the precise aim of promoting the Emirates as both a regional and international hub for virtual assets.

Sub-Saharan Africa

Sub-Saharan Africa accounted for only 2% of global crypto activity in the year ending June 2022. Nevertheless, in some countries, crypto adoption rates are now skyrocketing. Some of this is semi-legal activity meant to bypass relatively weak fiat currencies. In Kenya and Nigeria, for instance, where banks cannot legally deal in crypto, peer-to-peer exchanges are the focus of the most activity.[8]

It's significant that there seems to be a higher percentage of crypto retail activity, as measured in relative size of transfers, here than anywhere else in the world. (Smaller transfers of crypto funds tend to indicate retail usage.) Retail activity is estimated to account for 80% of the total crypto activity in the region. Increasing numbers of people in sub-Saharan countries such as Kenya, Nigeria, and the Central African Republic see crypto as a way to build wealth outside the system.

Figure 99[9] is a map showing where crypto is legal but regulated, banned implicitly, and banned outright.

CRYPTOCURRENCY REGULATION WORLDWIDE

GRAPHIC

fig. 99

■ Absolute ban
■ Implicit ban
■ Regulated

Overall, the number of countries limiting use of crypto doubled between 2018 and 2022 and continues to increase. Even where crypto use is legal, many governments are debating what steps to take next.

Figure 100 has a timeline with some of the major events in international crypto regulation.

In the years ahead, you can expect the position that countries take on cryptocurrencies to evolve. Bans will be levied and lifted. Regulations, not all of which will be enforceable, will proliferate. Governments will find themselves increasingly required to take a stance on a crypto economy that is simply not going away.

TIMELINE OF INTERNATIONAL CRYPTO REGULATIONS

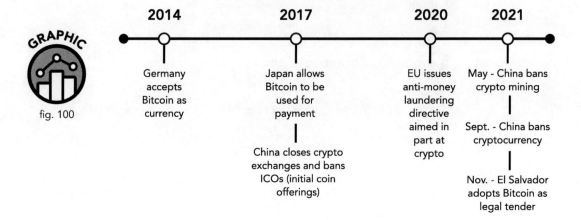

fig. 100

2014 — Germany accepts Bitcoin as currency

2017 — Japan allows Bitcoin to be used for payment

China closes crypto exchanges and bans ICOs (initial coin offerings)

2020 — EU issues anti-money laundering directive aimed in part at crypto

2021 — May - China bans crypto mining

Sept. - China bans cryptocurrency

Nov. - El Salvador adopts Bitcoin as legal tender

Crypto Taxation Worldwide

As might be expected, there is little consistency in crypto tax policies among countries. While the United States imposes a capital gains tax policy on crypto, certain countries have become thought of as crypto tax havens precisely because they do not impose such capital gains taxes. These countries include Singapore—where 22 percent of the population has invested in crypto—and Portugal, Switzerland, and Germany.

The Netherlands and Canada, among many other countries, work more on the American model, taxing crypto itself as an asset subject to short- and long-term capital gains regulations. Fees, such as those derived from proof-of-work and proof-of-stake validation, are taxed as income. Likewise, in the rest of the European Union, virtual currencies are generally viewed not as currencies but as assets.

Due to their very nature, virtual currencies pose many challenges for tax policy, such as valuation difficulties and decentralization, which makes digital assets less subject to oversight. Other challenges arise from the rapid evolution of both the underpinning blockchain technology and virtual currencies themselves.

Almost everywhere, taxation regulations have yet to catch up with the latest developments. For example, the status of DeFi transactions is for the most part yet to be addressed. These developments are taking place so quickly that more issues are raised than can be answered. Tax and other regulatory agencies are not only lagging but show every sign of falling even further behind.

The professional services firm PwC's in-depth Annual Global Crypto Tax Report 2022 acknowledges the market's turbulence and the resulting inability of regulatory agencies to keep pace with the speed of change. This is unlikely to resolve itself any time soon.

The Case For and Against Regulation

There are strong cases to be made for further regulation of crypto markets, and some reasons to be apprehensive about these regulations. Here's a quick look at often-cited pros and cons of regulating crypto, so you can decide what you consider most important as you weigh positions on regulation from government officials, politicians, or yourself.

GRAPHIC

fig. 101

CRYPTO REGULATION PROS AND CONS	
PROS	**CONS**
Increased investor protection: Crypto ideals are supposed to democratize digital money.	**Going against the spirit of cryptocurrency**: Crypto ideals espouse a trustless system that doesn't require government intervention.
Encouragement of more cautious investors: There may be investors who are hesitant to get involved in such an unregulated environment, but would feel comforted by greater government oversight.	**Limiting innovation**: Some bold future ideas derived from blockchain technology may not come to fruition if excessive regulation scares off more revolutionary thinkers.
Prevention of money laundering and tax evasion: Reduces the significant risk and ongoing challenges of criminal activity that hurts governments and consumers.	**An uneven playing field**: As more countries adopt regulations that serve their needs, barriers will go up between borders that go against the frictionless and global intent of crypto.
Limiting economic damage: A popular but unregulated crypto market could have catastrophic economic effects in the event of a major crash.	**Driving down crypto prices**: Part of cryptocurrency's appeal is its independence, and regulation could throttle its growth.

The Future of Crypto Regulation

What I hope is obvious from this overview is that the crypto regulatory landscape is tumultuous. There are so many different approaches that shift so frequently—sometimes 180 degrees—that it's hard to determine what an individual government's stance is going to be from year to year, or even from month to month.

Predictions are always risky, and particularly so in situations as volatile as that in which cryptocurrency finds itself. You can probably expect increasingly louder calls for regulatory clarity and cross-border consistency, along with little chance of governments' being able to heed such calls in a timely manner.

Such lack of clear direction may inhibit some crypto trading in the short and medium terms by those who feel such trading is too risky. But one thing that's virtually certain is that crypto and other virtual currency, and the blockchain technology that underpins it, are going to continue to be a force that governments will have to reckon with.

At the beginning of this book, I make the point that crypto and, by extension, blockchain are part of the much larger technologically driven global movement known as the Fourth Industrial Revolution. Within this revolution, the world is undergoing a digital transformation, and digital currency simply makes sense as every aspect of our lives evolves from analog to digital. How important is the digitalization of money and its underlying distributed ledger in this revolution? Klaus Schwab, founder of the World Economic Forum, best known for its annual conference in Davos, Switzerland, has said, "Blockchains are the heart of the Fourth Industrial Revolution."[10]

Just as fears about the possible repercussions of artificial intelligence and genetic engineering are managed with some level of regulation rather than stopping those advances entirely, national concerns about the potentially destabilizing impact of cryptocurrency are unlikely to halt its growing usage. Regulation, if properly applied, might bring some desirable order into the often chaotic proliferation of cryptocurrencies, but it's finding the right approach to regulating this emerging phenomenon that's proving challenging.

I doubt that these issues are going to be resolved any time soon. But it won't be from lack of trying. As the Fourth Industrial Revolution proceeds, the issues involved are going to become ever more pressing.

Chapter Recap

» In the US and other prominent Western democracies, the most common approach to crypto is what's called "regulation by enforcement" of current laws.

» In the US, cryptocurrency is currently taxed as an investment.

» It is likely the US Congress will pass further legislation regulating crypto.

» Some countries, notably China, have banned crypto entirely.

» Many countries have placed significant restrictions, such as forbidding banks from dealing in crypto.

» Blockchain and crypto appear to be poised to take central roles in the emerging Fourth Industrial Revolution.

| 14 |

What's Next

So much of the interest in cryptocurrency seems tied up in its status as a possible money of the future—a next step in the evolution of currency. It's natural, then, to speculate about where cryptocurrency may be heading. In this final chapter I provide a survey of ideas on the future of crypto. These are not necessarily iron-clad predictions, but they may help you consider how to approach crypto in the years ahead.

To the Moon or Bust?

Tyler Winklevoss, cofounder of the popular Gemini cryptocurrency exchange, has suggested that Bitcoin will supplant gold as the preeminent store-of-value asset and will reach prices as high as $500,000 per coin within the current decade.[1]

Other crypto enthusiasts, like tech entrepreneur Michael Saylor, cite the originality of Bitcoin as an asset class as reason for its inevitable endurance, both as an investment and a means of exchange. Saylor draws several contrasts between Bitcoin and other assets. Property, for instance, is inherently vulnerable to governmental action. It is not at all portable, can be easily taxed, and can even be annexed via eminent domain. Gold, he says, is a fine store of value, but it isn't nearly as transportable as the digital keys to a crypto wallet. Moreover, gold has a history of being confiscated by sovereign governments. And cash, which is barely an asset at all, is hopelessly inflationary. Saylor concludes that Bitcoin will prove to be the ultimate tool for the preservation of generational wealth.[2] I might add that Bitcoin holds an advantage over assets like property and gold in that it is more divisible (to the eighth decimal place).

If Winklevoss, Saylor, and similar enthusiasts are proven correct and Bitcoin appreciates to grand heights ($100,000 or even $500,000 per coin), then those who acquired significant quantities of the asset would be mightily rewarded. Another, less obvious, effect of such dramatic price appreciation could be inflation. Given Bitcoin's finite supply, if the market can command 500,000 US dollars for a single unit of this digital currency, then inflationary pressures could manifest, with too many dollars pursuing too few goods and services.

On the other hand, plenty of observers have urged more caution. Following the FTX scandal in late 2022, where $1 to $2 billion in investor funds went suddenly missing from the FTX cryptocurrency exchange,[3] The Motley Fool's Emma Newbery announced her decision to close out her account at the popular exchange crypto.com, citing her desire to not "keep *any* crypto assets on any crypto platform unless there's a compelling reason to do so."[4] Clearly, there are reverberations of concern over asset security in the wake of the FTX scandal.

In the days following the FTX revelation, the price of cryptocurrencies fell sharply, including a drop of about 20% for BTC. Some might point to scandals like FTX and others as evidence that even well-established, widely adopted cryptos such as Bitcoin could end up going to zero when it's all said and done.

Most crypto analysts agree that a total collapse in Bitcoin is unlikely. Andrew Button, also of The Motley Fool, argues that Bitcoin's first-mover advantage, broad institutional adoption, and general use as currency make it likely to stick around.[5]

Some others believe Bitcoin will endure but ultimately will need to be moved into a proof-of-stake (PoS) consensus mechanism in order to reduce its energy footprint. But skeptics decry the potential consequences of such a move. As stated by Prashant Jha at Cointelegraph,, "one of the major concerns with PoS networks is the level of centralization and its subsequent impacts on the security of the network."[6] Gerrit Van Sittert of CryptoVantage expands on Jha's concerns: "In this writer's opinion, it would never make sense to move Bitcoin to proof-of-stake, except if it was desired that Bitcoin whales take control over the network."[7] Sittert is referring to the outsized staking power wielded by a proof-of-stake currency's largest holders.

Prior to Bitcoin's decline in price following the FTX scandal, the coin's price point had stabilized around $20,000 for several months during the back half of 2022. This momentary lack of volatility seemed like a welcome sign of Bitcoin's maturity, and an indicator that Bitcoin and other cryptos might emerge dominant as authentic currencies capable of settling all manner of transactions at a global scale. The subsequent drop in Bitcoin's price in the wake of the FTX scandal is a handy reminder that nothing is set in stone.

Crypto as the Global Currency of Record

Today, the innovations of DeFi (which I discussed in chapter 12) have brought a multitude of crypto-based options to firms in the financial sector. Crypto can also be used at thousands of major retailers worldwide. Some already accept crypto payments directly; many others accept crypto indirectly by way of conversion products. BitPay, for example, indirectly facilitates payments via crypto through crypto-funded debit cards. These debit cards are powered by traditional payment networks such as Mastercard. Crypto in the cardholder's account is automatically converted to the fiat currency demanded by the merchant.

At any time, Walmart, Best Buy, McDonald's, or any business for that matter is free to start using crypto directly, assuming the currency is not banned by the government or so overregulated as to be unwieldy. There is nothing to stop them from rolling out crypto-compatible payment terminals to receive direct, verifiable, and cost-effective payments from customers. Employees of these businesses could even request wages denominated in crypto rather than in fiat, and employers, in the right circumstances, may be glad to make that accommodation.[8]

The technological prerequisites to widespread societal integration of crypto, then, are largely already in place. So what might entice a critical mass of society to opt for crypto over status-quo alternatives?

One factor could be the reduction of the risks that accompany the regular use and holding of a volatile asset. Intuitively, both consumers and businesses want confidence that a coin worth $1 today won't be worth 50 cents tomorrow.

Another issue standing in the way of more widespread adoption is ease of use. The know-how that goes into owning and using crypto isn't intuitive. As this book illustrates, the world of cryptocurrency is rather complex. Some research and learning are usually required to understand it and become comfortable using it. Progress has been made on this front in that cryptos are a lot easier to acquire and use now than they were in, say, 2010. That said, there are still learning barriers to entry that need to be addressed.

Despite the aforementioned headwinds, crypto has demonstrated an ability to embed itself within an economy when opportunities are present. Argentina offers an example of how a nation-state's economic and political circumstances can create a perfect storm for crypto adoption.

In recent years Argentina's unstable financial system and heavy-handed government economic intervention have led Bitcoin and other cryptos to become popular. Argentines earned $1.86 billion in crypto in 2021.[9] 60 percent, of Argentines believe that Bitcoin will retain its value over a two-year period, whereas only a third believe the same about their country's fiat currency, the peso.[10] Nations such as Argentina, El Salvador, and others may come to crypto under duress, as traditional financial systems collapse around them or because too many of their citizens remain unbanked. Such examples, however, don't preclude the possibility that other nation-states may one day be drawn to crypto merely for its merits.

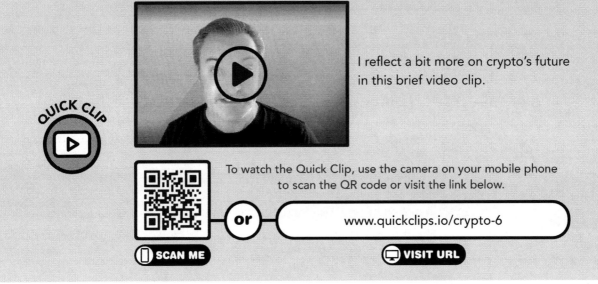

QUICK CLIP

I reflect a bit more on crypto's future in this brief video clip.

To watch the Quick Clip, use the camera on your mobile phone to scan the QR code or visit the link below.

or

www.quickclips.io/crypto-6

SCAN ME   VISIT URL

Friend or Foe: The Financial Establishment

For those of you worried about the biggest players of the financial industry lobbying to preserve the status quo, consider that it may be the ongoing adoption of crypto by that same establishment that fuels the big leap forward to mainstream adoption.

Take note, for example, of the ever-growing selections of crypto-based financial instruments (ETFs, mutual funds, trusts etc.) offered by legacy firms that seem to expand their offerings by the day[11] and show no signs of slowing down (even in the face of crypto-negative events such as the crypto market crash in spring 2022 and the FTX scandal).

Also noteworthy is the launch of new trading platforms backed by legacy financial brands, such as Fidelity Investments' crypto trading platform, called Fidelity Crypto, which will bring access to crypto and other digital assets to Fidelity's 40 million individual clients.[12]

If the financial establishment continues to warm to crypto—and government regulations prove more supportive than stifling—there could be a gradual but transformative adoption of crypto into every facet of economic life. After all, the mainstream attitude toward crypto has already been moved once, from conception of crypto as a *novelty* to conception of it as a speculative investment. Who's to say it can't be moved again, this time from a *speculative investment* to a *true alternative currency*.

Such a move may be helped along by yet another new kind of currency that's emerging as an alternative to fiat, this one brought to us by an ironic ally in the quest for a new money—the world's central banks.

Friend or Foe: Crypto Central Bank Digital Currencies (CBDCs)

When considering the entities best equipped to roll out a brand-new alternative currency, the question of resources comes to mind. Deeper pockets, broader influence, and a wealth of experience in the management of currency circulation certainly can't hurt. Perhaps this is why there is a growing consensus that the phenomenon of **central bank digital currencies** (CBDCs) will play a role in future currency revolutions.

As implied, CBDCs are issued by a nation-state's central bank as an alternative to that nation-state's fiat currency. They are similar to stablecoins (see chapter 6) in that their value is pegged to that of fiat currencies. But unlike stablecoins, CBDCs are not administered by decentralized ledgers but are digital currencies issued and regulated by a country's central bank or monetary authority.

From a monetary governance perspective, a digital currency offers both convenience and control. Their less cumbersome transfer protocols provide convenience for businesses and individuals looking for lower-cost options for transferring money domestically and especially abroad. Meanwhile, the centralized administration of the currency allows monetary authorities to control growth and inflation, making CBDCs less volatile than crypto.

At the time of this writing, according to Atlantic Council's CBDC tracker, 11 CBDCs have been launched, mostly in smaller nations, including several in the Caribbean. Fifteen nations have launched pilot programs, and many development and research initiatives are underway across the globe.[13] The Bahamas' Sand Dollar—a digital alternative to the Bahaman dollar (B$)—is among the most prominent of CBDCs to come along to date.[14]

The value proposition of convenience, simplification, lower cost, and stability put forth by CBDCs might entice more of society to part with their fiat currencies in favor of a digital alternative. Should such conversions come to pass at scale, then it could serve as a dam-breaker for the more widespread adoption of cryptos as a common means of exchange. CBDCs could become a gateway digital currency of sorts. Pierre Gildenhuys of Bitcoin Magazine, writing in September of 2022, puts it as follows:

It is likely that CBDCs are going to phase out the small amount of paper currency that still forms part of world economies today. This means that these countries will rely on technological education and word of mouth explanations as to how it works. This will cause a rise in technological know-how in these nations, meaning it should be ever easier to onboard otherwise unwilling members of society to Bitcoin once they realize the false value they are holding instead of a hard money.[15]

– PIERRE GILDENHUYS

Gildenhuys alludes to "hard money" as something distinct from fiat currencies. This means that fiat currencies, rather than being backed by hard, finite assets like gold, are ultimately no more than IOUs printed at whim by the nation-state.

The argument made here—CBDCs as the gateway digital currency—is comforting if you're hoping for a best-case scenario for crypto. But it's important not to overlook the reality of CBDCs as possible competitors to crypto. By replicating many of crypto's positive attributes, but with the resources of the world's central banks, CBDCs may one day render their decentralized counterparts wholly obsolete.

The Future of Crypto-Based Online Gaming

The video game industry is currently worth nearly $200 billion and expected to grow to around $340 billion by 2027.[16] It represents another significant avenue for future crypto growth. In chapter 7, I briefly discussed gaming tokens, which are NFTs that allow gamers (as opposed to the game publishers) to claim and verify ownership over various in-game assets. Such assets might include costumes, weapons, and skill sets, as well as characters and creatures—the type of entities you'd expect to be represented in an NFT. When demand for these NFTs increases, the gamers reap the rewards. Given the immense size of the gaming industry, there is a considerable amount of runway space for game developers wishing to incorporate NFTs and cryptocurrencies into their work. Crypto has enabled a new incentive structure for gaming to take root, one that could flourish in the years and decades to come.

In a crowded marketplace full of eye-popping products for gaming enthusiasts, video game developers have long sought to earn and retain devoted fans through the institutionalization of reward structures. In the past, these structures included *play-to-win*, whereby perks were given to frequent gamers. Consider, for example, the triple-A sports franchise *MLB: The Show* or the immensely popular *Fortnite* from Epic Games. Each of these titles provides in-game rewards to players for logging in on a regular basis. Log on to *MLB: The Show* seven days in a row and you might be rewarded with a powerful bat for your character that boosts your chances of hitting one out of the park during your next online matchup. The more controversial counterpart to play-to-win is *pay-to-win*, whereby digital assets, such as the aforementioned power-hitting baseball bat, can be purchased through the game's e-commerce storefront. The cryptocurrency phenomenon has brought in its wake a new and distinct incentive structure, known as **play-to-earn** or P2E, whereby digital tokens can be earned through gameplay.

Ninety percent of people will not play a game unless they are being properly valued for that time... [In the near future] you will actually value your time properly, and instead of being harvested for advertisements, or being fleeced for dollars to buy stupid hammers you don't actually own, you will be playing some on-chain equivalent game that will be just as fun, but you'll actually earn value and you will be the harvester.

— ALEXIS OHANIAN

cofounder of Reddit

The P2E model surged in 2021, in the wake of the global coronavirus pandemic. A wave of new games that came to be known as "NFT games" were rolled out by developers, so named for their tendency to feature collectible digital items that could be owned, traded, and even staked. Most of these games are developed to run their in-game economies on established blockchains like Ethereum, Solana, or the Binance chain, but use more game-specific tokens as in-game currencies.[17] Players can therefore acquire the in-game crypto as well as other assets that can be sold for ETH, SOL, BNB, or some other well-known coins.

NOTE

It is often the case that the tokens used as in-game currencies are themselves powered by the Ethereum network (see *Ethereum Token Standards* in chapter 7).

Though there are reports of devoted gamers and savvy NFT traders (as well as some scammers) bringing in significant windfalls through NFT games, these revenue channels are unreliable and vulnerable to sudden implosion.

Take, for instance, the case of the popular Axie Infinity NFT game, where users collect and own digital monsters. The monsters could be traded or pitted against one another in battles to earn Smooth Love Potions (SLP), the in-game currency. In the midst of the pandemic, a documentary followed the many Filipino gamers who had taken to playing Axie Infinity as their primary means of income.[18] Within a few short months, the average incomes derived from playing the game fell below the national minimum wage. The Axie Infinity gaming economy deteriorated further when the game's base blockchain, known as the Ronin Network, was hacked, leading to losses of over half a billion dollars, a fiasco that, at the time of writing, stands as the largest ever crypto heist.[19]

If you're interested in accumulating cryptos through gaming, seek out projects that have the highest potential for growth and mass appeal. For example, you might subject NFT games to a particular test:

1. If there was no play-to-earn incentive here, would the game still be capable of attracting a large fan base?

2. Would you still play it?

As with the cryptos themselves, most of these games publish white papers. You can look under the hood and assess the resumes of the development team members. You can and should subject these projects to the same type of fundamental analysis I outlined in chapter 10. It would be wise to do so before you invest significant amounts of your time and energy into becoming a competitive player.

The Role of Crypto in the Emergent Metaverse

According to some analysts, a multi-user 3D world, such as that found within a video game or an avatar-based chat venue, can only be considered a *metaverse* if it has a full-fledged digital economy.[20] All of the approximately 19 major metaverse projects in existence at the time of this writing run their own cryptocurrencies.[21] It stands to reason that a given metaverse, as it generally provides a platform for economic activity, naturally wants to create its own currency for use within its confines. Creating a cryptocurrency is not difficult (see chapter 6), and if a metaverse economy is being created out of thin air, it seems wise to create a native digital token to provide liquidity and a means of exchange for all the digital goods and services that will change hands within the metaverse economy.

Whereas internet commerce throughout Web 1.0 and Web 2.0 relied on the digital transactions of fiat currencies, in Web3—the decentralized Web—this won't be so. Web3 is where the metaverse is poised to flourish. Its promise is a platform that maximizes the autonomy, monetary and otherwise, of participants, including metaverse developers and denizens.

To the extent that the metaverse continues to form around blockchain-based platforms such as Decentraland and The Sandbox, it will be crypto tokens, such as Decentraland's MANA and Sandbox's SAND, that fuel these emergent virtual economies.

Cryptocurrency Rewards and the Crypto-Accumulative Model

Many investors see crypto as no more than another asset category that should be included in their larger portfolios. They are content to merely establish and maintain their 5%, 10%, or 15% targets and go on about their days as if crypto didn't exist. Distinct from this group is another segment of hodlers who really, really love the world of crypto and are willing to orient their routines and choices around the steady acquisition of coins and tokens. I call this frame of mind the crypto-accumulative model—and who knows, maybe they're onto something. Time will tell.

What follows are some of the avenues traveled by those devoted to the crypto-accumulative path.

» **Cryptocurrency Interest Accounts:** Major players in crypto, such as Crypto.com, Midas Investments, and others, now offer their customers cryptocurrency interest accounts. What you'll notice when exploring this space is that the interest rates offered are much higher than those offered by traditional fiat currency savings accounts. You're depositing (and staking) volatile assets and your interest will be paid to you in the form of those same assets. In exchange for that volatility risk, cryptocurrency interest accounts may offer customers APY (annual percentage yields) as high as 8.5% on their deposits of Bitcoin and ether, and even higher rates (upwards of 10% even) on stablecoins.

» **Credit and Debit Cards:** The crypto-accumulative model relies on the routine and, when possible, automated accumulation of cryptos. To this end, there are major credit cards, such as the Gemini Mastercard, The Crypto.com Visa card, and the Brex credit card, that offer customers an opportunity to claim the rewards they earn from card use in cryptocurrency rather than in cash back, airline miles, etc.

» **Altcoin Masternodes:** A *masternode* is a full node (discussed in chapter 2) that has additional functionality beyond maintaining a full copy of the blockchain in real time. Running a masternode requires more computing power to support the administration of the altcoin and its blockchain. Several altcoins allow members of the general public to invest in and reap the rewards of masternodes. You are typically looking at a big up-front investment, often in the thousands of dollars, and you will be rewarded via routine payments denominated in the altcoin you are supporting through your masternode. Syscoin (SYS), for example, offers a masternode for over $60,000 with yearly payments of $4,000.[22]

» **Games:** If your goal as a true believer is to steadily accumulate cryptos, then why not have a little fun while you're at it? As I discussed earlier in this chapter, opportunities abound for gamers looking to accumulate NFTs and crypto.

» **Mining:** See chapter 11 for more about how to mine crypto yourself. As with masternodes, if you want to mine from home at a smaller scale, then you'll find lower barriers to entry with altcoins.

> » **Learn and Earn**: The Coinbase exchange offers customers free crypto (altcoins) for taking free online courses about cryptocurrency.

NOTE

Faucets and airdrops, both discussed in chapter 11, can be counted among the tools used in the crypto-accumulative approach.

Expanded Applications of Blockchain

Though cryptocurrencies attract the most attention, the underlying blockchain technology may prove to be the most durable innovation that emerges from this period. To thrive, cryptocurrency requires widespread adoption, continued buzz, and sustained interest. Blockchain, by contrast, offers solutions to problems less glamorous than how to reinvent global finance—yet these problems, by virtue of their utility, may be the ones that make blockchain an enduring technological phenomenon. For example, blockchain can be used in the context of identity management.

Blockchain Use Case: Identity Management

The need to verify identity is routine in everyday life. In the offline world, this process involves tools such as driver's licenses and passports. Though generally effective for this purpose, these documents are issued and managed by central authorities, which can lead to bureaucratic delays and inefficiencies, as well as some risk of fraud, theft, or loss. Furthermore, their utility does not extend into the online world, a place where your identity must also be regularly verified—for many people, more often than in the offline world.

Of course, the online world is not free of its own threats. Hackers compromise the identities of millions of individuals each year. This occurs most frequently by the theft of credit card information and online passwords. In computing and online, being authenticated is part of *identity and access management (IAM)*. This consists of technologies and processes to digitally identify users and authorize access to systems and services.

Like offline identity management, IAM has vulnerabilities rooted in the centralization of authorities. A person's identity data is centralized, and to authenticate them, their data must be shared with yet another party, namely, the authenticator. Furthermore, current IAM is generally not very portable. For much of the internet's history, users haven't been able to employ a common set of login credentials on disparate systems. Instead, you have to enter separate usernames and passwords for each system accessed.

In the past few years, organizations have been deploying single-sign-on solutions. These enable the use of a single username and password that, once authenticated, can be used to access a variety of unrelated systems. These have created a great deal of convenience for users, but they've also concentrated the risk on a single point of failure. Fortunately, multifactor authentication (requiring additional confirmation of identity beyond a password, often involving a smartphone or another device) brings more security to this approach.

Blockchain has brought a new tool to the discussion that appears to address several of the weaknesses of current IAM. One concept called *self-sovereign identity (SSI)* gives the user control over their personal data and how it is shared. There is no central management, since identity information is coordinated and validated through the use of a blockchain, and it allows for a person's identity to be authenticated without the need for the approver to acquire any knowledge about the requestor. A person's identity information is held by them in a special type of digital wallet and the requestor only needs to trust a validation process rather than seeing the person's actual information.

The essential structure used in SSI is often referred to as a "trust triangle." The three components are the issuer, the holder, and the verifier (with a separate component being the verifiable data registry, a blockchain in this instance, where necessary authenticity information is stored) (figure 102). The issuer grants the credential. The Department of Motor Vehicles (DMV) is an example of an issuer. The holder is you, the user of the credential. The verifier is the party who requires the credential, such as the admin of your healthcare provider's online portal or the police officer that pulls you over for running a red light.

The verifier would not necessarily need to inspect the data within the credential, but only have a high level of confidence that it is accurate, which is derived from trust provided by special data stored in the blockchain-based verifiable data registry. This is known as zero-knowledge proof and it's a component of SSI.

TRUST TRIANGLE

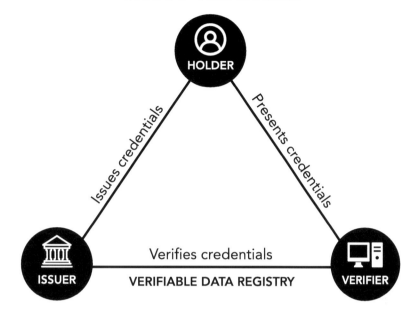

GRAPHIC

fig. 102

If you were pulled over by a police officer on the highway, you would be required to present your certificate from a digital wallet. Unlike traditional identification, you would retain control over what was shared with the officer. If, for example, the officer just needed evidence that you were licensed to drive, presenting the certificate might suffice. If more was needed, such as your home address, you could simply share that information from your digital wallet.

SSI still remains in its early phases but is growing fast. This elegant architecture may allow society to reap the benefits of a secure and portable digital identity.

Blockchain and Web3

Since the mid-1990s, the internet and the World Wide Web have had a significant impact on the way we work, live, and play. On balance, a more connected world has been a boon for humanity. The first generation of the web, version 1.0, provided access to a whole world of information at our fingertips. In the second generation, Web 2.0, the internet became interactive and provided the basis for e-commerce, social media, and so much more.

The success of the internet, and Web 1.0 and Web 2.0, has relied heavily on centralized systems and a great deal of trust in big tech. It has worked to a point, but it has come with a growing price over time. Today, too much of the internet and the web is controlled by a small set of powerful entities. Users are increasingly frustrated by their inability, for example, to control their own data and online autonomy.

A new, emerging version of the internet and the web, called Web3, is a nascent response to the frustrations felt by many and the limitations of powerful, centralized solutions. Web3 proposes an online world that is decentralized and controlled by users.

Intuitively, blockchain becomes a logical technology for a decentralized internet. Already having proven itself with crypto, blockchain has shown that it can democratize governance and the management of digital assets, improve identity management, and, through DeFi, reinvent the delivery of financial services. Blockchain has the potential to give power back to users and create a better internet.

Naturally, there's a strong possibility that crypto will play an important and increasing role in Web3, such as in the metaverse, but it's too early to make too many bold predictions.

An Epilogue: Which Forrest Family Member Are You?

When it comes to cryptocurrency, corporate lawyer Peter Forrest follows the archetype of the *conservative*. He's willing to divert just enough of his traditional investment portfolio to crypto to ensure he's not caught totally flat-footed should this strange asset take flight and soar for reasons he doesn't think he'll ever fully understand. Following his dabbles with NFTs and his reluctant setup of a crypto portfolio, he barely thought about crypto at all, content to let Mariana, his financial advisor, think about it for him. Eventually, Tori successfully convinced her father to move some of his crypto assets into the DeFi start-up she had joined. After a few quarterly reports, Peter is now quite content to have his daughter mind the bulk of his crypto assets, as she has proven quite adept at maximizing returns through on-chain asset management. Despite the healthiness of his recent returns, he still can't shake the fear that the whole industry might someday vanish in the blink of an eye. It's a concern centered more around his daughter's career choices than Peter's own portfolio.

Tori decided to go all-in with crypto. Hers is the archetype of the *believer*. Cryptocurrency, digital assets in general, and blockchain are the future in her mind and she's staking her career on it being so. The DeFi start-up Tori joined, though built on a sound technological foundation, still lacks the customer base Tori thinks it deserves. Having witnessed and abetted the softening of her own father's skepticism, she can't imagine that the rest of the world won't eventually be similarly convinced.

Lynn Forrest, the empty-nester psychologist and metaverse pioneer, follows the archetype of the *hobbyist*. For her, the world of crypto, metaverses, Web3, and so on is all fun and games. That's not to say she takes her hobby lightly. Lynn has become something of a celebrity in Decentraland. You can find her there most every day, either working at her practice, attending concerts, or trying her luck in the casinos. Thanks to the success of her practice and some winning at the blackjack table, Lynn has accumulated a healthy pile of MANA, quite in excess of what Mariana advised for the altcoin segment of the family's crypto allocations. For better or worse, Lynn keeps a secret wallet chock full of MANA on her phone with a seed phrase she's committed to memory. No one has to know, right? It's just for fun, after all.

Young Alan, also known as Alan the Great, follows the archetype of the *learner*. He's still working out how he feels about this emerging phenomenon that's so captivated his sister, baffled his dad, and *Mom's doing what exactly?* Alan continued to trade cryptos throughout his freshman year at college. Though he didn't end up making millions of dollars, he became quite interested in the crypto markets themselves. Following completion of his first year of undergraduate study at Stanford's School of Business, Alan successfully applied to spend a summer interning at a major cryptocurrency exchange. Through his internship, Alan learned more about how liquidity is maintained in the markets and how market makers profit within the small margins of every trade they broker. While the grind of real work wasn't as stimulating as the thrill of live trading, Alan was enthralled by the firm's ability to rake in huge profits. Fortunes shifted toward the end of the summer, as Alan's firm was caught up in a wave of SEC crackdowns on crypto exchanges. Several of the crypto derivatives and various DeFi products offered by the exchange were determined—via the Howey test (see chapter 7)—to be "investment contracts" properly subject to US securities laws. In the final weeks of his internship, Alan watched in disbelief as the firm downsized and restructured itself to accommodate the new regulatory burden. There were layoffs and an attempt to prematurely end a lease on an expensive suite in San Francisco's financial district. He was shocked to hear one C-suite exec say to another that they were lucky no one ended up in jail. Alan's not sure if he's done with crypto entirely—despite his turbulent experience as an intern—but he knows that if he does wade further into the waters of crypto, blockchain, and DeFi, he'll proceed with caution.

Chapter Recap

» Crypto enthusiasts envision a world where Bitcoin is priced in the hundreds of thousands of dollars, whereas even the most bearish of Bitcoin followers don't see a total collapse as likely.

» The technology exists to support widespread adoption of cryptocurrency. However, the public continues to hesitate for reasons that include concerns about the risks involved, the complexity of how to use crypto, comfort with the status quo, and resistance to change.

» Central bank digital currencies (CBDCs) are digital currencies issued by central banks. They carry some of the benefits of cryptos but are centrally managed.

» Hundreds of video games incorporate cryptocurrencies, tokens, and NFTs into their play-to-earn (P2E) model.

» The use of cryptocurrencies and tokens within metaverse environments is prevalent as developers aim to build virtual economies that depend on custom cryptos as their primary means of exchange.

» Financial and technical vehicles exist to support the *crypto-accumulative* habits of *hodlers* who want to amass as much crypto as possible at every opportunity.

» Blockchain applications, both present and future, exist outside of cryptocurrency.

Conclusion

After reading this book, no matter what you believe will be the fate of cryptocurrency, it's hard to deny what an incredible story it has been so far. Like you, I'm fascinated by the subject and have a deep curiosity about what comes next. If the past is any indication, it's conceivable that the future of crypto may be even more surprising and disruptive. Realistically, though, it's anyone's guess.

In 2008, the Bitcoin paper, a document barely nine pages long, boldly proposed a new form of money. Modestly written but consequential in its implications, the proposal suggested a digitally based currency that could exist independent of the world's financial systems. A year later, this new money was in circulation and a new era had suddenly arrived.

Now, a decade or so later, crypto has exceeded all expectations. Bitcoin launched a massive and complex cryptocurrency ecosystem that today supports a vast empire of participants and novel solutions. Unintentionally, even blockchain, the central enabling technology of cryptocurrencies, has become its own breakout hit and is the basis for a wide range of uses that extend well beyond its original purpose.

Crypto emerges and exists in a world in transition. Much evidence suggests we're in the opening years of the Fourth Industrial Revolution, characterized by hyperconnectivity and digital transformation. With so much of our world moving from analog to digital, it was likely just a matter of time before money would follow. Not simply in a digital form, but in a manner that would reinvent how it was created and used. In this regard, crypto has not disappointed. It may have started with money, but what has emerged is an entire platform for innovation.

To suggest crypto has been disruptive would be a gross understatement. Riches have been created, wealth has been destroyed, and governments and financial institutions are still among the many grappling with unresolved disorientation. And, curiously, for a high number of enthusiasts and detractors alike, crypto is an emotionally charged topic. Its surprise entrance into the world has created copious servings of mixed human sentiment.

The story of crypto so far features twists and turns, suspense and mystery, surprises and disappointments, and so much more. It's also an unfinished story that continues to unfold. I think it's one of the great human stories that must be told, no matter what happens next.

I wrote this book, in part, to tell the story to this point and to add to the historical record of the role of crypto in the current zeitgeist. In this effort, I hope I've done it justice. That said, my primary goal was to create a relatively easy guide to help more people understand crypto, to expand existing knowledge, and to enable readers to make an informed choice on whether to actively participate in the ecosystem.

To understand crypto you must understand money, but you are also required to understand a mix of computer science topics that are both unintuitive and intimidating to some. Documenting this in a way that was consistent with the promise of a simple guide, as well as keeping you engaged, was my challenge as an educator.

To help you learn, I created the fictional Forrest family as a proxy for questions and perspectives you may have or have experienced. It was a vehicle to make learning about crypto a more human-centric experience. Technology alone can too easily sanitize a topic and make it even more unapproachable.

My eyes were wide open from beginning to end, and it was my intent to capture the breadth and depth of the crypto industry and share it with you, warts and all. Whether you were bullish about crypto or a skeptic looking for validation in picking up this book, my goal was to inform and help you decide.

Over the course of my writing this guide, the world of cryptocurrencies experienced an extraordinary period. For example, Bitcoin and ether both lost substantial value, the world's second-largest exchange collapsed, and an increasing number of high-profile and influential individuals loudly questioned whether crypto had any merit at all. At times, it was hard for me to catch my breath keeping apprised of a volatile industry trying to find its footing.

Let me just say, I ended up rewriting certain sections of the book more than once. However, despite this period of turmoil, crypto expanded its footprint in many ways and the number of participants engaged in the crypto ecosystem continued to grow. For instance, innovation prospered through new developments and offerings in DeFi, creative uses of NFTs in a variety of industries emerged, and the role of crypto in both Web3 and the metaverse gained some clarity and traction.

Notably, the cryptocurrency roller-coaster ride keeps both optimists and pessimists equally engaged. No matter where you stand, there's nothing dull about this subject.

For some readers this book will be used as a step-by-step guide to engage in trading and investing. For others, it may confirm their worst fears about the validity and sustainability of crypto. Either way, caution and objectivity are advised. Jumping too eagerly into crypto carries substantial risks. Equally, prematurely writing off what could offer a reasonable return may limit opportunities.

If there's one lesson to take away, it's to fully understand the risks with each crypto-related decision you make. And make no mistake, the risks right now are extraordinarily high.

It's said that knowledge is power. This book has attempted to logically present the current state of crypto and, in doing so, provide you with essential insights and tools. That's your power now—to make informed decisions, to deliberate on what the future of crypto may bring, and to determine what your role will be.

I've provided you with that power. What happens next is up to you.

REMEMBER TO DOWNLOAD YOUR FREE DIGITAL ASSETS!

 **Major Cryptocurrencies Library**

 **Crypto Portfolio Management Workbook**

 **Crypto Research and Analysis Link Library**

TWO WAYS TO ACCESS YOUR FREE DIGITAL ASSETS

Use the camera app on your mobile phone to scan the QR code or visit the link below and instantly access your digital assets.

or

go.quickstartguides.com/crypto

SCAN ME   VISIT URL

Appendix I

Major Cryptocurrencies

NAME	SYM	CONSENSUS MECHANISM	LAUNCH DATE	KEY FEATURES	WEBSITE
Avalanche	AVAX	Snowman	9/2020	• Unique consensus • Fast transaction time	avax.network
Bitcoin	BTC	proof-of-work	10/31/2008	• Finite supply • Most well-known crypto	bitcoin.com
Binance	BNB	Proof-of-staked authority (PoSA)	7/2017	• Runs on the Binance Chain • Originally offered as a utility token for the Binance exchange	binance.us
Cardano	ADA	Proof-of-stake (Ouroboros)	2017	• Uses distinct processing layers for settlements and dapps • Unique PoS mechanism called Ouroboros	cardano.org
Dogecoin	Doge	proof-of-work	2013	• Iconic "meme coin" • Underlying technology derived from Litecoin	dogecoin.com
Ethereum	ETH	Proof-of-stake	7/30/2015	• Pioneered the use of smart contracts • The premiere blockchain for NFTs	ethereum.org
Litecoin	LTC	proof-of-work	10/2021	• Created from copy of Bitcoin source code • Faster transaction times than Bitcoin; runs a different mining algorithm	litecoin.com
Polkadot	DOT	nominated proof-of-stake	2016	• Uses "parachains" to optimize cross-chain compatibility	polkadot.network
Polygon	MATIC	proof-of-stake	2017	• A layer 2 protocol running on Ethereum • Boasts greater scalability and lower fees	polygon.network

Shiba Inu	SHIB	proof-of-stake	11/2020	• Self-styled "Doge" killer • Runs on Ethereum blockchain	shibatoken.com
Solana	SOL	proof-of-history	2017	• Fast transaction times • Low transaction cost	solana.com
Tether	USDT	none	10/6/2014	• A stablecoin with reserves in US dollars • Runs on multiple block-chains	tether.to
Tron	TRX	delegated proof-of-stake	7/25/2018	• No transaction fees • Ranks only behind Ethereum for total number blockchain transactions	tron.network
Uniswap	UNI	proof-of-stake	11/2/2018	• Utility token for Uniswap exchange • Solely a governance token to enable community ownership of Uniswap protocol	uniswap.org
UNUS SED LEO	LEO	proof-of-stake	5/2019	• Utility token on Bitfinex exchange • Burn mechanism will ultimately remove token from circulation	leo.bitfinex.com
USD Coin	USDC	multiple	9/2019	• A stablecoin with reserves in US dollars • Runs on Ethereum and several others	centre.io/usdc
Wrapped Bicoin	WBTC	proof-of-stake	1/30/2019	• BTC support on the Ethereum blockchain	wbtc.network
XRP	XRP	federated consensus mechanism	2012	• A product of Ripple Labs • Used to expedite cross-border transfers	ripple.com

Find an updated digital listing of major cryptocurrencies included with your digital assets at www.clydebankmedia.com/crypto-assets.

Appendix II

Consensus Mechanisms

Consensus mechanisms are methods by which participants in a blockchain network reach agreement on whether transactions can be trusted and are permissible. Through this, participants in the network validate the correct and current state of a blockchain at any point in time. Proof-of-work (PoW) and proof-of-stake (PoS) are the two most popular methods, but there are more options being introduced all the time.

CONSENSUS MECHANISM	DESCRIPTION
Proof-of-work (PoW)	Network nodes known as "miners" solve a difficult mathematical puzzle involving encrypted hashes of the data in the block to be validated. *Bitcoin, Litecoin, Dogecoin*
Proof-of-stake (PoS)	Validating nodes stake tokens for the privilege of earning transaction fees for blocks accepted into the blockchain. *Ethereum, Polygon, Shiba Inu*
Delegated proof-of-stake (DPoS)	Nodes pool tokens into a staking pool and then elect a delegate or delegates to validate the next block. *Tron, Eos*
Nominated proof-of-stake (NPoS)	Stakeholder voting determines which previously nominated nodes can validate new blocks; unlike in delegated proof-of-stake, nominators are subject to loss of stake if they designate a bad validator. *Polkadot, Cosmos*
Proof-of-authority (PoA)*	Nodes earn the right to become validators, so there is an incentive to retain the position and reputation they have achieved. *VeChai, Xodex*

Proof-of-history (PoH)	A cryptographic timestamp is attached to all transactions allowing them to be rapidly sorted and grouped into blocks. *Solana*
Snowman	In each round, a validator is selected randomly to propose new blocks, which the rest of the nodes then validate. *Avalanche*
Proof-of-activity (PoA)*	Combines mining (PoW) and staking (PoS) consensus mechanisms. *Decred*
Proof-of-capacity (PoC)	Hard drive space rather than computational power (PoW) is used to determine the right to mine. *Chia, Storj*

*Proof-of-authority (PoA) is not to be confused with proof-of-activity (PoA) despite the acronym they have in common

Appendix III

Cryptocurrency References

Data Aggregators

coinmarketcap.com
up-to-date price-tracking, charting, and data on all major cryptos

coingecko.com
aggregates price, market cap, community growth, and other data on cryptos

nomics.com
offers users access to APIs (application programming interfaces) to customize crypto data

coinapi.io
offers users access to APIs (application programming interfaces) to customize crypto data

lunarcrush.com/coins
uses AI to analyze price and social metrics surrounding crypto

stakingrewards.com
tracks staking rewards offered by cryptos

defillama.com
aggregates data on DeFi protocols

hedgewithcrypto.com/cryptocurrency-exchange-hacks
a comprehensive listing of cryptocurrency exchange hacks

Media

cointelegraph.com
news and analysis in fintech, blockchain, and Bitcoin

cryptoslate.com
source for crypto news, insights, and data

cryptopanic.com
aggregates crypto industry news

Cryptocurrency Research and Analytics

bitcoin.org/en/bitcoin-paper
Bitcoin white paper

ethereum.org/en/whitepaper
Ethereum white paper

tradingview.com/markets/cryptocurrencies
crypto charting platform

app.intothe block.com
price directional analytics on cryptos

Associations and Other Organizations

abcaonline.org
an American blockchain and cryptocurrency association

theblockchainassociation.org
a nonprofit lobbying group

bitcoinfoundation.org
nonprofit, oldest bitcoin advocacy group

ethereum.org/en/foundation
nonprofit, advocacy and support for the Ethereum platform

cardanofoundation.org
nonprofit, supports the Cardano ecosystem

global-dca.org
digital asset self-regulatory association

cryptoconsortium.org
issues crypto-related certifications

wsba.co
Wall Street Blockchain Alliance

Cryptocurrency Communities

reddit.com/r/CryptoCurrency
Reddit's cryptocurrency thread

reddit.com/r/Bitcoin
Reddit's Bitcoin thread

t.me/DeFimillion
a popular Telegram Messenger channel devoted to DeFi tokens

t.me/thebull_crypto
a popular Telegram Messenger channel for crypto trading

discord.com/invite/QbgHBnKwus
a smaller Discord channel devoted to Web3 learners and developers

discord.com/invite/bE6TTrAyNy [Surge Women]
a popular Discord channel devoted to promoting women in Web3

bitcointalk.org
one of the oldest online cryptocurrency communities, launched in 2009

minerstat.com/pools
a list of mining pools

crackingcryptocurrency.com/free-discord-walk-through/
a beginner-friendly Discord server

coindar.org
finds crypto-related events

thehiveindex.com/topics/crypto
an aggregator of crypto communities

Find an updated digital listing of resources by accessing our Crypto Research and Analysis Link Library included with your digital assets at www.clydebankmedia.com/crypto-assets.

About
the Author

JONATHAN REICHENTAL, PhD

Dr. Jonathan Reichental is the founder of Human Future, a global business and technology advisory, investment, and education firm. His previous roles have included senior software engineering manager and director of technology innovation, and he has served as chief information officer (CIO) at both O'Reilly Media and the City of Palo Alto, California.

In 2013 he was recognized as one of GovTech's Top 25 Doers, Dreamers and Drivers in government in America. In 2016, he was named a top influential CIO in the United States, and in 2017 he was named one of the top 100 CIOs in the world. He has also won a Silicon Valley Business Journal's Best CIO Award and a national IT leadership prize.

Reichental is a recognized global thought leader, a keynote speaker, and a business and government adviser on a number of emerging trends including urban innovation, smart cities, sustainability, blockchain technology, data governance, the Fourth Industrial Revolution, digital transformation, and many more.

He is an adjunct professor at the University of San Francisco and at Menlo College and instructs at several other learning organizations. Reichental regularly creates online educational video courses for LinkedIn Learning, which include highly successful courses on blockchain and cryptocurrencies.

Reichental has written several other books, including *Smart Cities for Dummies*, *Exploring Smart Cities Activity Book for Kids*, *Exploring Cities Bedtime Rhymes*, and *Data Governance for Dummies*.

You can learn more about his work at www.reichental.com.

» Twitter: https://twitter.com/Reichental
» LinkedIn: https://www.linkedin.com/in/reichental/
» Facebook: https://www.facebook.com/reichental
» LinkedIn Learning Videos: http://www.reichental.com/learn

About QuickStart Guides

QuickStart Guides are books for beginners, written by experts.

QuickStart Guides® are comprehensive learning companions tailored for the beginner experience. Our books are written by experts, subject matter authorities, and thought leaders within their respective areas of study.

For nearly a decade more than 850,000 readers have trusted QuickStart Guides® to help them get a handle on their finances, start their own business, invest in the stock market, find a new hobby, get a new job—the list is virtually endless.

The QuickStart Guides® series of books is published by ClydeBank Media, an independent publisher based in Albany, NY.

Connect with QuickStart Guides online at www.quickstartguides.com or follow us on Facebook, Instagram, and LinkedIn.

Follow us @quickstartguides

Glossary

Accredited investor
According to SEC regulations, an investor who has earned income exceeding $200,000 (or $300,000 with a spouse or partner) in each of the prior two years; has a net worth over $1 million (excluding the value of a primary residence); or has a Series 7, 65, or 82 license.

Airdrop
The sending out of newly minted, free coins or tokens to different crypto wallet addresses for promotional purposes, from blockchain developers, often hoping to promote new crypto initiatives.

Altcoins
Any cryptos that are not Bitcoin—a label that encapsulates thousands of digital coins.

Arbitrage
A trade where an asset is purchased from one market and near-instantly resold in another market where it's more expensive.

Asset
Property having some kind of value, owned by an individual or company, thought of as able to fulfill debts or legal commitments.

Backtesting
Evaluating behavior of buyers and sellers in the marketplace to gain a sense of how price action may be predicted, involving proposing a trading technique based on patterns and news cycles, then studying whether that trading technique would have worked based on historical data.

Bitcoin network
The worldwide collection of nodes that help to verify that each proposed blockchain transaction is permissible on the network.

Block header
A component of a block that forms the link from one block to another, containing information about the transactions contained in that block, also known as that block's metadata.

Block reward
The reward in Bitcoin that a miner receives for being the first to successfully complete a proof-of-work.

Blockchain
A distributed database that manages a continuously growing list of ordered and cryptographically linked records.

Blockchain trilemma
The notion that a single blockchain network cannot possess security, scalability, and decentralization at once, leading to the "layering" of blockchains.

Burning
A transaction made on a blockchain that deletes units of crypto, that results in limiting supply, boosting demand, and protecting the value of the currency.

Call option
The purchasable right (though not the obligation) to buy an asset at a specified price on or before a specified date in the future.

Candidate block
A block of data that hasn't yet been verified and appended to a blockchain.

Central bank digital currencies (CBDCs)
Digital money issued by a nation-state's central bank as an alternative to that nation's fiat currency (but still pegged to the value of fiat currencies).

Cold wallet
An offline approach and device to store public and private keys.

Consensus mechanism
A method to ensure blockchain transactions are valid and permissible, such as proof-of-work or proof-of-stake.

Cross-chain bridges
Protocols that permit different blockchains to interface with each other.

Cryptocurrency
Digital money enabled by blockchain technology.

Cryptocurrency exchange
A business that enables users to buy and sell cryptocurrencies through the exchange of cryptos for fiat currencies, or through the exchange of one crypto for another.

Cryptography
Methods of transforming data into formats that cannot be understood by unauthorized users.

Dapps
"Distributed applications," applications that are run on a blockchain-based distributed network. Ethereum is the most prominent example.

Day trading
The practice of making a high volume of relatively small transactions and then closing them out at the end of the market day.

Decentralized database
A distributed database without a server or administrative authority issuing permissions, also known as peer-to-peer architecture.

Decentralized insurance
A form of blockchain-based insurance that aims to streamline and cut costs on traditional insurance processes and procedures.

Decryption
The conversion of encrypted data, called ciphertext, into its original readable form, called plaintext.

DeFi
Short for decentralized finance, referring to solutions that provide blockchain-based financial services unmediated by such central authorities as banks and brokerages.

Derivatives
Contracts with specific parameters that oblige the sale or purchase, or give the option to make a sale or purchase, of a given asset, at a given price, at a given point in time (or over a given time period). Their value is derived from the value of the underlying currency, hence the name.

Distributed ledger
A database of records shared across a network of computers, with the exact same records on each of the computers in the network.

Double-spend problem
The question of how to prevent people from spending the same digital money twice without the involvement of a central clearing house such as a bank.

Efficient market hypothesis
The idea that markets are ever-rational and will ultimately create accurate, fair transaction prices for goods and services.

Encryption

The conversion of readable data, called plaintext, into an unreadable form, called ciphertext.

Exchange-traded fund (ETF)

A fund, traded on stock exchanges, that tracks the price of an asset or an index.

Faucet

In cryptocurrency, a website that spreads awareness of a new cryptocurrency, giving crypto to community members who perform simple tasks like filling out forms.

Fiat currency

Forms of money that are government-issued and not backed by an underlying commodity such as gold.

Fourth Industrial Revolution

A way to define the digital transformation currently taking place in our world, including how we learn, how and when we work, how we make things, how we move from place to place, and how we produce and use energy.

Fork

A new blockchain that branches off a previously existing blockchain, like a side road, to become the official ledger of record for a new cryptocurrency.

Full node wallet

A computer that hosts and synchronizes an entire copy of a blockchain and all its transactions. These nodes manage essential functions for ensuring that the blockchain network functions.

Fundamental analysis

Examining a particular asset through research and analysis, investigating whether that asset has long-term financial viability.

Fungible

Capable of mutual substitution; interchangeable. In financial terms, a $20 bill is fungible because it can be exchanged for another $20 bill with no loss in value.

Futures contract

The obligation to buy or sell an asset at a specified price, on a specified date in the future.

Gaming tokens

Digital assets that represent material within games like weapons, costumes, and skills. Some gaming tokens also enable token holders to participate in the project's governance.

Halving

The ongoing process of cutting Bitcoin's block reward in half, after every 210,000 blocks are added (which takes approximately four years).

Hard fork

A new blockchain, branched off from a previously existing blockchain, where the parameters of the network software are substantially revised to the point where entrants to that new blockchain are fully walled off from those using the old blockchain – creating an entirely separate, distinct blockchain.

Hash

A one-way cryptographic method that takes an input and produces a coded output that is nearly impossible to decipher.

Hierarchical deterministic wallet

A cryptocurrency wallet that uses a series of public-private key pairs, rather than just one, all generated in a predetermined sequence from a master root seed (which is recoverable through the wallet's recovery phrase).

Hodling

A term, originally derived from the misspelling of "holding" on a popular Bitcoin forum, that refers to the practice of buying and holding Bitcoin.

Hot wallet
A cryptocurrency wallet that is connected to the internet.

Identity and access management (IAM)
Technologies and processes (such as passwords or two-factor authentication) used to digitally identify users and authorize their access to systems and services.

Immutable
Unable to be altered or changed. In the context of cryptocurrency, a blockchain is immutable because no one can change blocks once they have been validated and linked.

Inflation
The ongoing loss of a currency's purchasing power, causing the price of goods and services to go up over time.

Initial coin offering (ICO)
A sale of tokens that crypto start-ups use to raise funds needed to launch, roughly the equivalent of a public company's initial public offering (IPO).

Interoperability
In terms of crypto, the ability of a blockchain to handle other crypto assets and decentralized applications.

Ledger
A record of transactions, whether handwritten or digital.

Light wallet
A piece of software that hosts and secures private keys.

Lightning Network
A second layer on the Bitcoin network that provides a separate space for transactions to be brokered in order to increase the processing speed of transactions.

Limit order
An order that allows you to declare the price at which you want to buy or sell an asset.

Margin
The use of borrowed money to trade, also referred to as leverage.

Market capitalization
A measurement commonly used to describe the total value of a given asset by multiplying its share value by the total number of outstanding shares. With cryptocurrencies, the market cap refers to the total units of a currency in circulation multiplied by its value per unit.

Market order
The most basic order type, indicating that you want an asset bought or sold on the market at the prevailing price at the time of the order's execution.

Masternode
A full node that has additional functionality beyond maintaining a full copy of a blockchain.

Memory pool
A holding area where transactions from the blockchain are sent to await assignment to a potential new block.

Merkle root
A hash of all transactions in a given block on the blockchain, included as metadata for the block and used to speed up transaction verification.

Micro-transactions
Exchanges of currency involving smaller available units than typical fiat currency. Instead of a penny (one-hundredth of a dollar), the smallest unit of Bitcoin is one hundred-millionth of a bitcoin (also known as the satoshi).

Miner
In proof-of-work cryptocurrency, this refers to a computer node that does the work of solving problems required to approve blockchain transactions.

Network effect
Value bestowed upon a product or service due to widespread usage.

Non-fungible token (NFT)

A token representing a unique asset that cannot be substituted, such as a work of art.

Nonce

Short for "number used only once," an unknown quantity that the miner needs to discover by completing the proof-of-work calculations in a blockchain transaction.

Open source

Software that anyone may inspect, modify, or distribute.

Opportunity cost

The term used to describe benefits that are lost when choosing one option over another.

Oracle

A service that connects non-blockchain systems (off-chain) to smart-contract-based blockchains (on-chain) enabling data to flow in either direction.

Paper trading

A method of practice trading that does not involve putting real money at risk.

Peer-to-peer database

See *decentralized database*.

Perpetual swaps

Contracts with no expiration or settlement date that allow traders to manage risks and hedge positions without having to continually open new positions every time an option expires or a futures contract comes due.

Play-to-earn

An incentive structure within video games, where digital tokens can be earned through gameplay.

Position trading

Holding trading positions for a month or more, often while waiting for a newsworthy event to play out.

Proof-of-history

Used in conjunction with proof-of-stake, PoH is a protocol that attaches a cryptographic timestamp to all transactions allowing for them to be sorted rapidly and grouped into blocks, resulting in faster overall transaction times.

Proof-of-stake

A form of blockchain validation where validating nodes stake tokens for the privilege of earning transaction fees for blocks accepted into the blockchain.

Proof-of-work

The most common type of consensus mechanism, originally developed to validate Bitcoin transactions, where network nodes known as "miners" solve a difficult mathematical puzzle involving encrypted hashes of the data in the block to be validated.

Pump and dump scheme

In the context of cryptocurrency, this is when influencers or promoters buy into a cryptocurrency, promote it heavily, and then sell their own coins while other people are bidding them up—and before the new buyers realize their holdings are worthless.

Put option

The purchasable right (though not the obligation) to sell an asset at a specified price on or before a specified date in the future.

Recovery phrase

A string of 12 to 24 words generated by a wallet that can be used to regain access to your wallet and keys on a digital device.

Relational database

Software that organizes data in tables and maintains relevant and logical relationships and links between those tables.

Replication
A process in distributed databases where changes to one copy of the database are also updated to all connected copies.

Scalping
A trading style that involves making a series of small profits by buying and selling within the span of short-term price movements.

Security token offering (STO)
A public offering that issues security rather than utility tokens, and must comply with security laws administered in the jurisdiction in which they are issued.

Seed phrase
See *recovery phrase*.

SegWit
Short for "Segregated Witness," a soft fork on the Bitcoin network that reduces the size of transactions stored on a given 1MB block. It accomplishes this by storing digital signature records ("witness" records) in a separate space outside the block, freeing up space to store more transactions.

Self-sovereign identity (SSI)
An approach to establishing identity that enables an individual to control the information that is used to prove who they are to third parties.

Smart contract
An agreement in computer code that automatically executes once certain conditions are met.

Soft fork
A new blockchain, branched off from a previously existing blockchain, where the network software changes are still backward-compatible with the previous blockchain.

Spoofing
The criminal creation of fake buy or sell orders in the marketplace without the intent of having them filled, aiming to influence market trends in one direction or another.

Stablecoins
Cryptos that are pegged to the value of an established fiat currency or non-digital asset like gold, designed to enable crypto users to enjoy blockchain-based, peer-to-peer payments without weathering the volatility of the cryptocurrency marketplace.

Statutory trusts
Trusts whose shares can initially only be sold to institutional and accredited investors. Following a period of 12 months, shares may be sold in secondary markets to the general public. This describes the majority of trusts that hold cryptocurrencies.

Stop limit order
An order that uses a predetermined price as a stop, which then switches to a limit order, to buy or sell at the limit price (or better).

Stop order
An order that uses a predetermined price as a trigger for a market order for a particular asset (even if that price is no longer available by the time the order is completed).

Swing trading
The practice of traders holding their positions overnight or for a few days.

Token
Something that stands for, or can be exchanged for, something else; a representation of an asset that can be bought.

Tokenomics
A term describing the study of anything that determines a cryptocurrency's value, addressing supply, mining issues, and potential uses.

Trustless system
An organization where the underlying process/code ensures security and integrity, eliminating the need to personally trust any of the individual participants.

Yield farming
A cryptocurrency investment strategy that involves lending crypto out to others who are attempting to maintain a liquidity pool, for compensation. Also known as *liquidity farming*.

References

CHAPTER 2

1. Roose, Kevin. (2022, March 18). "The Latecomer's Guide to Crypto." *New York Times*. https://www.nytimes.com/interactive/2022/03/18/technology/cryptocurrency-crypto-guide.html

CHAPTER 3

1. Gnu, Tippy. (2022, August 20). "Review: The Blockchain Code, Part 5: Mining Bitcoin." *Chasing Unicorns*. https://unicorniks.com/2022/08/20/review-the-blockchain-code-part-5-mining/

CHAPTER 4

1. Bitcoin.org. "Bitcoin Core Requirements and Warnings." https://bitcoin.org/en/bitcoin-core/features/requirements

2. Lewis, Anthony. (2021). *The Basics of Bitcoins and Blockchains: An Introduction to Cryptocurrencies and the Technology that Powers Them*. Mango Publishing.

3. Southurst, Jon. (2021, January 3). "12 Years Since the Genesis Block: A Reminder of What Bitcoin Is Really About." CoinGeek. https://coingeek.com/12-years-since-the-genesis-block-a-reminder-of-what-bitcoin-is-really-about/

4. Wintermeyer, Lawrence. (2022, March 13.) "What Does the Future Hold for Bitcoin Mining?" *Forbes*. https://www.forbes.com/sites/lawrencewintermeyer/2022/03/13/what-does-the-future-hold-for-bitcoin-mining

5. Tully, Shawn. (2021, November 6). "Offsetting Bitcoin's Carbon Footprint Would Require Planting 300 Million New Trees." *Fortune*. https://fortune.com/2021/11/06/offsetting-bitcoins-carbon-footprint-would-require-planting-300-million-new-trees/

6. Murez, Cara. (2022, October 10). "Patient Care Delayed at Large Hospital Chain After Ransomware Attack." *NBC News*. https://www.nbcrightnow.com/lifestyles/health/patient-care-delayed-at-large-hospital-chain-after-ransomware-attack/article_29315541-3adc-5820-a678-b954499a2138.html

7. Department of Justice. (2021, June 7). Press release: "Department of Justice Seizes $2.3 Million in Cryptocurrency Paid to the Ransomware Extortionists Darkside." https://www.justice.gov/opa/pr/department-justice-seizes-23-million-cryptocurrency-paid-ransomware-extortionists-darkside

8. Alper, Alexandra. (2021, September 21). "Biden Sanctions Cryptocurrency Exchange Over Ransomware Attacks." *Reuters*. https://www.reuters.com/business/finance/biden-sanctions-cryptocurrency-exchange-over-ransomware-attacks-2021-09-21/

9. Coinbase. "What Is Lightning?" https://www.coinbase.com/learn/crypto-basics/what-is-lightning. Accessed May 13, 2022.

10. Breedlove, Robert. (2021, April 20). "What Is Money?" *Show*. https://whatismoneypodcast.com/

11. Asli Demirgüç-Kunt, et al. (2017). Global Findex Database white paper, World Bank.

12. Silver, Laura, et al. (2019, March 7). "Mobile Connectivity in Emerging Economies." *Pew Research*. https://www.pewresearch.org/internet/2019/03/07/mobile-connectivity-in-emerging-economies/

13. PwC. (2018, September 27). Press Release: "PwC Study Shows Four Out of Five Executives (84%) Surveyed Report Blockchain Initiatives Underway." https://www.pwc.com/jm/en/press-room/blockchain-initiatives.html

14. Mitchell Capital Management. (2020, December 11). "Three Challenges Standing in the Way of Bitcoin Adoption." https://mitchcap.com/what-can-you-do-for-me-bitcoin

15. Mehta, Neel, et al. (2019). *Bubble or Revolution? The Present and Future of Blockchain and Cryptocurrencies*. Paravane Ventures.

16. Phillips, Daniel, and Scott Chipolina. (2021, April 20). "What Will Happen to Bitcoin After All 21 Million Are Mined?" *Decrypt*. https://decrypt.co/33124/what-will-happen-to-bitcoin-after-all-21-million-are-mined

CHAPTER 5

1. Lielacher, Alex. (2018, November 20). "Smart Contracts Aren't Contracts — and Other Crypto Legal Puzzlers." *Brave New Coin*. https://bravenewcoin.com/insights/smart-contracts-aren't-contracts-and-other-crypto-legal-puzzlers

2. Dapp Radar. (2022, April 6). "Dapp Industry Report: Q1 2022 Overview." https://dappradar.com/blog/dapp-industry-report-q1-2022-overview

3. See https://deepdao.io/organizations

CHAPTER 6

1. Siglaos, MacKenzie. (2021, May 7). "How Dogecoin Went from a Joke to One of the World's Top Cryptocurrencies." *CNBC*. https://www.cnbc.com/2021/05/07/what-is-dogecoin.html

2. Tretina, Kat. (2022, December 6.) "Ten Best Cryptocurrencies of 2022." *Forbes Advisor*. https://www.forbes.com/advisor/investing/cryptocurrency/top-10-cryptocurrencies/ Accessed December 10, 2022.

3. XRP Ledger. "Your Questions About XRP, Answered." https://xrpl.org/xrp-overview.html Accessed December 15, 2022.

4. Analytics Insight. (2022, March 13). "Solana, Cardano, Avalanche, and Bitgert – Which Has the Fastest Blockchain?" https://www.analyticsinsight.net/solana-sol-cardano-ada-avalanche-avax-and-bitgert-brise-which-has-the-fastest-blockchain/

5. Schroeder, Stan. (2018, February 24). "Cardano: A Rising Cryptocurrency That Wants to Change the World." *Mashable*. https://mashable.com/article/cardano-hoskinson-interview#M7WXfcgYIkq2

6. Kiayias, Aggelos, et al. (2019). "Ouroboros: A Provably Secure Proof-of-Stake Blockchain Protocol." International Association for Cryptologic Research.

7. Forbes. "Profile of Changpeng Zhao." https://www.forbes.com/profile/changpeng-zhao/ Accessed December 7, 2022.

8. Binance Academy. (2022, January 12). "What Is BNB Auto-Burn?" https://academy.binance.com/en/articles/what-is-bnb-auto-burn

9. Geron, Tomio. (2021, September 21). "Here's Everything Going Wrong at Binance, the World's Biggest Crypto Exchange." https://www.protocol.com/fintech/binance-regulation-crypto

10. Trading Education. (2022, December 28.) "Pros and Cons of Binance Coin in 2023." https://trading-education.com/pros-and-cons-of-binance-coin. Accessed February 7, 2023.

11. Mishra, Sarvottam. (2022, June 24.) "The Cons of Polkadot: The Dots Connected." https://www.cmnnews.live/the-cons-of-polkadot-the-dots-connected/

12. Van De Carr, Kedric. (2022, May 31). "Foundations of Decentralized Finance." *LinkedIn Learning*. https://www.linkedin.com/learning/foundations-of-decentralized-finance-defi/stablecoins

13. US Dept of Treasury. Report on Stablecoins white paper

14. Brown, Dalvin. (2021, September 30). "Crypto Tax: 'MiamiCoin' Has Made the City $7 million So Far, a Potential Game-Changer for Revenue Collecton." *Washington Post*. https://www.washingtonpost.com/technology/2021/09/30/crypto-miamicoin/

15. Mitra, Mallika. (2022, April 8). "The Total Value of the Crypto Market More Than Doubled in One Year. What Happens Next?" *Money*. https://money.com/crypto-market-doubled-value-whats-next

16. Lewitinn, Lawrence. (2022, January 9). "2021: The Year of the Alts." *CoinDesk*. https://www.coindesk.com/markets/2022/01/09/2021-the-year-of-the-alts/

CHAPTER 7

1. Frankenfield, Jake. (2022, August 18). "Initial Coin Offering (ICO): Coin Launch Defined, with Examples." *Investopedia*. https://www.investopedia.com/terms/i/initial-coin-offering-ico.asp

2. Alexandre, Ana. (2018, July 13). "New Study Says 80 Percent of ICOs Conducted in 2017 Were Scams." *CoinTelegraph*. https://cointelegraph.com/news/new-study-says-80-percent-of-icos-conducted-in-2017-were-scams

3. Sykes, Jay B. (2018, August 31). "Securities Regulation and Initial Coin Offerings: A Legal Primer." *Congressional Research Service*. https://sgp.fas.org/crs/misc/R45301.pdf

CHAPTER 8

1. Cryptopedia Staff. (2022, March 17). "The Early Days of Crypto Exchanges." *Cryptopedia*. https://www.gemini.com/cryptopedia/crypto-exchanges-early-mt-gox-hack. Accessed June 17, 2022.

2. CoinMarketCap. "Top Cryptocurrency Spot Exchanges." https://coinmarketcap.com/rankings/exchanges/ Accessed June 23, 2022.

3. Schoenberg, Tom, et al. (2022, June 6.) "US Probes Binance Over Token That Is Now World's Fifth Largest." *Bloomberg*. https://www.bloomberg.com/news/articles/2022-06-06/us-probes-binance-over-token-that-is-now-world-s-fifth-largest

4. Binance. "Why Can't I Withdraw or Trade?" https://support.binance.us/hc/en-us/articles/360047428953-Why-Can-t-I-Withdraw-or-Trade- Accessed August 19, 2022.

5.	Khatri, Yogita. (2020, October 2). "Coinbase Now Offers 'Instant' Withdrawals via Visa and Mastercard." *The Block*. https://www.theblock.co/linked/79729/coinbase-instant-withdrawals-visa-mastercard

6.	Leondis, Alexis. (2022, January 13). "Banks Are an Odd Place to Keep Your Crypto." *Bloomberg*. https://www.bloomberg.com/opinion/articles/2022-01-13/bitcoin-and-banks-make-an-odd-couple

7.	Rooney, Kate. (2022, April 1). "As Wall Street Banks Embrace Crypto, High-flying Start-ups Look to Lure Top Finance Talent." *CNBC*. https://www.cnbc.com/2022/04/01/as-wall-street-banks-embrace-crypto-start-ups-look-to-lure-top-finance-talent-.html

8.	Levy, Adam. (2022, July 28). "What Gives Bitcoin Value?" *The Motley Fool*. https://www.fool.com/investing/stock-market/market-sectors/financials/cryptocurrency-stocks/value-of-crypto/

CHAPTER 9

1.	Mahmadov, Murad. (2019, September 11.) Interviewed by Jacob Canfield on CryptoTrader podcast.

2.	Ibid.

3.	Pisani, Bob. (2020, November 20.) "Attention Robinhood Power Users: Most Day Traders Lose Money." *CNBC*. https://www.cnbc.com/2020/11/20/attention-robinhood-power-users-most-day-traders-lose-money.html

4.	Duggan, Wayne. (2021, July 31). "If You're Day Trading, You Will Probably Lose Money: Here's Why." *Business Insider*. https://markets.businessinsider.com/news/stocks/if-you-re-day-trading-you-will-probably-lose-money-here-s-why-1030667770

CHAPTER 10

1.	Malone, Richard. (2018, July 22). "The 'Hodl' Investment Strategy - From Bitcoin to Altcoins." *The Daily Hodl*. https://dailyhodl.com/2018/07/22/the-hodl-investment-strategy-from-bitcoin-to-altcoins/

2.	Statista. (2022, March 22). "Number of Cryptocurrencies Worldwide." https://www.statista.com/statistics/863917/number-crypto-coins-tokens/ Accessed August 24, 2022.

3.	N.A. (n.d.). "List of Dead Crypto Coins." *Coinopsy*. https://www.coinopsy.com/dead-coins/ Accessed August 24, 2022.

4.	Packin, Nizan Geslevich. (2022, July 22). "Bankruptcy and Crypto." *Forbes*. https://www.forbes.com/sites/nizangpackin/2022/07/15/bankruptcy-and-crypto/?sh=739193fe7df5

5.	Disparte, Dante Alighieri. (2018, July 21). "Beware of Crypto Risks – 10 Risks to Watch." *Forbes*. https://www.forbes.com/sites/dantedisparte/2018/07/21/beware-of-crypto-risks-10-risks-to-watch/?sh=7a07da455f17

6.	Ibid.

7.	Curry, Rachel. (2020, December 21). "How the Price of Bitcoin Affects Other Cryptocurrencies – For Better or Worse." *Market Realist*. https://marketrealist.com/p/how-does-bitcoin-price-affect-other-cryptos/

8.	Decentraland. (2020, February 20). "The Gates to Decentraland Have Opened!" *Decentraland Blog*. https://decentraland.org/blog/announcements/decentraland-launch/

9.	Ravenscraft, Eric. (2021, December 26). "The Metaverse Land Rush Is an Illusion." *Wired*. https://www.wired.com/story/metaverse-land-rush-illusion/

10. CoinMarketCap. "Top Cryptocurrency Spot Exchanges." https://coinmarketcap.com/rankings/exchanges/ Accessed June 23, 2022.

CHAPTER 11

1. Tezos Agora Wiki. "Tezos Energy Consumption." https://wiki.tezosagora.org/learn/baking/tezos-energy-consumption. Accessed December 8, 2022.

2. Schwarzer, Lyn Alden. (2021, August 6). "Bitcoin's Energy Usage Isn't a Problem. Here's Why." *Seeking Alpha*. https://seekingalpha.com/article/4452010-bitcoin-energy-usage-isnt-a-problem-heres-why

CHAPTER 12

1. Galileo Platforms Limited. (2021, January 28). "Galileo Platforms Offers Tools to Help Thai Insurers Manage Costs and Create New Products in Post-Covid World." https://sg.finance.yahoo.com/news/galileo-platforms-offers-tools-help-091000832.html 1.

2. Gans, Nicholas. (2021, November 15). "How Decentralized Finance (DeFi) Is Disrupting Active Asset Management." *Forbes*. https://www.forbes.com/sites/nicholasgans/2021/11/15/how-decentralized-finance-defi-is-disrupting-active-asset-management/?sh=2306556d67aa

3. Chainalysis. (2022, June 6). "DeFi-Driven Speculation Pushes Decentralized Exchanges' On-Chain Transaction Volumes Past Centralized Platforms." https://blog.chainalysis.com/reports/defi-dexs-web3

4. Synthetix. https://synthetix.io/. Accessed February 7, 2023

5. Graffeo, Emily. (2021, April 2). "Warren Buffett Warned 18 Years Ago About the Financial Instruments That Triggered the Archegos Implosion." *Markets Insider*. https://markets.businessinsider.com/news/stocks/warren-buffett-archegos-implosion-warning-derivatives-total-return-swaps-lethal-2021-4-1030272114

CHAPTER 13

1. Godbole, Omkar. (2021, November 19). "Crypto Could Destabilize Nations, Undermine Dollar's Reserve Currency Status, Hillary Clinton Says." *CoinDesk*. https://www.coindesk.com/markets/2021/11/19/crypto-could-destabilize-nations-undermine-dollars-reserve-currency-status-hillary-clinton-says/

2. White, Kathryn, et al. (2022, July 20). "Cryptocurrency Regulation Is Changing. Here's What You Need to Know." *World Economic Forum*. https://www.weforum.org/agenda/2022/07/cryptocurrency-regulation-global-standard/

3. White House Press Office. (2022, March 9). "Fact Sheet: President Biden to Sign Executive Order on Ensuring Responsible Development of Digital Assets." https://www.whitehouse.gov/briefing-room/statements-releases/2022/03/09/fact-sheet-president-biden-to-sign-executive-order-on-ensuring-responsible-innovation-in-digital-assets/

4. Berry-Johnson, Janet. (2022, July 9). "Cryptocurrency Tax Calculator." *Forbes Advisor*. https://www.forbes.com/advisor/taxes/cryptocurrency-tax-calculator/#:~:text=Generally%2C%20the%20IRS%20taxes%20cryptocurrency,other%20capital%20gains%20and%20losses

5. Quiroz-Gutierrez, Marco. (2022, January 4). "Crypto Is Fully Banned in China and 8 Other Countries." *Fortune*. https://fortune.com/2022/01/04/crypto-banned-china-other-countries/

6. Jha, Prashant. (2022, September 23). "El Salvador's Bitcoin Decision: Tracking Adoption a Year Later." *Coin Telegraph*. https://cointelegraph.com/news/el-salvador-s-bitcoin-decision-tracking-adoption-a-year-later

7. Crawley, Jamie. (2022, September 21). "Crypto Exchange CoinCorner Eyes Middle East Expansion Via Partnership With Emirates CEO's Private Office." *CoinDesk*. https://www.coindesk.com/business/2022/09/21/crypto-exchange-coincorner-eyes-middle-east-expansion-via-partnership-with-emirates-ceos-private-office/

8. Adeyanju, Oluwaseun. (2021, September 14). "Bitcoin Opportunity: Africa Adoption Rate Is Highest Globally." *Forbes*. https://www.forbes.com/sites/oluwaseunadeyanju/2021/09/14/bitcoin-opportunity-africa-adoption-rate-is-highest-globally/

9. Buccholz, Katharina. (2022, March 18.) "Where the World Regulates Cryptocurrency." *Statista*. https://www.statista.com/chart/27069/cryptocurrency-regulation-world-map/

10. Gil-Pulgar, Julio. (2016, October 7). "Bitcoin: Welcome to the Fourth Industrial Revolution." *Bitcoin.com*. https://news.bitcoin.com/bitcoin-fourth-industrial-revolution/

CHAPTER 14

1. Olowoporoku, Muhaimin. (2020, November 30). "Winklevoss Twins Predict Bitcoin Price to Hit $500K." *Cryptopolitan*. https://www.cryptopolitan.com/winklevoss-twins-predict-btc-to-hit-500k/

2. Saylor, Michael. (2022, November 3). "The Future Is Bitcoin with Michael Saylor." Interview with Peter H. Diamandis. https://www.youtube.com/watch?v=v4na2pycrcc

3. Dore, Kate. (2022, November 20). "'There Is No Such Thing as a Free Lunch.' 4 Lessons for Crypto Investors from the FTX Collapse." *CNBC*. https://www.cnbc.com/2022/11/20/4-lessons-for-cryptocurrency-investors-from-the-ftx-collapse.html

4. Newbery, Emma. (2022, November 22.) "Here's Why I'm Closing My Crypto.com Account in 2023." *The Motley Fool*. https://www.fool.com/the-ascent/cryptocurrency/articles/heres-why-im-closing-my-cryptocom-account-in-2023/

5. Button, Andrew. (2022, January 11). "Bitcoin: Could It Go to $0?" *The Motley Fool*. https://www.msn.com/en-ca/money/topstories/bitcoin-could-it-go-to-0/ar-AASFKiX

6. Jha, Prashant. (2022, May 6). "Eager to Work: Bitcoin Switch to Proof-of-Stake Remains Unlikely." *Coin Telegraph*. https://cointelegraph.com/news/eager-to-work-bitcoin-switch-to-proof-of-stake-remains-unlikely

7. Van Sittert, Gerrit. (2022, June 29). "Will Bitcoin Ever Move to Proof-of-Stake?" *CryptoVantage*. https://www.cryptovantage.com/news/will-bitcoin-ever-move-to-proof-of-stake/

8. Dhue, Stephanie. (2021, December 20). "More Businesses Offer Pay in Cryptocurrency in a Bid to Lure Young Workers." *CNBC*. https://www.cnbc.com/2021/12/20/more-businesses-offer-pay-in-cryptocurrency-in-a-bid-to-lure-young-workers.html

9. Gildenhuys, Pierre. (2022, September 12). "The Only Potential Benefit of Central Bank Digital Currencies: Bitcoin Adoption." *Bitcoin Magazine*. https://bitcoinmagazine.com/culture/cbdcs-will-lead-to-increased-bitcoin-adoption

10. Toppa, Sabrina. (2022, June 16). "Why Argentina Is Increasingly Adopting Crypto." *TheStreet*. https://www.thestreet.com/crypto/news/why-argentina-is-increasingly-adopting-crypto

11. Adams, Michael. (2022, November 1). "Best Bitcoin ETFs of 2022." *Forbes*. https://www.forbes.com/advisor/investing/cryptocurrency/best-bitcoin-etfs/

12. Rosen, Andy. (2022, November 28). "Fidelity's Crypto Platform Is Now Open. Is It Any Good?" *Nerdwallet*. https://www.nerdwallet.com/article/investing/fidelity-crypto

13. Atlantic Council. "Central Bank Digital Currency Tracker." https://www.atlanticcouncil.org/cbdctracker Accessed October 14, 2022.

14. Digital Bahamian Dollar. https://www.sanddollar.bs/ Accessed November 23, 2022.

15. Gildenhuys, Pierre. (2022, September 12). "The Only Potential Benefit of Central Bank Digital Currencies: Bitcoin Adoption." *Bitcoin Magazine*. https://bitcoinmagazine.com/culture/cbdcs-will-lead-to-increased-bitcoin-adoption

16. Mordor Intelligence. (n.d.) "Gaming Market Share Size, 2022-27." https://www.mordorintelligence.com/industry-reports/global-gaming-market. Accessed November 25, 2022.

17. Tan, Zyane. (2022, June 1). "Top Crypto Games in 2022." *Finder*. https://www.finder.com/crypto-games. Accessed July 17, 2022.

18. Nunley, Christian. (2021, June 14). "People in the Philippines Are Earning Cryptocurrency During the Pandemic by Playing a Video Game." *CNBC*. https://www.cnbc.com/2021/05/14/people-in-philippines-earn-cryptocurrency-playing-nft-video-game-axie-infinity.html

19. Tsihitas, Theo. (2022, December 14). "Worldwide Cryptocurrency Heists Tracker." *Comparitech*. https://www.comparitech.com/crypto/biggest-cryptocurrency-heists/ Accessed December 20, 2022.

20. Rossolillo, Nicholas. (2022, September 20). "The Metaverse and Crypto." *The Motley Fool*. https://www.fool.com/investing/stock-market/market-sectors/information-technology/metaverse-stocks/metaverse-crypto/

21. Scholz, Michael. (2022, August 31). "Why Crypto and the Metaverse Can't Exist Without Each Other." *Fast Company*. https://www.fastcompany.com/90781389/why-crypto-and-the-metaverse-cant-exist-without-each-other

22. Knight, Richard. (2022, April 6). "Top Masternodes for Passive Income in 2022." *Altcoin Investor*. https://altcoininvestor.com/masternodes-for-passive-income

Index

Bitcoin versus, 75–77, 79, 82, 84–86
blockchain of, 78–79, 82, 84, 98, 196
characteristics of, 77*f*, 265
DAOs, 83
dapps, 82, 84
as DeFi blockchain, 216–217
definition of, 53, 76
description of, 83, 265
ERC-20, 98, 108, 119–120
ERC-721, 119–120
ERC-1155, 119–120
gas, 83–84
initial coin offering, 116
miner revenue by month, 207*f*, 208
non-fungible tokens based on, 129
proof-of-stake used by, 85–86, 203, 213–214, 220
smart contracts, 78–81, 83, 87
Solidity, 81–82
tokens, 108, 119–121, 219
transaction per second rate for, 94
value of, 77*f*
white paper for, 76, 78, 81, 270
Ethereum Foundation, 76, 81, 84
Ethereum network, 84
Ethereum Request for Comments, 120
Ethereum Virtual Machine, 81–82, 85, 87
EVM. *See* Ethereum Virtual Machine
Exchange
    cryptocurrency. *See* Cryptocurrency exchanges
    money used as means of, 15*f*
Exchange-traded funds, 179, 185–187, 225
Extortion, 61

F

Facebook, 213
Faucet, 212, 255
FBI, 61
Fear, 177
Federal Reserve, 11, 16, 63, 106
Fee(s)
    bank, 149
    cryptocurrency exchange, 139
Fee tokens, 221
Fiat currency
    central bank digital currencies and, 249
    cryptocurrency versus, 20*f*, 20–22, 64, 200, 218
    description of, 11, 15
    as fungible, 114
    as records, 28
    withdrawal lock for, 144
Fidelity Crypto, 249
Finance. *See* Centralized finance; DeFi
Financial establishment, 248–249
Financial regulations, 231–232
Fintech, 215–216, 222
First Industrial Revolution, 8, 9*f*
Fishermen, 103

Forbes Advisor, 235
Fork
    Bitcoin Cash, 64, 66
    definition of, 63, 74
    formation of, 63–64
    hard, 63–65, 67, 74, 108
    list of, 65*f*
    origin of, 57
    soft, 64–65, 74
Fortnite, 251
Fourth Industrial Revolution, 7–9, 11, 242, 261
Fraud/fraudulent schemes, 45, 116, 184, 228, 233
Fraudsters, 109
Free-market capitalism, 161
FTX, 99, 232–233, 246
Full node
    definition of, 29
    hosting of, 55
    Full node wallet, 134, 136
Fundamental analysis, 196–200, 252
Fungibility, 197
Fungible assets, 114
Fungible tokens
    definition of, 115
    description of, 128
    governance tokens, 115
    initial coin offerings, 116–117, 130
    non-fungible tokens versus, 115
    security tokens, 115, 117–118, 128
    transactional tokens, 115–116
    utility tokens, 115, 130
Futures contracts, 176–177, 186

G

Galileo Platforms, 223
Gaming, online, 251–253
Gaming tokens, 119, 251
Gas, 83–84, 152
Gemini, 140, 245
Generational wealth, 245
Genesis block, 56, 60
Genetic engineering, 242
Gensler, Gary, 234
Gildenhuys, Pierre, 250
GitHub, 107
Gold, 14–15, 245
"Gold-Bug, The," 40*f*, 40–41
Gold coins, 13–14, 14*f*
Gold standard, 15
Goldman Sachs, 228
Good till cancelled, 169
Google, 213
Governance tokens, 102, 115, 221
Government-issued paper currency, 14–15
GPUs. *See* Graphical processing units
Graphical processing units, 210, 212*f*
Grayscale Bitcoin Trust, 188

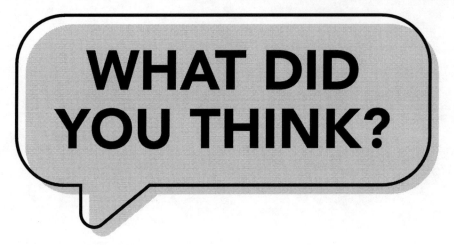

WHAT DID YOU THINK?

We rely on reviews and reader feedback to help our authors reach more people, improve our books, and grow our business. We would really appreciate it if you took the time to help us out by providing feedback on your recent purchase.

It's really easy, it only takes a second, and it's a tremendous help!

—— NOT SURE WHAT TO SHARE? ——

Here are some ideas to get your review started…

- *What did you learn?*
- *Have you been able to put anything you learned into action?*
- *Would you recommend the book to other readers?*
- *Is the author clear and easy to understand?*

TWO WAYS TO LEAVE AN AMAZON REVIEW

Use the camera app on your mobile phone to scan the QR code or visit the link below to record your testimonial and get your free book.

or

www.quickstartguides.review/crypto

SCAN ME   VISIT URL

GET YOUR NEXT
QuickStart Guide®
FOR FREE

Leave us a quick video testimonial on our website and we will give you a **FREE *QuickStart Guide*** of your choice!

RECORD TESTIMONIAL   **SUBMIT TO OUR WEBSITE**   **GET A FREE BOOK**

TWO WAYS TO LEAVE A VIDEO TESTIMONIAL

Use the camera app on your mobile phone to scan the QR code or visit the link below to record your testimonial and get your free book.

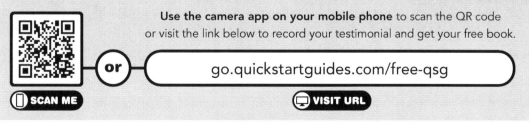

or

go.quickstartguides.com/free-qsg

SCAN ME   **VISIT URL**

SAVE 10% ON YOUR NEXT

QuickStart Guide®

USE CODE: QSG10

www.quickstartguides.shop/business

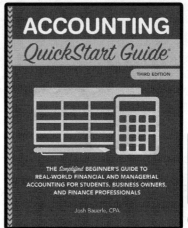

www.quickstartguides.shop/accounting

www.quickstartguides.shop/investing

www.quickstartguides.shop/html-css

Use the camera app on your mobile phone to scan the QR code or visit the link below the cover to shop.

Get 10% off your entire order when you use code 'QSG10' at checkout at www.clydebankmedia.com

LISTEN TO *QuickStart Guides* ON THE GO

NEW AUDIBLE MEMBERS GET THEIR FIRST AUDIOBOOK
FREE!

DIGITAL MARKETING *QuickStart Guide*

FLIPPING HOUSES *QuickStart Guide*

INVESTING *QuickStart Guide*

FOREX TRADING *QuickStart Guide*

REAL ESTATE INVESTING *QuickStart Guide*

TWO WAYS TO SELECT A FREE AUDIOBOOK

Use the camera app on your mobile phone to scan the QR code or visit the link below to select your free audiobook from Audible.

or

www.quickstartguides.com/free-audiobook

 SCAN ME

 VISIT URL

CLYDEBANK MEDIA

QuickStart Guides®

PROUDLY SUPPORT ONE TREE PLANTED

One Tree Planted is a 501(c)(3) nonprofit organization focused on global reforestation, with millions of trees planted every year. ClydeBank Media is proud to support One Tree Planted as a reforestation partner.

Every dollar donated plants one tree and every tree makes a difference!

Learn more at www.clydebankmedia.com/charitable-giving or make a contribution at onetreeplanted.org.

Made in the USA
Columbia, SC
28 October 2024

45179348R00176